FALLING
PALACE

FALLING PALACE

A Romance of Naples

DAN HOFSTADTER

Alfred A. Knopf, New York 2005

THIS IS A BORZOI BOOK PUBLISHED BY ALFRED A. KNOPF

Copyright © 2005 by Dan Hofstadter

All rights reserved. Published in the United States by Alfred A. Knopf,
a division of Random House, Inc., New York,
and in Canada by Random House of Canada Limited, Toronto.

www.aaknopf.com

Portions of chapter six previously appeared, in slightly different form, in Smithsonian. The
story of the concierge Abinotto, as related by Gigi Attrice in chapter one and chapter nine, is drawn
from Mr. Attrice's screenplay Un posto all'ombra; the lyrics to the song "The Life of the
Octopus" ("La vita del polipo"), quoted in chapter thirteen, are also by Mr. Attrice.

Knopf, Borzoi Books, and the colophon are registered trademarks of Random House, Inc.

Library of Congress Cataloging-in-Publication Data

Hofstadter, Dan.
Falling palace : a romance of Naples / Dan Hofstadter. —1st ed.
p.   cm.
ISBN 0-375-41440-1
1. Hofstadter, Dan—Travel—Italy—Naples.   2. Naples (Italy)—Description and travel.
3. Naples (Italy)—Social life and customs—20th century.   I. Title.

DG844.2.H63   2005
914.5'730493—dc22   2005044079

Manufactured in the United States of America
First Edition

For Will

CONTENTS

FALLING
PALACE

PROLOGUE

Falling Asleep in the City

Whenever, after a long absence, I return to Naples, that beautiful and wounded city, I find myself looking forward to bedtime, to the first few moments of falling asleep. I always stay in one of the more populous quarters, in a room overlooking a steep, narrow street, and as I throw open my window a vast wave of sound floods over me. Settled in bed, I'm disconcerted at first by the sheer volume, by my feeling of floating helplessly in a tide of half-drowned voices, people calling or quarreling, snatches of jokes, television commercials, soccer games, ghosts of song twisted by the wind; footfalls mingle with rasping scooters, a baby's crying with the honking of horns. Yet soon the noises soothe me, and suspended between wakefulness and sleep I enjoy a sensation of homecoming, of rejoining a crowd of kindred spirits, faces I have always known. The sounds summon up mental pictures, and in my mind's eye I can see the one-way street beneath my window, I can see the *bassi,* those tiny street-level flats, with their open windows and monumental, tomblike beds, and gold-embossed icons of the Madonna. I can see the old ladies gossiping in chairs along the sidewalk and the kids revving up their bikes at the corner, I can see the *circolo sociale* where grizzled gents play *scala* under a neon strip, smoking, coughing, trading affectionate insults.

Naples is one of the world's noisiest cities, yet by night those noises form a pillow of sound. They relieve me of a childhood fear, reassure me that in some sense I never sleep alone. In Naples sleep is crowded, full of faces, gestures, winks, and warnings—I feel that I drowse in a room packed with people. Yet only after I'd lived in Naples for the better part of a year did it occur to me that to be half asleep here, half exposed to a world of wanton fantasy, was to be perfectly in tune with the city's truest nature. For Naples was, and, I believe, remains, a place best or perhaps only grasped through myth and memory and half-remembered dream.

When I first came to Naples, alone, in my late teens, I felt as though I'd seen it before. Not all of it, of course, but certain pockets around the cathedral and the northwest quadrant. I had the sensation that I was visiting a place I had once dreamed about, and maybe I was, though a less fanciful explanation suggested itself. A few years earlier, I had been rescued from a charmless childhood by a band of friends, New Yorkers like myself, some of whom, for family reasons, spoke Italian fluently. There was a girl I liked, her flaxen-haired twin sister, a boy who played the guitar like an angel—and there were others. Those evenings spent in pizzerias or cheap restaurants, those walks along dark streets lined with salami shops and bridal stores, mom-and-pop bakeries, newsstands selling *Oggi* or *Gente*—I felt them returning whenever I strolled around Naples. My contentment grew partly from a sense of deliverance, and partly—more viscerally—from a sense of acceptance. Not that Naples was purely beautiful or welcoming—it was also dirty and devious. Yet I recall feeling flattered by the kindness of strangers. Young men of my age would guide me through casbah-like neighborhoods, refusing a tip. Giggling girls with glazed hair would sit close to me on hideous sofas, trying to pronounce my name. And workers I passed in the street would casually offer me part of their lunch, which was hard to decline, considering how appetizing it looked. When I discovered, around the church of Materdei, an especially congenial neighborhood, apparently untouched by the uglier sort of modern construction, it seemed that an entire civilization was proposing to take me in.

Often I'd walk there just before nightfall, when the wall shrines with their statuettes and electric candles and plastic flowers bloomed out of the gathering darkness. I passed the butcher and the wine merchant, the local headquarters of the Communist Party, the man on the corner who talked to himself. I glanced down alleys at half-derelict palazzi, and peeked into courtyards where one wistful palm curved into the sky. Often I'd smell a pot of *genovese,* the ambrosial Neapolitan sauce (quite foreign to Genoa, despite the name) made with beef and onions and white wine simmered for half a day. I peered into the windows of minuscule shops that sold buttons or notions or children's underwear, shops as cozy as a mother's lap.

Looking back through the haze of the years, I think it was actually the crowdedness of Naples that seduced me. The city clasped me in a warm, maternal, slightly musty embrace. I remember that during one of my many later sojourns, I tried explaining this to Benedetta. I tried telling her that the sheer close-packing of people and objects delighted me—how every street and piazza was so amazingly congested, so wildly overstocked with physical and emotional inventory. I had felt this in a reliquary chapel contrived like a chest of drawers, each bearing a tiny bronze bust of the bishop whose ashes it contained; and again when I saw the bridal stores beside the cathedral, with their tempests of tulle and white lace; and yet again in a *salumeria* from whose ceiling an abundant fruitage of hams, sausages, and mortadellas overhung a banner-draped altar to the Napoli soccer club. Wherever I went, I told her, I felt swathed by textures that seemed to breathe, as if animated by some magical force.

"Your wet-kiss theory of Naples," Benedetta called this, curling her upper lip in derision. This always unnerved me a little, because of that lip's heartbreaking curve. She looked rather like the country girl in Pontormo's fresco at Poggio a Caiano, which I'd discovered a year before. She had the same narrow mouth tucked neatly under the base of the nose, the same playful eyes. Sometimes I pictured her climbing over a stone wall like Pontormo's *contadina,* revealing a winsome calf; I pictured her in a torn peasant dress, barefooted and thorn-scratched, clambering up a hillside fragrant with thyme. So I was not very happy when Benedetta told me that my ideas were silly.

We talked in a scruffy bar in Via San Biagio dei Librai, convenient to the university where she studied. There, most afternoons, she would take my hands in hers, dominating arguments always conducted in her language. Tongue-tied, I would listen with rueful excitement: only later would I understand that our hours together added up to a fairly typical international romance, a romance that conjoined one lover's pronunciation handicap with the other's bafflement over the subjunctive.

We had met at a gathering in somebody's parents' apartment (Italian students, I noticed, almost always lived at home). As I came in, a voice called out my name and said, "There's a somebody here who wants to ask you something." A short, pretty girl with a face full of raillery was threading her way toward me through the crowd, and then, looking up at me with one arched eyebrow, she demanded, in Italian, that I pronounce the English word "mirror."

"Mirror," I said.

"Caspita!" Benedetta exclaimed, an expression of amused surprise. "Can you say that again?"

"Mirror," I repeated, a little perplexed—and then, all at once, I understood. The girl with the raised eyebrow adored, for whatever reason, the American *r.* "Horror," I said, expelling a gusty *h,* and again she let a *"caspita"* slip out. Craving to master these sounds, she tried her luck for a while with *r*'s and *h*'s, moving her lips in quaint ways. But Neapolitans, as I was learning, find English impossible, and she made no progress at all.

And then—how did it happen?—we were out on the street together, just the two of us, looking down toward the bay, and a tower by the harbor caught fire. A burst of gold sparks sequined the black sky, and the tower, a campanile, began to glow blood-red. It threw out bombs like a powder magazine hit by a shell.

"Oooh!" said Benedetta, insinuating her body next to mine as though taking shelter. Of course she must have known that the conflagration was only a fireworks display for the Festa della Madonna Bruna, an event as dependable as the solstice.

Like many Italians, she had studied English for years under teachers who spoke it incompetently, who couldn't even pronounce it. Neither could she. Though she needed English for her degree and was amused by its childish sound, the only language we ever used was Italian. And face-to-face with someone so talkative, and also so articulate, I grew aware of my discomfort with the subjunctive. This iffy mood, which suggests what *might* happen or *would* happen or is downright "contrary-to-fact," had already bamboozled me in my grade school Latin classes. But there at least I hadn't needed to impress a female—hadn't needed the "mights" or "woulds" on which flattery and seduction depend. Now, spellbound by Benedetta, I found that my tongue turned to wool, causing me to forgo some of the initiative I otherwise might have (would have?) taken. For chatterbox Benedetta not only ruled our conversations, she also corrected my grammar.

Was our interlude iffy in itself? Was it viable, or essentially contrary-to-fact? I suspected the latter, and any hint of this wounded her vanity, understandably—her faith was greater than mine. Yet that wasn't our only bone of contention, for she was annoyed by my perception of her city as a beacon of maternal warmth. Naively, I envisioned the great southern metropolis, in which so many of the old Italic ways persisted—the sprawling families, the spontaneous intimacy, the love of song—as a sort of fertility goddess with whom I might gently commune. And this, Benedetta thought, was absurd. The real Naples, she told me, was deeply *borbonico,* stuck in the prejudices of the pre-1860 Bourbon monarchy. *Borbonico,* she said, was a key word in Naples. It suggested obese walnut furniture, leafy ironwork running riot, and a decorative irony that dodged any forthright emotions. The famous Neapolitan cordiality, she insisted, was a sham, especially among those whom she termed "the parasitic bourgeoisie." Above all, Neapolitan society was a masculine fortress, a stronghold of bullies who despised the feminine spirit.

Benedetta had strong views on the war between the sexes. "Listen," she said one afternoon in the bar in Via San Biagio, "do you know what a *mammone* is?"

"I know that I've heard it," I said. "I'm not quite sure what it means."

Not true: but I wanted to hear it from her.

"A *mammone* is a boy who's too attached to his mother," Benedetta said, elaborating a basic term in the glossary of Italian pop psychology. A *mammone* lived with his mother till he was practically middle-aged, and without her he could scarcely cope. If he was considering marriage he asked her advice, but also if he needed new socks. He was forever comparing his fiancée or his wife to his mother, naturally to the poor girl's disfavor—especially in the kitchen. Many of Benedetta's male friends were *mammoni*, I gathered, from the face she made when she talked about them. "So I'd like to know," she said, in a very firm voice, "are you especially close to your mother?"

I considered not replying. But Benedetta, who talked with her whole body, had assumed one of her more fetching poses. She stretched her bare arms out in front of her on the café table, hands joined. She rested her head on a forearm so that her river of dark hair cascaded all to one side. She gazed up at me, arching one eyebrow.

"My mother died when I was three," I said.

She pulled herself up and stared at me, eyes wide with wonderment. "Of course, of course," she said softly. "Now I know why I like you."

It was an unforgettable moment. Never before had it occurred to me that this circumstance might be considered an advantage; half touched, half offended, I didn't know how to respond. The unintended humor of the remark eluded me. I felt, obscurely, that she had violated the conventions of an amorous conversation, but as usual, I didn't know quite how to reply. There was, in those days, that problem with the subjunctive.

Later, as we walked along Via San Biagio, Benedetta said, "Do you think Italian girls are aggressive?"

That summer I discovered that the Neapolitans liked to go out walking about an hour before sundown, when the air has usually cooled off. As a tide of shadow washed over the city, mounting higher and higher on its domes and bell towers, crowds would stroll about the streets, eating sfogliatelle and saluting one another; and Benedetta and I would also wander through the crowds. Every two minutes she would exchange embraces with some passerby, for at some time, so it seemed, every mouth had to touch every cheek.

This performance of a ritual *passeggiata,* which lasted until dark, reminded me of that other nightly transition, the crossing from wakefulness into the region of dreams. Naples, I began to feel, was a city of trespasses, of people who disliked boundaries and made a point of ignoring them. I remember a compelling instance of this. Toward closing time, Benedetta and I often poked into a shop in the Via Chiaia where a couple of her female chums sold women's clothing. Usually a group of friends had gathered there over a tray of coffee and apéritifs, and all of them talked simultaneously, with great animation. Every now and then somebody would make a move to go home, but the leave-taker, to my astonishment, would continue talking while heading out the door. He, or more likely she, would keep conversing over her shoulder, be pulled back inside by the force of the rejoinders, then head outdoors again, then be pulled back; and this shuttle would be repeated, Jimmy Durante–style, any number of times. Hesitating on the threshold seemed a pleasure in itself.

Benedetta, however, unlike so many Neapolitans, was not a threshold figure. She didn't straddle; you could count her in or out. And though in the years that followed I would often dream about her, in life there was nothing dreamlike about her—she stood out sharply against her slightly spectral surroundings. Her family, however, was not like her. They dwelt at the margin of the spirit world.

Benedetta's people occupied two apartments in a crumbling palazzo notable for the peculiar, ungraspable shapes of its rooms. One apartment was on top of the other, and both overlooked a pleasantly decrepit square. In the upstairs apartment, vacant save for a bed, a table, and a piano, her old uncle, Zi' Ippolito, had lived alone until his death a few weeks before my arrival; the rest of the family resided downstairs. Ippolito had a small income from some obscure source (certainly not his avocation of wedding singer) with which to meet his bachelor expenses, and he was not disposed to spread it around. "For many years," Benedetta told me, "he worked as a bank officer, but he was seized by whims that distressed his superiors. During the warm months, he liked to stay in his pajamas all day long. My God, those horrible striped pajamas!—I think we still have them somewhere. Anyway, my uncle began to turn up at the office in his pajamas, and since nobody had the heart to fire him—his performance, I suppose, was acceptable otherwise—they got him a trailer so he could work out of sight. They parked the trailer in a side street beside the bank, and he would sit there at his desk, in his pajamas, doing whatever bank officers do."

"I wish I could have met him," I said.

"He was charming," she replied, "from a distance—with people who didn't know him very well. He had been friendly with a famous singer named Salvatore Papaccio, and he loved all the old Neapolitan songs, which he sang at weddings for a pittance. Then one day, out of the blue, he was indicted—don't ask me why, I never found out. The judge called him into his chambers with his lawyer to work out a deal, and he had to leave the rest of us behind in the antechamber. We all waited there, including his mother, Nonna Immacolata, who was crying loudly and was generally inconsolable. But after a while we heard singing coming out of the judge's room—"

"He was actually singing to the judge?"

"No, no, the judge was singing to him—I guess he loved the same tunes. My uncle had started it, just humming a few bars, and then the judge broke into full-throated song."

"Did he beat the charges?" I asked.

"I actually don't know," she replied. "Nobody ever told me, and I guess I forgot to ask—" Benedetta screwed up her brow and thought for a moment. "When Zi' Ippolito died," she went on, "many girls and women flocked to his funeral chamber. All of them wept profusely, but nobody in the family knew who they were. A florist, though, an acquaintance of ours, had been engaged for the funeral, and he knew them all, at least by name. He ran a concession in the flower market by the Castel Nuovo, and he told me some things about my uncle. He told me that every time Zi' Ippolito fancied another woman, he sent her enough flowers to fill up her room."

To me this sounded merely like another instance of the Neapolitan love of cramming things into confined spaces; but the women, Benedetta said, were enchanted. "They accepted the flowers as proof of his passion—they simply couldn't resist him, don't you see? What they didn't know—what the florist explained to me—was that he and Zi' Ippolito had a standing arrangement. My uncle always bought the flowers at five in the morning, cut-rate."

The rest of her uncle's funeral arrangements, Benedetta told me, were left in the hands of an ageless lady, gnomelike and bewhiskered, named Eufemia. Eufemia took charge of all such rites, but she wasn't blood kin and indeed Benedetta couldn't explain her relation to the family. (She may have been the daughter, if I can trust my diary, of Nonna Immacolata's sister-in-law.) Her principal office, though, and this Benedetta knew firsthand, was to hold converse with the dear departed. Such interviews, Benedetta explained, served a serious purpose, because the period just after a funeral could torment the living, who had so many unpaid debts to the deceased, so many gripes and regrets. Luckily, dead souls could be easily contacted when they had newly migrated to the next life, and Eufemia reached them efficiently, without delay. She functioned as a kind of otherworldly radio transmitter, and in this, I came to realize, she was like many other Neapolitan women, both old and young.

Mulling over what Benedetta told me about her family, I began to see that the whole city still subscribed, though only half consciously, to some very old ideas—ideas that probably went back to Greek antiquity. There was the Orphic idea that music can propitiate or even disarm our enemies, and there was the idea, equally Orphic, that we can induce the gods of the underworld to put us in touch with the dead. Mainly there was the assumption that none of life's many chambers were totally sealed off from any of the others—everything communicated with everything else. Judges burst into song in front of defendants; old bachelors carried on like young lovers; and florists took the place of funeral orators, even if what they said could hardly qualify as a eulogy.

Before meeting me, Benedetta, like most townspeople, had little call to explore her surroundings, and besides, the backstreets were more menacing in those days than they are today. But together we walked long hours, and our walks taught both of us a good deal. Alone, I sometimes had trouble penetrating from one district into the next, for certain quarters appeared to turn their backs on each other, like villages set at odds by some ancient feud. On our rambles, though, I learned that this wasn't really the case, because we discovered plenty of shortcuts no maps deigned to divulge. Often such a shortcut consisted of a long, winding flight of stone steps which steered us this way and that, disorienting us. As we climbed, and climbed higher, landmarks shifted about, towers and domes disappeared, and even the bay might suddenly well up in some unexpected place—perhaps in the notch between two palazzi, or behind a stand of parasol pines. Then, overcome by the pure blue expanse, I could hardly keep from holding Benedetta. We had stolen several times into Zi' Ippolito's deserted apartment, and once, slipping an arm around her waist, I began to suggest that we go down and use it again.

"*Se tu vorresti—*" I began.

"*Se tu volessi,*" she corrected me, then twice murmured the correct form: "*Se tu volessi, se tu volessi . . .*"

If only you wanted, if only you wanted . . .

Then twilight came, our favorite hour, and a strange silence hung about those heights where we passed arm in arm into a different, more rarified world. The roar of Naples subsided into a distant sibilance, the stillness broken only by the occasional mewing of a cat or the sound of two boys with a ball, and spiked grilles closed off jungle-like gardens, and the streets bent away into the shadows. Yet as we climbed still higher, shafts of sunlight washed the fronts of broad palazzi, illuminating tiny figures at the windows, and we vied with each other in pointing them out. Look, that old woman reeling in her wash . . . that child gazing at the sky . . . And when Benedetta told me that she would never let me leave her, that she would be sure to "walk away first," I pictured her moving briskly down a long stone stairway, her bare arms swinging, her hair lifted lightly by the breeze.

Now, more than two decades later, I am reminded of something strange she once said. She loved America mostly because of the movies she had seen, but she did in fact visit America once, staying for a week in a borrowed Manhattan apartment. And there she was unable to get a good night's sleep. She had observed in horror films that such apartments had a second front door (what we New Yorkers call the "service entrance"), through which assailants and monsters broke, and she would wake up repeatedly, as the hours ticked away, compulsively checking that this ingress was secure. "A second door!" she exclaimed to me, shaking her head—flats in Naples had only one door, surely all that anybody needed. And it strikes me now that the way I felt about Naples was precisely the opposite. In Naples I slept easily amid apocalyptic noise because I wanted not to protect myself but to dissolve in my surroundings, like a bar of soap in the bath of the night.

Since those days with Benedetta, I have been back to Naples some fifteen or twenty times, once for the better part of a year. After each sojourn, I come away with a mind drenched in the same persistent reveries. Obliged by the primacy of gesture to pay more heed to the set of a chin or the turn of a wrist than I would elsewhere, I tend to see people as figures draped or posed against a background—at times it's like living in a theater. Meanwhile the backdrop too possesses my thoughts—the somber gray-and-rose of the palazzi; the blue sea; the islands, low-lying or craggy; the volcano sliding into view in the gaps between buildings or at the end of winding streets. One's consciousness, like that of the natives, brims over with the landscape, which never quite forfeits its spicy hint of malediction. *I curse you with fiery clouds, I bless you with the richest soil in Europe:* curses and blessings, blessings and curses . . .

Perhaps that is why I have rarely ended a day in Naples without a luminous sense of where I am, a vision of the place floating lightly on my brain. And perhaps because the city is already so dreamlike, the process of falling asleep leads into a world not so different from the waking world, a realm where things can almost be touched or hefted, like a little collection of objects—here a castle, there a volcano, farther away a town felled by ashes. In Naples I still waken, on those mornings when I remember some fragment of my dream, with a sense of mysteries half understood.

PART ONE

I

Sidewalk-ology

The Caffè Gambrinus, in Piazza Trieste e Trento, was the most convenient meeting place in Naples. Inside, politicians rehearsed the deals they would later strike in the city council chamber, the Sala dei Baroni; visitors and greenhorns from outlying towns staked out the sidewalk tables; and carabinieri gadded about in the streets, receiving their dole of female admiration. The café's interior was lined by mirrors full of shifting lights and decorative panels by painters of the Belle Epoque. Two gigantic Venetian chandeliers romped overhead, as though inviting you to do the same on the floor.

Benedetta with her unique blend of affection and defiance inevitably claimed a lot of my time; but once, when she had to study for one of her "soul-destroying" examinations, I decided to embark on a study of my own, of the people's gestures in the Gambrinus. For several nights I took up a station at the bar and watched the patrons, and soon I began to recognize many of their gestures. I could say that I recognized them from Arthur Avenue, in the Bronx, or from Havemeyer Street, in Brooklyn, but really I recognized them from everywhere. I say this because so many gestures are actually universal, signals the body dictates and the mind passively ratifies. To signify money, for instance, we rub a thumb against a pointer; to show exasperation, we fold our arms and cock our heads. Other gestures, though not necessarily unknown to us Americans, seemed more intrinsically Mediterranean. These included nose-tapping, to signify the odor of something fishy; the pulling down of an eyelid, to suggest that one ought to keep one's eyes open; and the upward jerking of the lower jaw to indicate refusal, like an animal jibbing at suspect food. Still others were typically Italian, such as the hands pressed prayerfully together and shaken at someone who was behaving unreasonably, or the sign for "later," an index finger twirling around in front of the speaker's nose, like the hand of an imaginary clock. Some gestures enacted an entire social role, such as the hand held edgewise and palm up, rocking back and forth at shoulder height, pretending to threaten a blow. To understand this one, you had to remember that the classic Italian grandmother had two prime insignia, the *matterello,* or rolling pin, and the *spianatoia,* or pasta board. The hand held edgewise stood for the *matterello.*

There was never a time when I conceived of Neapolitan mimicry—that rolling-pin gesture, for instance—quite apart from Benedetta. For all her chattiness, she was the archetypal enunciator of body language. Words came second for her: when she spoke, speech glossed gesture, rather than the reverse. Her body never stopped doing its wry little pantomime, her smile archly informing me that nobody's words could be fully believed, not even hers. "They can't fool me," she seemed to be saying. It never occurred to her that she might be fooling herself.

In those days, prowling the historic Neapolitan bookshops— Treves, Colonnesi, Pironti—I found, at Colonnesi, I think, a book titled *La mimica a Napoli,* by a learned Neapolitan abbé named Antonio De Jorio. It made a big impression on me. Writing in the early nineteenth century, De Jorio had thoroughly researched his city's gestural vocabulary, and he furnished amusing plates to support his contention, showing standard types of quarrels and domestic calamities. De Jorio was a French-style positivist, and his writing was as ponderous as today's social science jargon, but he also championed the nifty idea that conversational mimicry had a grammar much like that of spoken language. He claimed that such mimicry had its nouns and verbs, its adjectives and expletives, even its metaphors. I made heavy weather of the abbé's prose, but in time I came to enjoy him, responding to the sly humor lurking within his long-winded arguments. Sometimes I wished I could talk to him and put a few pointed questions to him. If you whistled and drew a feminine curve in the air, I wanted to ask him, was that synecdoche, "the part for the whole"?

In the Gambrinus I saw De Jorio's catalogue of gestures come alive, plus others he hadn't dreamt of. Waiting at the gelati counter, some women moved their whole bodies in unconscious arcs, even pointing with a foot to illustrate a point. The difference between the patrons here and those in, say, an American café wasn't so much the air pictures themselves as their frequency, their relentless articulation. Wrists, ankles, necks, and waists spiraled in a constant ballet, but the most interesting moves belonged to no known language. They were personal and abstract, like abstract art; and it occurred to me that such intimate gestures were as intrinsically mysterious as the movements of serpents or parrots. In Naples, I was learning, the body spoke the mind. Watch the hands, I would remind myself, as I listened to people talk; keep your eyes always, always on the hands.

~⇌~

My very first test, you might have said, was Gigi in Al Portico, telling me a story in his bizarre lingo, a staccato mix of Italian, Neapolitan, and lots of white wine. Gigi was a theater person, a comic and a poet, and he was unlike anyone I knew in this town. I didn't know anyone else who, flinging himself down opposite me with barely a salutation and no preamble, would launch into an anecdote, a harangue, a routine. Gigi had dyed-blond, porcupine-like hair, and always had a three-day beard. With his tommy-gun stutter and opaque, coffee-bean eyes, he flaunted a vaudeville version of shiftiness, and he habitually glanced around as if to jump up at any moment. Gigi talked mainly with his hands, which flew in all directions, like startled birds, but when he wanted to make a point he slowed down and molded the air, kneading it, cutting it like a baker. Drawing a distinction, Gigi gave you two loaves of air, pushed neatly apart with both hands.

Benedetta had recently introduced me to Gigi, who seemed the answer to my difficulties with the Neapolitan dialect. I had originally studied in central Italy and was used to Italian with a Tuscan sound; when I started spending time in Naples, talking at a normal clip, people answered me at the same speed, but in a language I hardly recognized. Many expressions were new to me, while others were old friends in outlandish disguises. Most words ended in a faint generic vowel, a sort of primal "uh," or they simply dropped their final syllables. Down here those syllables seemed expendable, like the outer leaves of an artichoke.

I hoped that Italian-without-words would offer a way out of my difficulties. Since the Neapolitans were renowned for the graphic precision of their gestures, I had set about studying the patrons in the Gambrinus, hoping to appropriate the gestural vocabulary, but naturally my study went beyond that café. I had resolved that whenever I encountered a dialect speaker, I'd follow his gestures as an aid to gathering his meaning.

That was where Gigi came in. I thought he could unwittingly help me learn what I needed to know. Listening to his stories, watching his simultaneous manual elaboration, I'd gradually absorb a basic gestural lexicon. This evening, for instance, I was trying to follow him carefully without letting him see that I was copying his hand motions under the table.

Gigi had the habit of resuming old conversations as if we had left off chatting the evening before, and sometimes he resumed conversations we had never begun. This time we had run into each other by accident. The weather that fall was so balmy that people couldn't keep off the streets, and toward nightfall, when the traffic fumes had settled, many wandered idly about, performing the *passeggiata* or dropping into a café for an aperitif. Some restaurants were serving dinner outdoors, and this balmy evening, at about ten-thirty, I had followed my nose to a table at Al Portico, a place that served food on a terrace out back. At one of those tables Gigi had spotted me.

That was where I usually met Gigi. The first time he ever saw me, he said, hearing that I was an American, "Do you know Joe Pesci?"

"Not personally," I answered. "I know who he is."

"Well, I'm an actor, too," he said, forgetting all about Joe Pesci, "and I'm famous, too. My name is Gigi Attrice." He extended his hand as though responding to applause. Gigi is a male name in Italian, a diminutive for Luigi. Gigi told me that he specialized in comic routines and could sometimes be seen on television. I'd never seen him on television, but Benedetta had—she told me later that she'd seen him trying to push a car uphill, with what success she couldn't remember.

This evening Gigi was telling me a long story about a friend of his who worked as a concierge. Like most men in the service trades in Naples, Gigi said, this fellow had to hustle to make ends meet. The story illustrated the *arte di arrangiarsi,* the technique of occupational improvisation, but it was meant no less to say something about Gigi himself.

As Gigi talked his hands went faster and faster, but soon I lost track of the sign language, because I got drawn into the tale. The concierge's name was Abinotto, Gigi said, and his building had some unusual tenants. Among them were a transvestite, a secretive old widower, and a smuggler of contraband cigarettes. There were also three illegal Arab immigrants and a pair of elderly sisters, one of whom had two beautiful daughters who'd been deluded into thinking they were fashion models.

"Those girls," Gigi said, "went constantly to fake interviews and beauty contests, events they had to pay for. One of them got pregnant and didn't know who was the father. But my friend Abinotto knew. Being the concierge, he knew all there was to know about her, and all about the other tenants as well."

Gigi was a nervous raconteur. If it's true, as they say, that comedians are angry deep down, then Gigi exemplified that truth. Maybe because of his stutter, he had a bilious way of telling a joke. Shakily he lit a cigarette, then lost his grip on it, bobbled it in the air, and rescued it—all without burning himself.

He told me that Abinotto had a porter's lodge off to one side of the building's entrance. In the lodge Abinotto kept nothing but an old service revolver his father had given him and seven hundred condoms.

"Gigi, why seven hundred condoms?"

"Listen," he said, dragging on his cigarette, "Abinotto wasn't so young anymore, okay? His wife had died a few years earlier, and just before that he'd bought a job lot of condoms on the black market. He'd calculated the number of times he was likely to have sex with her before one of them died, and it was seven hundred. Of course he'd been wrong, poor guy, so now he was stuck with the merchandise, which he thought he might as well dispose of. At a profit, if possible."

Maybe Gigi was embellishing this tale, but I was so intent on memorizing at least a few of his gestures that I didn't question its veracity. And anyway his delivery was distracting. He kept sticking his hand—the one holding the cigarette—under his shirt collar to scratch his neck. And every time he introduced a new character he would wring his own features into a version of that person's face—you wouldn't have thought his own could contain so many others.

Around us on the terrace, tables were being claimed. Parties of diners, overdressed, with glittery watches, were sitting down and confabbing with the waiters. Many of them glanced over at Gigi as he rattled on, waving his arms, and some couldn't help smiling as they recognized him. The air vibrated with the clinking of tableware and the laughter of women. At intervals I could hear the snarl of a Vespa on the other side of the arbor that screened the terrace from the street. When a waiter came, Gigi asked for more wine and I ordered ziti.

"My friend Abinotto is basically a good person," Gigi said. "But his concierge's salary wasn't enough to live on. He needed more money, okay? So he began to run errands for the people in his building. They'd give him money to buy things for them, and of course he skimmed off a percentage for himself. *Così si arrangiava*— that was how he got by. And, well, as he ran these errands, his lodge began to fill up with merchandise—the old pistol and the condoms had company now. There were boxes full of contraband cigarettes for the smuggler, who was afraid of keeping them in his own place, and porn videos for the old widower, and in the end Abinotto's lodge was packed with all this stuff—the pistol, the condoms, the cigarettes, the videos."

I thought Gigi's tale had the neatness, the brilliant illumination, of a story by Boccaccio, who lived in Naples for eleven years and adored the city. In Boccaccio's stories the people acted the way you'd expect them to act, with direct, inescapable consequences—everyone was bathed in a high, searching light that left nowhere to hide. I was smiling at Gigi's story, but I could already see the police sniffing around Abinotto's lodge, making the obvious connection between the porn videos and the seven hundred condoms and the beautiful girls upstairs; the pistol and the contraband cigarettes wouldn't help matters any. So Abinotto's arrest wasn't about to surprise me. What did surprise me was that Gigi, as he was wrapping up his routine, stuttering and nervously scratching his chest, bobbled a lighted cigarette and dropped it right down his shirtfront. Retrieving it just above his belt, he fished it out from under his shirt, inserted it in the corner of his mouth, and kept on talking, unscathed.

Later, I asked him point-blank to show me some Neapolitan gestures. He said, "What do you mean? What gestures?"

~~~

Gigi was one of many friends made in Naples that year, friends I didn't so much look up, each time I arrived, as run into within a matter of hours. The city was that convivial, our social circuits that intertwined.

In the months following my first encounter with Benedetta, I came as often as I could. Arriving at Piazza Garibaldi and dodging the sundry confidence games proposed to me there, I would deposit my suitcase at whatever lodgings I could find and begin to nose around town. I was struck by the mixed dignity and playfulness of the architecture, and inevitably I noticed where our bombs had fallen in 1942–43—in the port zone, around Piazza Cavour, wherever some monstrous tower block had risen to fill a gap. Yet no degree of damage could have blunted Naples's topographical splendor. As in other Mediterranean cities, the ascending streets and waterfront promenades offered a variety of marine views, but this coast was unique in its way of curling lazily back upon itself. For here the empty, anxiety-inducing horizon of the sea was truncated by the farther shore of the bay, and I felt cheered when, peering across the water, I saw only more dwellings, stirrings, signs of life. There could be nothing more full of expectancy, I felt—of renewed initiation into the mysteries of Latin civilization—than to walk just after sunset along the marina, among the crowds of young people taking their evening stroll, and watch a vast dusting of lights, like an earthbound Milky Way, blink on in the headland of Posillipo.

My dominant emotion was a kind of excited puzzlement. I was like a person happy to be lost, for the metropolis was so involuted, so multilayered, that my mind could not begin to discern any spatial logic in it. The facades of magnificent palazzi fronted on alleys so narrow that they would never again be seen in their totality. The gray walls of conventual compounds screened superb churches from any common awareness of their existence. And certain interiors had been subject to infinite subdivision, a crypt turning into a maze of chapels, the chapels into a host of even tinier tombs, the tiny tombs into cookie tins filled with human skulls, scapulars, broken tibia, rusty ex-votos. The kaleidoscopic impression continued to work on me even as my visits grew longer, and then, late that winter—about half a year after I'd met Benedetta—I decided to stay on indefinitely.

I found a sublet in a crowded, run-down district where lines of wash flapped overhead and baskets were lowered from windows to receive bread or wine. This district was the Quartieri Spagnoli, built in the mid-seventeenth century to "quarter" the troops of the Spanish viceroy but otherwise unconnected to Spain. Most of the Quartieri consisted of low, tenement-like buildings, some of whose outer walls were still braced by tubular scaffolding, a vestige of the earthquake of 1980. These structures stood packed together like dominoes in a box, but among them rose a number of fine palazzi, mottled, peeling, and ostentatiously neglected, their courtyards shrouded in tangles of clotheslines. The Quartieri, I believe, more than any other neighborhood, had spawned Naples's reputation as a raggedy sort of place.

I knew of the district's reputation for violence, caused by rival camorra clans, but I never felt menaced in the streets. Actually I was rarely alone in the streets, which teemed with people of all ages, including some super-sociable pensioners who did little but talk: you could pass two old ladies talking on a corner and come back later, when the shadows were twice as long, and they'd still be planted there, talking. The poorest residents lived in the tiny *bassi,* or street-level flats, and as I passed their wide-open doors or windows I'd glimpse intimate yet completely unself-conscious scenes: tired housewives fanning themselves under pictures of Padre Pio; muscular youngbloods shining up their Vespas next to their beds; groups of girls sewing or basting skirts and dresses. All over the Quartieri, teenagers and children worked, and worked hard. The seamstresses were known for their ability to counterfeit the most finely tailored Milanese garments, and local gossip had it that they actually produced, at substandard wages, a fair proportion of the real thing.

In Naples the rich and the poor did not, and still do not, live as they do elsewhere. The rich did not stake out the center of town, as in most European cities, leaving the suburbs to the poor, nor was it the other way around, as in America. What counted in Naples—at least, in the traditional quarters—was (more or less) how far above ground you dwelt. The *bassi,* which had no windows besides those that gave on the street (many back rooms had none at all), were inhabited by the less fortunate. Wealthier residents lived higher up in the same buildings, in breezy apartments with tall windows and arbor-shaded terraces. Yet generally the poor and the middle class were on good terms, sharing a common culture and ancestry and saluting one another cordially in the vernacular dialect. On stifling summer evenings, some occupants of the *bassi* casually furnished the pavement in front of their homes with tables and chairs, turning them into rooms without walls, and this arrangement felt normal to everyone.

My own tiny flat—one room on top of another—was at the back of a courtyard as high and narrow as a ship's funnel; I never once saw sunlight enter this shaft. Piranesian staircases, a Neapolitan commonplace, climbed around its walls. A person walking upstairs might first be visible from the back, disappear for a moment, reappear as a bust in an oval window, then turn into a pair of feet beneath a railing before vanishing altogether. Just off the courtyard, in a cupboard-like space, a curly-headed youth would sit for hours on end, drowned in soft blue light; I supposed he was studying something.

Inside my flat, I felt engulfed by the reverberant noise of the courtyard. Early each morning I'd hear the same sounds: a big dog panting and panting, like someone whispering nonsense; two women ceaselessly chatting, their voices fruitily intertwined; and a young man, whom I judged to be afflicted by some mental disability, exchanging courtesies with the concierge on her balcony.

"Good morning, Donna Concetta," he would say.

"And good morning to you, Peppino."

"I wish you a fine day, Donna Concetta."

"And I return the wish, Peppino."

During the daylight hours I was away as a matter of course, interviewing people or reading in the Biblioteca Nazionale; but at night, as I lay on the verge of sleep, the words and cries of a thousand families wove a blurry, somniferous tapestry of sound. This fabric was frequently rent by hollering and honking—an orchestra tuning up in a barnyard might have produced the same effect—but none of it bothered me much. I was resigned by now to the cacophony of the south.

Outside, in the streets, I noted a casual but disconcerting erasure of the joints between things. Where, I would wonder, out on a stroll, did that police station end and that fish market begin? Could it really be true, as it certainly seemed, that one side of the church of Montecalvario metamorphosed into a graffiti-scrawled tenement? And that open parlor with rows of chairs along the walls—was it an old folks' home or a *bisca,* a clandestine gambling parlor? Often I couldn't tell what was what, or what belonged with what: laundry racks sat out on the pavement, doorposts served as soccer goals, and one genial fellow in a sleeveless undershirt—I passed him evening after evening—would set up a chair in the street facing his *basso* and watch television through the open window. The chaos of the Quartieri flattened my powers of discrimination.

Nightfall brought out crowds of people. Most wanted to catch the breeze, and stood chattering in the street or hung in profusion over the gates of their dutch doors like hats on a hat tree. Ladies, not necessarily old, sat for hours in rows along the lanes, saluting the passersby, a custom known as *fa' a vita* (which can also, secondarily, mean "turning tricks"); they had estimated the pavement so exactly that vans passed within an inch of their toes. Walking in a lane where all the doors and windows had been thrown open, I saw a *basso* where transvestites played tombola, another entirely filled by a bed piled high with romping children, and another that doubled as a shop selling—I couldn't say what, exactly. Was it blocks of ice or contraband cigarettes? Wardrobe-sized shops jostled one another on both sides of the streets, and their windows, packed with gaudily colored diminutive goods (cheese graters, frying pan sets, celluloid sponges, plastic tableware), dissolved into blizzards of brilliant color. Overhead, the clotheslines, billowing like the sails of a clipper ship, seemed sacred somehow, a declaration of thrift and progenitive power; and in the pork butchers' shops the displays of tripe and offal, neatly sliced open so that the insides of the insides might be rendered manifest, formed tall, dripping altars.

Around the corner from my place was an excellent pizzeria, equipped with the usual woodburning oven and stocked with firewood. Outside, every evening, a host of teenagers gathered, mounted on Vespas and mopeds and surrounded by their friends and younger children. Some of the teenagers struck carefully studied poses on their saddles, preening in front of the windshields as if before a boudoir mirror, while others wove flirtatiously through the crowd, alone or in twos and threes. Apparently any number of kids could squeeze onto a moped. I saw one carrying three shrieking hussies of about thirteen cruising the alley at regular intervals, charging the boys. I saw a Vespa-borne family of four—teenage papa, mamma, and two infants, plus bulging grocery bags—sidewind nimbly through the knots of loiterers. I saw tiny tots whiz past, wedged between their papa's knees, helmetless heads uptilted, eyes dazzled by the world streaming by.

'A *munnazzella,* in dialect, means he who's always dirty or grungy, something like "Smudgy-Face." That was the childhood nickname of Donato Casillo, who became my pal in the Quartieri. He had grown up mostly near the Largo Baracche, where an underground bomb shelter long survived, a dreary reminder of the war. As a kid he lived on the street, fooling around with boys who would later become thugs or jailbirds or get themselves murdered, casualties of the district's clan strife. But Donato, who was not a casualty, had warm memories of his childhood, especially of his grandmother's *basso,* which served as a sort of improvised social center for the neighborhood, much as fast-disappearing storefronts do today in Little Italy, in Manhattan. Handsome in a typically Neapolitan way—chubby build, chocolaty eyes ever ready to give you the benefit of the doubt, brow framed in thick, dark hair—Donato was, I always felt, a sort of audience of one: when his day was done, nothing pleased him more than to contemplate the pageant of life. His father had been a goldsmith—not rich, an ordinary artisan—and Donato, too, was drawn to manual arts and trades. As an adolescent he taught himself to play the piano and the organ, and he hung around with artists and musicians, including the great popular singer Pino Daniele, whom he knew through Pino's little brother. Then he got interested in photography and bought himself an enlarger; working for *Il Mattino* as a photoreporter, he began to range all over the city.

Only a few photographers in Naples can avoid the necessity of freelancing. The rest do news stories and catalogues, wedding albums and hotel brochures—whatever happens their way. Donato did all these things, but nuptials, a big source of cash in Naples, offered the most consistent revenue, and in the end he stuck to wedding photography. His studio consisted of a small commercial storefront surmounted by an office of the same dimensions reachable by a narrow stairway. Blowups of blissful brides half covered the walls, and sometimes the former brides, looking notably less blissful, dropped by for a chat. During Donato's frequent absences the place was tenanted by his nephew Aldo, a tall boy with mischievous eyes who was taking a course in photography. Late in the afternoons, Donato's pretty teenage daughter, Monica, might also pass the time there, waiting for her father to finish the day's assignments and tormenting Aldo if there was nothing better to do; he would respond in kind. When asked by patrons if they were related, they would answer, in unison, "He's my cousin, unfortunately," and "She's my cousin, unfortunately."

Donato knew that in Naples, among the popular classes, the most important moment in a woman's life was when she felt the marriage band slipping onto her finger. The second most important was when she stood with her new husband in front of the Duomo, in a blaze of white, and had her picture taken. She and her mother and her sisters (and presumably, one day, her daughters) would revere the wedding album as a sort of holy book, and in that sense every Neapolitan girl was a fundamentalist. Nothing that subsequently happened in the marriage, no heresy, apostasy, or schism, could desanctify this testament, which confirmed that the bride had assumed her rightful place in the cycle of life. In Naples, then, at least in the more traditional quarters, the métier of wedding photographer served an almost priestly purpose.

A lot of the brides Donato photographed were very young— young enough for him to remember having photographed their mothers' weddings when he was getting started. Time and again, in his upstairs office, he would tell me of his dismay at having to deal with girls who so closely resembled their mothers, usually in their most socially doubtful points. "Carolina at sixteen had a shotgun wedding," he would say, sighing, "and now Teresa's having one, too." These girls, he felt, with their "fiancés" and gold jewelry, their designer tops and flashy scooters, were allowed no time to develop; they masqueraded as adults without an adult's understanding of life.

Aware that his wedding albums would become his clients' most treasured possessions, Donato proceeded with the utmost care. Like a film director, he had to organize the entire wedding day as a sort of montage, from the moment the bride emerged from her dressing room to the end of the festivities late that night. Without turning into a martinet, he insisted on marshaling a flattering yet plausible record of the unfolding marriage rite. The process, he told me, required unfailing diplomacy, and listening to his stories, I came to see him as a sort of Talleyrand of the Quartieri Spagnoli.

Because of his background and natural discretion, Donato had entrée where practically nobody else did. He was frequently called upon, for instance, to photograph fugitives from justice. Naples was full of them. Since they couldn't leave their lodgings and didn't want to attract attention, they invariably wore track suits, even when posing for a photograph. Some were powerful camorristi, mafia bosses, but like the young brides, they deferred to Donato's judgment, timidly following his instructions to smile pleasantly or refrain from sidelong glances. These appointments sometimes made Donato nervous, especially since the authorities might intervene at any moment. Once a police commissioner requested the negatives of a fugitive's wedding pictures, and Donato had to turn them over.

Donato photographed the wedding of Vincenzo Maresca, known to all as Babà. At the glittering reception Sergio Bruni sang and also Nino D'Angelo—the same Nino D'Angelo who later recorded so many songs about kids going wrong. As it happened, Nino was a singer-songwriter, not a *cantante di giacca*—the sort of wedding singer who wore a jacket and silk scarf and sang about the sorrows of crime—and he bridled at the guests' heedless chatter through the pieces he had written. After three numbers he said, "Thank you and good night," and he was just walking off-stage when Babà slapped him, hard, and pointed imperiously at the microphone. Nino sang about twenty more songs, but it gave Donato gooseflesh to think of Nino, a genuine artist whether or not you liked his music, being slapped in front of everybody, and standing there sobbing and sobbing.

Donato had the good fortune to be amazed at his own surroundings. Unspoiled by his youthful discovery of his city's vitality and exoticism, he remained captivated, too, by the characters in the neighborhood, who often dropped by his studio for a chat at the end of the day. Of course it's a custom, this business of visiting a friend's shop or office at closing time—people gather to gossip, to rejoice or complain, to smoke, to have coffee or an aperitif—and since I was soon dropping by Donato's about three times a week, I can say I'd contracted the bug. The place was tiny, as I've said—just one room on top of another—but in my imagination it was expansible as a concertina. If I'd been away for a week I never knew whom I might find there, what backdrops might cover the walls, or how the furniture might be arranged. One evening I came by to discover, upstairs, a stage set of a manorial library; another time it was a forest of tree boles and toadstools—a Carnival scene for children.

Usually out during the day, Donato would seat himself toward closing time behind his desk, facing the street. Plate glass had been let into the whole wall opposite him, so that each evening he could watch a sort of movie or parade consisting of all the tradespeople, the pretty girls, and the local oddballs on their way home, in addition, of course, to his own friends and clients. Often, just as I was arriving, one or two such clients would be leaving the studio. And often, too, when they had gone, he would look at me with an expression of comical despair.

"That," he would say (finger tapping skull), "is one of the craziest women I have ever met."

Or (the praying gesture): "What can I do to get her to raise that neckline?"

Or (eyes rolling heavenward): "That couple act like they're five years old."

But Donato's job was to mirror the world around him, not to judge or improve it; and he seemed content.

That neighborhood, a confluence of byways paved in black, lava-like slabs, always thickened with dawdling people before the siesta and at closing time. The shops, already employing any number of superfluous relatives, doubled as venues for business sidelines and amorous byplay after hours. The general sensation of delay, of eddying circularity, was compounded by off-street meanders and courtyard lagoons, where hoarse-voiced, snaggletoothed traders peddled knockoff shoes and shiny watches and polyester ties, while in the crossings itinerant fishmongers and pushcart men hawking vegetables from the volcanic slopes around the curve of the bay provoked scrimmages of housewives, rendering the streets impassable.

Like all districts, this one had its tutelary figures. Each week a pensioner named Armando made the circuit of the streets, his wooden case strapped over his shoulder, ringing a bell. Armando knew that certain elderly Neapolitans could no longer play lotto, the time-honored passion of Naples, usually because they lay stranded at home. So he had decided to launch his own numbers game, which he operated with his meager retirement savings, permitting the infirm to avail themselves of the pleasures of fortune. He was, you might say, the Saint Francis de Sales of the gambling world, devotedly making his charitable rounds.

Every once in a while a balding, unkempt man drove by Donato's on a motorcycle, at a perfectly peaceable speed, exciting talk in the streets. They called him Agostino 'O Pazzo, or Crazy Agostino. Years earlier he had mastered the art of riding his rebuilt Gilera 125 through the quarter faster than seemed humanly possible, climbing even the flights of stone stairs at top speed. He was then eighteen, fueled by adolescent fury at the absence of jobs for young men just out of school. Squad cars and motorcycle carabinieri chased him all over the Quartieri, but his technique was so exquisite, and the map of the casbah branded so precisely in his memory, that he always eluded capture. Since then he had calmed down and become a curio dealer over in Piazza dei Girolamini, like his father and grandfather before him, and I used to go there sometimes and try to induce him to talk. At first he demurred, for by now he had three children and wore a chastened, embarrassed look; but finally he did tell me a thing or two. He told how the authorities had thrown up barricades across all the streets of the old city to catch him. He told how for the better part of a week three thousand young men and boys had occupied those streets to defend him against a contingent of seven hundred police and carabinieri, and how, though he was never captured on his bike, eventually he was apprehended in a car, in Piazza Gesù, and did a little "time served," waiting for his trial. When I asked him the secret of his success, which meant, as far as I was concerned, the technique of taking corners at ninety miles an hour, he said, "Tomatoes—I eat a lot of tomatoes." Since this could be said of everyone in Naples, I decided to leave it at that.

It was striking how many people Donato knew: singers, comedians, painters, journalists, chefs, small businessmen, fixers, eccentrics from all over town. When drifting through the neighborhood, they always looked in on him. It was the eccentrics, men of bright eye and loose tongue, who interested me most, stirring my nostalgia for the run-down Manhattan of my childhood, the Manhattan of street-corner wiseacres, ranting émigré barbers, and cafeteria philosophers.

I recall that on an evening of intermittent rain, a small, grizzled, fit-looking man dropped by the studio for a moment's conversation. He enunciated his vowels unusually well and had the faceted facial bones of a poet or an aristocrat, but he turned out to be an ambulance driver.

"This may not be the best city in the world for my profession," he told me, with a wry smile, "but I've been at it for over forty years."

"Oh, really?" I said. He looked no more than fifty. "How old are you, then?"

"Sixty-four," he replied, "and in all my time I have always shut the rear door of my ambulance myself, with these hands."

He held out his hands in the demonstrative Neapolitan manner, as though I'd never seen a pair before.

"Tell him the story," Donato said.

"Once," the man said, "when I was starting out in this job, I let someone else close the rear door, and, well . . . I lost my patient. I looked around and he just wasn't there. I drove back and found him, lying on his backboard in the middle of an alley and surrounded by a crowd of hysterically weeping people."

"Did he die?" I said. The question was crude, but I couldn't help asking it.

"No, he didn't, but I almost did. He sat up, shouting 'Assassino!' and pulled a knife on me. He was quick with that knife, I can tell you."

The ambulance driver smiled his wry smile and gazed out the shopwindow at the ragtag column of people heading home, all the faces we would see again and not see again. Then a distant thunderhead rumbled, and the pavement grew dark with rain, and I thought about the man lying in the lane, outraged, drawing his knife.

On another evening a hungry man entered Donato's office, preceded by a sfogliatella. As the man devoured the pastry he scattered flakes on the floor in front of him, and also on his shirt and jacket. After saluting us both, he said to me, "You look like a foreigner."

I said, "I am a foreigner."

As he loosened his jacket, something saurian about his appearance, about the folds and pores of his jowls and neck, sprang into prominence. The man sank into a chair and looked about him with lazy satisfaction. Folds of fat bunched around his broad, powerful nape; he had, I thought, the sagging strength of an aging zoo reptile, and his bulging dark eyes swiveled in their sockets and fixed me with ominous solicitude.

"Do you live here?" he asked me.

"I do," I said.

He considered this. "Do you walk around alone in the Quartieri at night?" he asked, in a tone of commiseration.

"I do not walk around in the Quartieri at night," I replied.

"Do you wear a Rolex?" he asked.

"I do not *own* a Rolex," I said.

"And you know what a *pacco* is?" he went on. "I would be very ashamed of my city if you were to fall for a *pacco*."

"I am super-careful not to fall for a *pacco*," I replied. "Believe me," I continued, foolishly, "I have a second sense that warns me off falling for a *pacco*."

"Oh? You have a *second sense?*" he said, amiably, but with the barest hint of sarcasm. "I wish you'd teach it to me." The last of the sfogliatella had vanished into his mouth, leaving traces of powdered sugar on his stubbly chin. "Do you know what I am— my profession, I mean?"

"He's a scalper," said Donato, using the Italian word, *bagarino*.

"*Bagarino, bagarozzo,* it's all the same to me," said the scalper. "I am a scavenger animal. But I have a doctorate in science as well! My science is sidewalk-ology. And what sidewalk-ology has taught me is—*this!*"

With astonishing nimbleness the scalper jumped to his feet, thrust out his rump, and backed tightly into the corner of the room, where he wriggled from side to side.

"May I invite the two of you to my favorite pizzeria, up where I live, in the hospital district?" he asked us, wriggling. "This would give me very great pleasure." He smiled at us lewdly, exultantly, as he showed us how he sharpened his rear to the finest possible point.

My initial impression was that the scalper, whose name was Luca Corsaro, wished only to tease me for being a tenderfoot. But in time his various offers, chiefly that of showing me how to protect my back in a city known for deceit, would turn out to be genuine, however hammily put forth. I was to see a good deal more of Luca the *bagarino*.

Because the Quartieri slanted uphill onto fairly high ground, it was possible to make out, from the street corner nearest my *basso*, the summit of the Vesuvius. Few days went by when I did not see it, now snowcapped, now wreathed in mist or lit by the setting sun. And this, I felt, was in the order of things: it belonged to the genius of the Italian city to represent itself with a single emblem, derived, as the case might be, from some monument, pastime, or natural feature. If Rome had Saint Peter's, Siena the Palio, and Pisa the Leaning Tower, Naples had that great gray blister, star of innumerable calendar photos and pizzeria murals. Yet the matter did not end there. For the city was volcanic not only in substance, being constructed largely of igneous stone, but also in temperament, since the clouds of the volcano, active until 1944, had been poetically absorbed into the population's inner life. There was something of brimstone and pumice in the Neapolitan spirit, and this every citizen sensed in his or her own way.

Sometimes, as I gazed across the water at the dormant cone, I wondered whether geography had left such a forceful impress on the society of any other land. If Naples had long been celebrated as one of Europe's most beautiful cities, that was partly because its bloom was so clearly blighted by mortality. It lay, almost literally, in shadow, and this very condition had attracted artists for hundreds of years. During the nineteenth century, a sort of painting had come into vogue in which a frivolous vision of the Campanian landscape, embodied by vine-laden walls and barefoot girls, was invariably offset by a crater smoking somewhere on the horizon. Wandering around the streets, I saw, in gallery and antique shop windows, hundreds of these sentimental canvases. They conjured up an age of romantic pathos, when this region stood as the geographic counterpart to the lovely dying courtesan of popular literature. Naples was a lily whose petals flaunted the rust spots of corruption: a memento mori.

And it was true that the people of Naples had had to accept the fact that civilization exists only on geological sufferance, subject to sudden caprices. They had to concede that threatening formations like volcanoes tend to mold the mores of the societies around them. So they had long ago observed, whether rightly or wrongly, that just as a volcano extrudes lava and ash, they as individuals tended to turn themselves inside-out through constant playacting and the venting of confessions. They thought themselves fatalists and high-strung, too keenly aware of the brevity of life, and of course this disposition was not unique to them, shared as it was with other peoples of the south. But in Naples it had been consciously formalized—aestheticized, you might say—toward the end of the seventeenth century.

This much I learned: that as the Baroque age neared its convulsive triumph, a number of talented architects came to the city and filled it with domes, swooping pediments, and strange composite inventions. I saw them wherever I walked, those church facades like stage sets, those towering stone pinnacles at the center of public squares. To my sense, the pinnacles, crawling with grotesque carvings, had issued a license for theatrics: they had silently proclaimed that everyone—the priest in his biretta, the lace-draped lady of fashion, the bravo with his dueling knives—was henceforth onstage. And this Baroque staginess, though certainly now ebbing, had never completely disappeared. Even the piazza beneath Uncle Ippolito's window, with its shopkeepers and street traders and beggars and loiterers, often impressed me as a sort of psychodrama: people leaned out of balconies to call across the square to each other, but might just as likely poke out of opposite ends of the same building and shout to each other along the wall. Of course there were Neapolitans—skeptical Benedetta among them—who claimed that this theatricality was no more intrinsic to Naples than to any other city. But she made her point twirling her hands.

Nothing better expressed the local fondness for display than the frequency of street processions, which took place on important saints' days. Chief among these was the Feast of San Gennaro, when the martyred bishop's blood was promenaded through the city in a tall, ornate vial disconcertingly reminiscent of a hookah. But San Gennaro had become a formality; it scarcely resembled its rowdier cousin in Little Italy, in Manhattan. That late September affair, wildly popular and thoroughly commercialized, I had slogged through several times, always a little unwillingly, in my teens and early twenties. (To attend, as a well-wisher, a crowded Mass celebrated in honor of a saint decapitated by the Romans, only to enter, ten minutes later, the booth of the Amazing Two-Headed Lady, was a distinctly unnerving transition.) Now that I was in Naples, though, I remembered that millions of Americans had roots in this part of Italy, and I began to look for parallels between Italian-American festivals and Neapolitan ones. I found them aplenty, though not during San Gennaro; rather at the feast of the Madonna dell'Arco, on Easter Monday, or at the Feast of the Madonna del Carmine, in July, or at any number of other popular celebrations held in towns in the outlying province. I would notice the irrepressible affection for *luminarie,* those decorative lightbulbs strung across streets. I'd notice the overfed children, the vendors of watermelon slices and corn on the cob and fried batter (*zeppole* in New York, though this means "doughnuts" in Naples), the stands hawking sausages and sodas; about the only thing I do not recall from Naples is the ouchless tattoo.

Living in my *basso* was like having my ear to the seashell of the world, and this applied especially to those recurring street processions. I could hear them approaching from a distance, always straight at me as if fired from a cannon; their din was ferocious. Originating from one of the many small churches in the Quartieri, these processions would parade a float of the Virgin or some saint up and down the district, stopping at every crossing to wheel in all four directions, with a trumpet blast toward each cardinal point. The jolly, potbellied bruisers who carried those floats were another transatlantic replication. They looked just like their counterparts in Brooklyn, right down to their sweaty T-shirts stamped with a haloed countenance.

Once—it was the evening of an important saint's day—I heard a knock at my door. This surprised me, first because you usually had to ring at the outer portal of the building in order to reach my *basso,* and second because nobody knocked at my door, ever. I made appointments to meet people in cafés or bars, where I sat and listened, taking notes on my spiral notepad for some article or the book I was hoping to write someday. But this time when I opened the door I saw Benedetta standing there, in jeans and a cotton blouson top with tiny nacre buttons. She had never seen my place, and as she took it in she granted me one brief glance. No Lombard contessa on her first visit to Naples could have held her nose more disdainfully high. I wanted her to look at me, but all she could see was my *basso*.

She went right to work, full of scorn. She kicked off her shoes and found the broom closet—I didn't even know I had one—and filled a pail and mopped the floor. Pushing me out of the way, she cleaned the entire *angolo cottura,* or kitchenette, and the floor of the tiny bathroom. Holding her back straight, she scrubbed with fury. She was almost done (I stood, mortified, in the window embrasure) when the racket started outside. And then, as it drew nearer and began to crawl inside our ears, she did what I usually did when a procession came by: she squirmed into her shoes and ran out. It was, after all, a marching band: irresistible.

The outside portal was closed for the night, but from my window I looked across the courtyard and watched Benedetta lean out the pedestrian hatch that swung open in one of the double doors. I saw her blouson catch the breeze and ripple as she watched the procession go by. I heard the wild discordant music pass up the street. Then, in the half-light, I watched Benedetta stride back toward my door. Her eyebrows gave her a determined look. They were like a boy's eyebrows, but some boys' features look even better on girls.

She was shaking her head as she came in. *"Bestiale,"* she muttered: "Ghastly." "That sort of thing is why this damned city never gets anywhere." Again she kicked off her shoes, and looked at me slyly. "What are you doing in this dump, anyway?" she said. "I mean, what is this, some sort of anthropological exploit?"

"You tell me," I replied.

2

In Uncle Ippolito's Room

*I*f as I often think there is something vestigial about the city of Naples, then Uncle Ippolito's bedroom was a relic within a relic. Lofty, fairly spacious, it had two tall windows overlooking the piazza, and its coved and frescoed ceiling, though much ravaged by moisture, suggested a canopied pavilion. Most of the room's furniture, including its curtains, had long since been carted away, and in the resulting emptiness time seemed to stand still. Needing something to look at, I was drawn to the windows, where I would stand and gaze at the scene below. I would study the people in the piazza, their faces and gestures, how they gathered and drifted apart.

I had been away for months, and had recently come back. Ippolito's flat was up for sale now, along with his piano, and Benedetta was camping there till a buyer could be found. In due course she invited me in more and more often, leaving me alone sometimes while she went out on various errands. Though her stated intention was usually to borrow a book or do research for a paper, I grew used to seeing her return with a spring in her step and a trophy in hand from one of her favorite secondhand shops—

some craquelure-veined tile, perhaps, or a chipped but pretty faience pitcher. Since I had never known her late uncle, being in the denuded flat did not sadden me, and I came to associate it only with Benedetta, with her form silhouetted against its bare walls. Though I could not decide what name to attach to my feelings for her, I liked being at Uncle Ippolito's, whether in her company or simply alone, unreachable and able to work undisturbed. For there, I was certain, no one but Benedetta could find me.

The first time it happened I was alone, idling by one of those tall windows, looking down at the piazza. In any other Italian city such a square—a formal garden enlivened by six or eight palm trees and surrounded by weathered palazzi of ocher and reddish hue—would have been pristinely beautiful. But here the buildings were missing chunks of their intonaco, many of the balconies' wrought-iron railings had fallen off, and the palms stood at eccentric angles to one another. Misbegotten and ill tended, the garden was like a purpose that had slipped somebody's mind: there being no clear way to walk through its maze of hedges, pedestrians would enter it, soon get confused, and beat a muddled retreat. I had been considering it for a while with a practical, improving American eye when the telephone rang.

"Is this Benedetta's friend?" said a female voice.

I hesitated, and then I said, "Yes." It was the easiest answer. The expression "Benedetta's friend" seemed to imply some exclusivity in our attachment, but perhaps that was not so inaccurate. I didn't recognize the voice.

"I'm Loredana, dear," the voice said. "Maybe she's mentioned me to you." The voice, wavering and solicitous, sounded middle-aged, maybe older.

"I'm afraid she hasn't," I said. "She's out. If you want to talk to her, she'll be back very soon."

"Actually I wanted to say hello to you, dear. I wanted to find out how you're doing. Do you like it here? Are you enjoying yourself? They say our city isn't an easy place to adjust to—not that I'd know, really. I've never been anywhere else."

The unexpected familiarity of these phrases troubled me only slightly. Loredana's tone conveyed abstract benevolence, and though I had no idea who she was, I didn't see any reason to be on my guard. I had the odd sensation that she knew me.

"I do like it here," I said. "The food, of course." Nobody who said a thing like that was giving much away about himself.

"I'm so glad," said Loredana. "We're proud of our cuisine—perhaps too proud. It can be awfully heavy. But don't you love Giuseppe's sfogliatelle?"

"Of course," I said. Giuseppe—Beppe, we called him—was Benedetta's father; he kept a pastry shop on a commercial street in the old city. Now that I'd told one sociable fib—as it happened, I didn't care for sfogliatelle—I resolved not to tell any more.

My resolve was unnecessary. As our chat continued, somewhat uncomfortably, Loredana turned out to be a shrewd conversational bargainer, always appearing to pay out as much as she took in but in fact stating only commonplaces while eliciting quite earnest responses. Was her slyness even conscious? She had a knack of mentioning popular novels or plays that prompted decided opinions from me, which I tried and failed to repress. Increasingly humiliated by my verbal incontinence, I found myself growing impatient.

"Listen," I said, perhaps a little curtly, "I'll get Benedetta to call you. She should be back any minute now." I peered down at the people in the piazza, searching for Benedetta's tidy little figure—at this season she usually wore jeans and a sweater with fashionably overlong sleeves—but I didn't see her. "She's just gone around the corner for a moment," I said. "Something must have detained her."

"Don't trouble her," Loredana said. "I'll call back later myself."

As I hung up, still wondering who Loredana was, a bluish cloud-shadow bathed the piazza, giving it an alien look. For a moment it was as though I'd never seen it before—those scruffy people drifting helplessly around the garden, those bits of trash scuttering along the pavement . . . But of course it wasn't alien, which I knew when I concentrated on any one thing: the gypsy girl sitting with her cup out; the toy vendor hawking his mechanical birds. Then I spotted Benedetta, walking briskly toward me, her arms folded across her chest for warmth. She looked up, smiled, and waved.

Despite my absence, Benedetta and I had soon fallen back into the patterns established by our earlier periods together. Her schedule was elastic, and she always found time to spend with me: we walked, visited churches, went to antique fairs and junk shops. For some reason, however, I thought of her as a friend, and only after some weeks did I admit to myself that mere friends do not have morning coffee together as often as we were now doing. We had, without discussing it, become lovers again—it was almost as if the city itself, dimmed by Baroque cloudbursts and illumined by equally sudden flashes of sunshine, had wished this closeness upon us. Then, too, from a practical standpoint, living in Naples did not inconvenience me. I had brought along some freelance work, and I was pleased to observe that the Vesuvius, with its last scumble of snow, had never looked more pictorial. Day after day I walked through rain- or sun-washed alleys to one of Benedetta's favorite churches, the Santissimi Apostoli, where almost flat on my back I scrutinized the tortures of Lanfranco's martyrs. It did not for the moment occur to me to live in any other way, nor to question the nature of my feelings for Benedetta—or of hers for me.

When Benedetta came in, I said, "Who's Loredana?"

"Why, did she call?" She sat down on her uncle's piano stool, shivering and rubbing her shoulders.

I said, "A few minutes ago."

"What about? Anything special?"

"She called to welcome me back, she said. I'm sure it was you she really wanted."

"Why do you say that? If she told you she wanted to welcome you back, I'm sure that's what she wanted to do."

"Possibly, but I don't know her," I said. "Why don't you tell me who she is?"

Benedetta drew a deep breath. Her hands slunk inside her sleeves, where they often hid, like bashful animals. Then she told me about Loredana.

Loredana, she said, was an older lady who was very fond of her and her sister Tina. She served, you might say, as their guardian angel, and surely there was nothing unusual in that. Didn't certain families everywhere, she plaintively asked, have such a figure in their lives? Childless women often grew attached to a friend's or a relative's children. These auntie types babysat the little ones and took them on outings or to kids' afternoon shows of one sort or another, and though Loredana herself did not do any of these things, she filled much the same role in other ways. She had no blood connection to the family, but it had seemed for years as if she did. Once, when Benedetta was still very small, Beppe had spent a month in hospital, and Loredana had helped out during his illness—that was how the relationship had started. After that her attentions became regular, a sanctified habit, and she kept in constant touch with the sisters. Sometimes she did considerable favors for them and sometimes she merely embarrassed them, but at bottom they accepted her implicitly, lovingly, as one does a benign older relative: she was part of the climate of their lives. Always the soul of tact, she never distressed or seriously discomfited anyone in the family.

One thing, though, was unusual about Loredana—indeed, extremely unusual. "She's afraid to go out," Benedetta told me. "She never leaves her apartment." Of course this wasn't strictly true, because certain circumstances—emergencies, doctor visits, the odd wedding or confirmation—compel any able-bodied person to go out; but Loredana very seldom left home. "Her heart races terribly whenever she has to step outside," Benedetta explained. "She hates open spaces, she's afraid the worst will happen. She suffers horrible panics if she has to walk across the piazza to the greengrocer." Benedetta supposed that Loredana suffered from a phobia, whatever exactly that was, though Naples, if truth be told, positively fed phobias, especially in women. In Naples women might be trapped inside moving walls of traffic, pickpocketed, exposed to obscene propositions, pursued by strange men; their purses might be snatched. Though Loredana's species of phobia might have frustrated any other auntie, might have clipped, so to speak, her angel wings, Loredana found ingenious ways to sidestep it. If the girls' mother was away, she would send over large platters of sartù di riso or pasticcio di maccheroni. She would explain ablative absolutes or irrational numbers in long letters to Tina, who had problems with her schoolwork. And she would buy the sisters sentimental but useful gifts, such as boxes of letter paper, scented soaps, scrunchies, diaries, and for birthdays jewelry of real gold. Above all, she talked to them regularly on the telephone, calling every few days to find out how they were faring.

"The poor dear pesters us with well-meaning questions," Benedetta said, her eyes misting over. "If she does that to you, be nice, okay?"

"I'll try to, but . . . I don't even know her," I said.

"Just be nice. I know you will be."

In the sacristy we sat off to one side, along the wall. We were waiting for Gemma, Benedetta's mother, to finish teaching her catechism class, but she had wandered off on one of her tangents.

"We're going through a very difficult time in this beautiful city of ours," she was saying to the group of twenty or so fidgety children. "A couple of days ago, a boy was stabbed just because he looked at the wrong girl in a discotheque. I'm sure you've heard your parents or your older brothers and sisters talking about it— it's the sort of thing that happens fairly often these days. But here, children—here we are different. We try to be gentle, to be polite. And we're certainly not members of a gang, unless it's Jesus' gang. But we do commit sins sometimes, don't we, children? What are a few of the sins we commit?"

Silence.

At length a little girl whispered, "Watching too much television."

"Being rude to your mamma," said two boys in unison.

"Fighting!" A boy cuffed another on the shoulder.

The children looked tired, and many were sniffling or coughing.

To reach the sacristy, Benedetta and I had passed through the church, a soaring, mostly Gothic building off Via Duomo. The nave lay swathed in darkness, with three or four pews luridly lit by the beams of the waning sun, and in the gloom the sacristan flitted about like a sociable phantom, greeting parents as they arrived and escorting them to the catechism class and the kids' painting class, which were about to end. The sacristy could not be sufficiently heated, and Gemma's pupils sat huddled in their quilted jackets. Gemma was a short, squarish woman with a patient, forbearing manner.

"Now read the next paragraph of your book to yourselves," Gemma said to the children. The overhead light was dim, and the children hunched over their books and read to themselves in a loud, bee-like buzz.

"Okay, that'll do," Gemma said. "Now then, Francesco"—a small boy with tangled hair looked up—"what does it mean when it says here that Jesus is 'good like the Father'?"

"You see, that's just the problem," Benedetta whispered in my ear as the boy struggled to come up with an answer. "Half their dads are on drugs, so this image of the Father—well, you see what I mean."

Gemma talked, but we barely listened. We whispered back and forth as the lesson drew toward its close. I had accompanied Benedetta to pick up her mother here once before, several weeks earlier, and I'd liked the church so much that I'd returned several times on my own, to Benedetta's horror—she detested priests. This parish, I had discovered, included one of the most ill-reputed districts in Naples, which was why at least one family member often came by to walk Gemma home after catechism class. But the parish volunteers were enterprising, I thought, with their painting and dance and theater classes for children. Befriended by the sacristan, a gaunt, abstracted fellow who spent half his time loping across the vast nave to retrieve some forgotten object, I had also come to know the younger of the church's two priests. He spoke anxiously of his desire to rescue as many of the quarter's families as possible from drugs and crime, and had a role in a clever dialect play some young parishioners were rehearsing. Yet the church steps were defiled with trash, and sometimes, even as the priest sat talking to me, street urchins threw pebbles at his window.

Now Gemma had come to the passage in Mark where Jesus cures the paralytic and forgives him his sins. "But what *is* a paralytic?" she was asking her pupils.

At first nobody ventured to answer.

"Somebody who can't move," offered a small girl.

"Really?" said Gemma. "Who can't *move*? . . . Anybody else?"

"Who can't *walk*!" shouted a larger girl, emboldened by the small girl's error.

"That's right, Antonella—a person who can't walk. Now remember that they didn't have wheelchairs in Jesus' day. That's why four men were carrying the paralytic on a pallet, which is a sort of cot. And, well, the crowd was so big that the men couldn't get the paralytic into the house where Jesus was preaching— Francesco, I'm talking!—so in order to get into the house, they had to do something special? Now then—what did they do?"

This time the children had no doubt about the answer. In an explosion of pent-up energy, laughing with delight, they screamed in unison, "They removed the roof!" Up went their arms in a pantomime of that wild, rough-and-tumble, unheard-of act. Gemma forced out a smile and held up her hands.

Benedetta looked at me. She rolled her eyes heavenward.

"You're being unfair," I whispered.

"You don't get it," she replied. "My mother's a torturer."

I sensed that she was only half joking. "This is torture?" I said. "This cute little class? These laughing children?"

"You dummy," she said. "This is the moment when the torturer gives the victim a drink of water. Before the torture starts up again."

As we walked Gemma home that night, she and Benedetta conversed at telegraphic speed about various household matters. Somehow, in the course of life, Gemma's neck had disappeared, so that her head seemed to rise directly from her shoulders. The unfortunate, tortoise-like effect suggested someone who was permanently ducking, shielding her face to avoid some imminent blow. I didn't know whether Gemma believed in the catechism word for word or had, like most churchgoing Italians, certain private reservations; but none of that seemed important—she was dedicated to helping the people of her quarter. I had also assumed that her pupils' hard-pressed parents sent them to the church, at least in part, so that someone could keep an eye on them, but Benedetta had disabused me of that idea. "It works the other way around," she said. "The kids come to Mamma and tell her what's going on at home. You know, *He knocked her down;* or *She never came home last night*—that sort of thing. So Mamma's sending the parents an indirect message. *Statevi bene, mi raccomando*—you'd better be good, and I mean it, or we're going to know all about it. Mamma's like, you know, the secret police . . ."

⥺

As time went by I forgot all about Loredana, dismissing her call as an isolated gesture of duty or perhaps merely whimsy. About a week later, though, one gloomy evening, while Benedetta was downstairs talking to her sister and I was standing at the window of Uncle Ippolito's flat looking at a band of street musicians, the telephone rang.

"It's me, Loredana."

"Good evening, Loredana, how are you?"

"Just fine, so kind of you to ask. And you?"

"I'm fine, too," I said. "Though this weather is getting me down."

"I know, dear, it's enough to try the patience of a saint." Her tone was melting, maternal. "But this isn't our real Neapolitan weather, you know. Naples is a sunny city. The sun is the best thing we've got—oh, sometimes I think it's the *only* thing we've got. I'm sure that Benedetta wants you to enjoy a lovely Neapolitan spring. But tell me, how is your flat working out? I understand it's in the Quartieri?"

"Well, it's a little noisy, I suppose. But I'm getting used to it."

"And you've got your bearings all right?"

"Pretty much."

"Listen, dear, you do know there are some dangerous districts over there, don't you? Around Montecalvario, for instance. Some unsavory people frequent the Quartieri—those misguided youngsters they call baby gangs—it pains me to have to admit this, but it's best to speak plainly, don't you think? Forewarned is forearmed, after all." My attention slipped as she filled me in on the dos and don'ts of Naples, a lengthy ledger of imperatives and prohibitions which had no other purpose than to enhance her fairygodmother status. Surely this speech was superfluous—how could she imagine, for example, that after so many visits to her city I would actually buy a radio in Forcella?

"But listen to me go on," she concluded. "I know you have other things to do. Do tell Benedetta—"

"Do you want me to get her for you?" I asked.

"No, dear, that won't be necessary. But by all means tell her I called."

This conversation (if the word applies) left me uneasy and a little annoyed, and I resolved to tell Benedetta nothing of what Loredana had said. On the heels of this resolution the strong conviction came over me that Loredana would now be calling me regularly. Half touched, half offended, and in need of answers to questions I couldn't even formulate, I slumped down on Uncle Ippolito's bed and stared up at his scarred and discolored ceiling. Often, after our long walks, Benedetta and I had sprawled on this bed, and laughing, pointing, entwining our fingers, we'd invented little tales to explain the scenes depicted overhead. The frescoes were a paltry nineteenth-century addition to the bedchamber: fruit-laden wreaths (much the worse for wear) converged at the summit, and around the canopy-like coving, in a decorative border, figures of hunters and hounds could be seen in a faded procession. This time my mind turned not to these beings, however, but to Uncle Ippolito himself. I knew that he had never been a favorite of Benedetta's, but in secret I honored his memory. I pictured a movie Neapolitan in a pair of striped pajama pants and a sleeveless undershirt, a debonair, unflappable bachelor who would have known just how to handle a busybody like Loredana. Surely Uncle Ippolito would have put her gently in her place with some pointed dialect joke.

As I lay there it occurred to me that as far as Benedetta and I were concerned, Loredana probably played the rather disconcerting role of confidante: who knew what they said to each other? I tried to imagine her appearance from her voice, but no convincing picture cohered in my mind. Perhaps she was thin and wan, swimming in grannyish frocks with round collars . . . perhaps she had a large mole beneath one nostril. Always in my mind's eye she wore a hat, something old-fashioned like a cloche or a pillbox . . . but of course that was virtually impossible. I tried to put myself in her shoes, tried to envision what it would be like to stay indoors every day, watching the sunbeams inch around your flat, watching the dusk creep over your windowsills, but in the end I couldn't. I couldn't work up any genuine sympathy for Loredana, a person I'd never set eyes on.

Later, when Benedetta got back, I asked her whether I could meet Loredana, for surely that would help me to appreciate her. Benedetta's brow furrowed with apprehension.

"I don't think you should try that yet," she said. "I told you, she's terrified of being with new people."

She hadn't actually said that before; but I had to accept it.

Benedetta was the middle of three sisters. The eldest, Luisa, whom I was never to meet, had married a manufacturer of animal feed and moved to somewhere near Sarno. The youngest, Tina, who was sixteen, lived at home, and something in Benedetta's tone, when she talked about Tina, suggested that her arrival in this world had been a surprise. "Unplanned" though she may have been, however, Tina was indulged by her parents in a way that Benedetta clearly disapproved of. Her delicate beauty, phenomenal even in Naples, surely had much to do with this. Slender as a jonquil leaf and taller already than Benedetta, she had streaky blond hair and topaz-colored eyes that gave her an elf-child's otherworldly look. Physically she had not quite filled out, and she glided coltishly and a little shyly through the family's oddly shaped rooms. Attempting to conceal her curiosity about her big sister's latest, foreign boyfriend, she kept herself at a discreet distance from us. Between peeks in our direction, she busied herself with the telephone, into which she twittered at regular intervals in a mixture of dialect and teenage slang. Her laughter brought to mind a chandelier set atinkle.

I saw Tina and the rest of Benedetta's family rather seldom, since Benedetta herself tended to circumvent them. She had, after all, the key to Ippolito's flat, so we could easily slip in there and keep to ourselves. Despite a standing offer, Benedetta did not, except on Sundays, take meals at home, yet all the same Gemma's domestic spirit hovered about us at dinnertime. If by chance we arrived at the family's building toward nine in the evening, for instance, Benedetta would half consciously murmur "rigatoni impasticciati" or "acquapazza" or something of the sort as soon as we pushed open the portal. Her nose for Gemma's cooking twitched infallibly, with perfect olfactory pitch. Once I wondered aloud whether she thought of her mother as a torturer even when these aromas were wafting down the stairwell.

"Yes," she answered, "I do. It's her way of fretting about everything. She drives me crazy. *Turn down the lights, they're hurting my complexion. Go find out why your sister's wearing that guilty look. Uh-oh, you're not watching those onions.* Mamma's always killing herself in the kitchen. One weekend, to lighten her workload, I made ragù for the family. And what was her reaction? *Benedetta sweetheart, I can't eat this, it has lard in it.* I made it without lard, Mamma, just for you. *Without lard! But you know a real ragù has to have lard in it*—and so on. I tell you, she's a torturer . . ."

The household was ruled by one simple, inalterable fact. As a baker, obliged to wake up and retire early, Beppe lived out of phase with the rest of the world. Neapolitan conviviality tended to crank up toward midnight, not so many hours before he usually rose for work, and this discordance, which another baker might have managed with aplomb, had pitched him into chronic melancholy. Short, balding, and muscular, Giuseppe had a way of canting forward as he walked, his arms slightly outstretched, as if to grasp whatever paddle or mixing bowl lay nearest to hand. His ferocious energy equaled his gloom. Once, as a little girl, Benedetta, who sometimes helped out in the bakery, had asked him what to do when her forearm cramped from whipping cream. "Just keep on whipping anyway," he had gruffly replied, a maxim that decided her at once against a career of pastry-making. Beppe's intractable duel with the clock, his prison of permanent untimeliness, had undermined his relations with his family. He was always coming in the door as they were leaving, or leaving as they were coming, which aroused Benedetta's pity—she habitually referred to him as "my poor father." Beppe, for his part, so often addressed Tina as Benedetta or Benedetta as Tina (or even as

Luisa) that he had given up correcting himself, and would stand there helpless as the two girls giggled at the befuddled look that overspread his massive head. ("I'm Benedetta, Papà, *that's* Tina.") Good in the end for very little besides baking, at which he excelled, Beppe had decided well before my arrival that he wanted not to knead and bake, a waste of a lifetime, but rather to buy and sell. Securities had become his passion: he spent his spare hours studying financial gazettes and deciding whether to call his broker. Yet his stock market trades had never, to Benedetta's knowledge, either improved or damaged the family finances.

Possibly it was Beppe's schedule that had turned his wife into a "torturer." Gemma taught grade school, and having also assumed every domestic responsibility, especially that of bringing up three headstrong girls, she had become a patient and relentless nit-picker. To hear Benedetta tell it, Gemma did not so much nag as sweetly argue the finer points of every matter pertaining to household chores, deportment, courtesy, health, hygiene, religion, and schoolwork. According to Gemma, most articles of clothing and most culinary preparations were badly, even malevolently, made. Inexplicably opposed to many common idioms ("I hate that expression 'He doesn't mince words'"), she couldn't abide even hearing the names of Italy's Communist politicians. In response, Benedetta, who had vaguely radical notions, would launch into philippics of her own. At mealtimes the quarrels between the mother and the girls tended to mount toward the boiling point until, providentially obeying his own private schedule, Beppe would blunder onto the scene, carrying a magnificent tray of left-over sfogliatelle and babà. Duly admired, these would be left untouched.

What were my "intentions" toward Benedetta? One might have supposed that curiosity with regard to this question would be proper to the instincts of Neapolitan parents. If so, however, Gemma and Beppe concealed it—or repressed it. Perhaps they were resigned to their daughter's independence—resignation, after all, was the hallmark of their life—and feminism had swept the more furiously through their social milieu for being an alien force. Benedetta would soon be closer to thirty than to twenty; I could only assume that she had already had her fair share of admirers and engagements broken off. And perhaps there were other, deeper reasons for their refraining from prying into her emotional life, reasons I could not yet fathom.

I secretly suspected that Gemma and Beppe had entrusted their natural anxiety about their daughter's future to Loredana. She certainly appeared to keep tabs on me. With apparent benevolence, yet as if to spite me, she began to call more and more often, plying me with casual questions. She asked me if I'd liked provola, a dairy product of Campania whose flavor peaked in early spring. She asked me if I admired Al Pacino. She complimented me—mystifyingly, as she had never actually seen me—on my blue eyes.

"Loredana, my eyes are brown," I lied.

"For me they are blue, dear," she said.

And so it went. Soon, deftly deterring my attempts at evasion, she found ways to imprison me in long conversations. Still I wanted to preserve my privacy, and so, to avoid revealing anything further, I began to prevaricate more fulsomely, indeed with breathtaking audacity. I told her that my favorite meal was steak with a glass of Scotch; that I had once worked on Wall Street; that I had a brother who owned a ranch in Wyoming. It was slapdash American material, completely unconvincing on its face, and by the end of each fib I despised myself slightly and wondered if that weren't her covert aim. She, however, never sought to turn this transparent blather against me. Instead, she took it as a form of flirtation—perhaps a charming American custom—and flirted back, in a seraphic, asexual way.

One afternoon she asked me whether I preferred American or Neapolitan coffee.

"I prefer American."

"No you don't!" She gave a merry little laugh, infuriating me.

It was another rainy evening, and we were stuck in traffic. Benedetta was driving, having borrowed Beppe's Cinquecento to pick up Tina after a kids' party in the heights of the Vomero. I sat next to Benedetta. Tina, in back, seemed a little juiced-up, which had thrown Benedetta into a black mood. Benedetta despised all drugs and alcohol.

"You didn't tell me you smoked," Benedetta suddenly said, addressing me. "It's a disgusting habit. Italians do it. Not Americans."

"I don't smoke," I said. "What put that idea into your head?"

"What put that idea into my head, *amore,* is what I found in your trousers at the bottom of Ippolito's bed this morning."

"Benedetta," I said.

"Tina's not listening," said Benedetta. "Look at her."

I turned around and looked. Tina was singing softly along with the car radio and snapping her fingers. Actually Tina had sung along with every single song that had come on the radio since we'd started out. She had sung along with so many that I'd stopped hearing her.

"I wish there was at least one stupid song you didn't know!" Benedetta called back to Tina. "There are only two reasons"— Benedetta turned to me—"for carrying a Bic lighter around in your pocket. One is to light girls' cigarettes for them, which of course you don't do, because you have me. The other is because you smoke."

"And what is the reason," I asked, huffily, "for going through a gentleman's pockets? Especially when you have Loredana on my case." I knew at once that I shouldn't have said it.

"Some gentleman!" Benedetta snorted.

"I can't tell you how many boys I've kissed while this song was playing," said Tina dreamily from the back.

"Spare us," said Benedetta.

"Benedetta, I smoke cigars," I said.

"God, I love this song!" Tina moaned. "I love the way Nino's mouth looks when he sings it."

"Zip it, Tina."

"I guess I'm just crazy," said Tina, giggling.

"Not crazy—silly," Benedetta said.

"No—crazy—insane!" said Tina. "My problem is that I'm always in love. Though I am going through an antisex period right now."

"Okay, Tina, that's it!" said Benedetta, abruptly flipping off the radio.

"Discreetly. Outdoors," I said quietly. "Maybe three or four a week, tops. That's not what I'd call smoking."

After Benedetta had extricated us from the traffic gridlock and dropped off Tina, she stuck the car in Beppe's prepaid slot.

"Okay, I understand you don't smoke," she said, as she cut the engine, "but I happened to be upset. You see, Tina does smoke."

"She does?" I said. "I've never seen her."

"I haven't either, but she does. I know she does."

"Oh. How do you know?"

"If you reach right down to the bottom of her book bag," Benedetta said, "past all the other disgusting junk that's in there, you'll find her pack of cigarettes. Along with a lighter, like yours."

"So you go through her things, too?" I said, with irritation.

She glanced at me and made a gesture.

No firm offers had come in yet for Uncle Ippolito's apartment, and Benedetta had decided to make it look a bit more homey. One evening she began to hang curtains in his nearly blank bedroom. "Also I'm afraid people can spy on us," she said, winking at me. She had found some crimson brocaded material in a curiosity shop off Piazza dei Girolamini. Now, having gathered the fabric on a rod, she climbed onto a chair in order to attach the rod to the hooks I'd already fastened over the window. The window being tall, she stood on tiptoe, barefoot for surer footing. She was wearing a bathrobe, and as she stretched upward the robe rose to mid-thigh.

"Get your hand off my knee," she said, laughing. "You're going to make me fall!"

When she had adjusted the curtains she hopped off the chair and looked up to examine the effect. "Isn't it nicer that way?" she asked. As she arched her back, her hair, which she had just washed, fell down her shoulders in a glossy, violet-scented cascade.

I agreed that the curtains suited the room; and then, seeing that my remark had pleased her, I seized the advantage. Slipping my arm around her waist from behind, I blurted out what I'd been meaning to say for so long.

"Tell me something, Benedetta. Why does Loredana call me all the time?"

"All the time?"

"At least twice a week."

"I guess she likes you, sweetheart." She wiggled out of my embrace and faced me.

"You know that's ridiculous. She has some hidden motive."

"Oh, sure, she must have. *Dio mío,* you should hear yourself."

"You think I'm being cynical?"

"Well, how can you talk about Loredana that way? Such a loving, faithful, doggy sort of person. Look, do me big favor, okay? Don't try to understand her!" A hectic flush bloomed in Benedetta's cheeks. "Don't try to fit her into some story that isn't hers—like you do with me."

"Oh? What's the story I've made up about you?"

"How should I know? I only know it's not the real one. From your way of talking—from your whole way of *being.*" She flounced down onto Ippolito's bed, twisting her face into an ugly frown, and drew her knees up to her chin. Her robe had slipped to one side, exposing her thighs and her panties, but she seemed not to notice or to care.

We stared at each other, both amazed at the flare-up of this quarrel. My heart pounded and my breathing grew urgent—she seemed so remote, so resentful. She had said that I knew nothing about her, and this assertion, though painful, was true.

"Benedetta," I said, as calmly as I could, "I want you to do something for me. I want you to get Loredana to stop calling me. She can call you as much as she wants, of course, but when she calls me it makes me feel nervous. She's inquisitive—maybe without meaning to be. Besides, we have nothing in common."

"Nothing in common!" Benedetta growled. She was furious now, and she raked up her hair with her fingers so that it flew in all directions. Confronted with this vision of feline savagery, I recoiled a few steps and tried hard to think. But by the time I realized the blunder I'd made, she had softened—she had risen to her full, not-very-great height and encircled me with her arms.

"Don't ask me to say that to Loredana," she pleaded. Tears welled in her eyes. "I can't . . . I can't and I won't!"

So she wasn't going to do it—I saw that. But where was it written that I had to talk all the time to Loredana? I could always put her off by saying I was busy. I could be so cool and surly that she would never try to call me again. I was considering this idea, wondering how I could accomplish it without wounding Benedetta, when suddenly—silently—the curtain fell. It collapsed with a leisurely crumple, and lay stiffly in a pile by the windowsill. One of my hooks, ill fated, sat cushioned in its folds. Benedetta burst out laughing again and sank back onto the bed.

"What?" I said. "What's so funny?"

Already she was half weeping. "If people are spying on us now," she said, "they're not seeing anything very sexy."

How it annoyed me, this vision of the world peeking in at our window! "Benedetta," I said, "if only I didn't have the feeling of being checked out all the time—"

She made a despairing gesture and drew a finger under her eyes. "But Loredana's not checking you out," she said, heaving a sigh. "I'm the one whose behavior worries her. Don't you see that? Don't you see?"

It was around this time that I first did begin to see something. What I began to see was that Benedetta, however lively, was also rather unhappy.

We often had morning coffee at a café on the ground floor of a building adjacent to hers. I never ordered anything but black espresso, while Benedetta took hers with sugar—three spoonfuls in a demitasse cup—along with a cream-filled cornetto. Together we would listen to the lady at the cash register complain about the local school, or to the other habitués exult over the latest exploits of the then-triumphant Napoli soccer club. And as we stood at the bar one morning, it occurred to me that I had become something like the sugar in Benedetta's coffee, the mitigating or abating element in an otherwise too-bitter medium: her social ambience, which suited her well when I was in Naples, became, I suspected, almost unbearable in my absence. I sensed that Benedetta was up to her neck in some sort of trouble, though I could not guess what it was. I didn't feel entitled to ask her about it—she certainly hadn't volunteered to tell me—but I supposed she needed a diversion to make her woes seem less real. And as a creature right out of her Italian moviegoer's conception of America, I fitted the bill.

One evening I arrived alone at Uncle Ippolito's to find the front door ajar. Usually Benedetta bolted it shut with four turns of her latchkey, but this time it had been left open, obviously by someone in a hurry. As I stepped into the empty sitting room I heard a voice speaking in the bedroom and realized that it was Benedetta on the telephone with Loredana. Apparently she had heard the phone ringing and had rushed in to answer it. The call was surely intended for me, because Loredana usually reached me at this time of day; but since Benedetta had picked up the receiver, they had started to talk.

I stopped where I was, and breathed deeply: earlier it had rained, and from the streets rose the heavy, bittersweet smell of a wet spring evening. Benedetta was talking excitedly, but in the affectionate, respectful way in which she always addressed Loredana. After a while she fell silent, and an interval followed during which I heard nothing but sounds from outside—a constant dripping, the spray of passing cars, the tread of feet in puddles. At length she spoke again, and I realized that I'd been standing there for ten minutes or more. Rooted to the spot, I went on eavesdropping with anxious fascination.

"I couldn't bear it," Benedetta said at one point.

Later she said, "No, he doesn't."

And she said, "He wouldn't understand."

As I heard more references to "he" and to "him," I decided not to disclose my presence. Were they talking about me? The circumstances—and my vanity—suggested that they were.

By now it was twilight, and the colors of the room had drained away, so that nothing remained to be seen but two tall open windows framing patches of glimmering sky. The damp clamor of the city drifted through the windows, and on this ever-shifting ocean of sound floated Benedetta's silvery voice, passionately rising, fluctuating, at times disappearing. The effect was hypnotic, and, unable to move, I breathed as softly as I could until at last, taking care to make no noise, I turned and walked out the door.

Loredana continued to contact me about twice a week, but after this episode of shameless eavesdropping I stopped lying to her on the telephone. Though I cannot say that I particularly welcomed her calls, I did nothing to avoid them and answered her questions sincerely. As talkative as Benedetta and almost as pert, she began to amuse me, and I came to enjoy humoring her. At last I admitted to myself that it had been foolish of me to think that I could hide, like an outlaw in a western movie, in Uncle Ippolito's apartment.

I also gave up all hope of meeting Loredana in person, of matching her voice to a face and a body. It wasn't only that such an encounter lay beyond her horizon of possibilities, or that Benedetta saw no grounds to encourage it: I, too, came to view it as undesirable. With each passing week, I grew more accepting of her incorporeality, which was the very quality that made her angelic, or almost. Loredana was Loredana—I would have to live with that. I would never get to see her so long as I lived.

And then, one day, I did see her.

I had gone outside with Benedetta on a leisurely walk to have a look at one of her secondhand shops. We were sauntering along a convent wall near her home when I saw that her gaze had fastened on a piazzetta, a little square, just ahead of us. The piazzetta, though flanked by an ornate church, was also encumbered by dumpsters and partly staked out by street traders, whose battered merchandise lay strewn on the ground. On the alley nearest to us stood a line of blocked traffic.

All at once Benedetta grabbed my arm. *"Guarda un po'!"* she said, smiling broadly. "Do you want to see Loredana?"

"Where? Show me where!" I exclaimed.

"See that van, the blue one? Now look at the Vespa right behind it."

"But there's a *man* on that Vespa," I said, bewildered.

"Yes, that's Massimo, her husband," she said. "She's the woman riding behind him."

I had not at first noticed her, this passenger riding sidesaddle, almost hidden behind the man and clasping him tightly, crouching forward with her eyelids lowered. She wore a pleated navy skirt and a cardigan and looked about sixty, with silvery hair caught up in a tight chignon.

"That's her?" I blurted out, incredulous. "You never told me—"

"Massimo!" Benedetta shouted. "Loredana!" She was dragging me forward.

But just then the Vespa sprang ahead, whisking the couple around a corner, and though we threw ourselves after them, calling and calling, they soon sped completely out of sight.

Breathless, I struggled to comprehend what I had seen: a still-pretty lady hanging onto a robust, grizzled fellow in a brown leather jacket who jockeyed his scooter through traffic in the usual devil-may-care Neapolitan fashion.

She had a husband, then, did she? And she rode with him on his Vespa when obliged to go somewhere? And this husband served as her contact with the outside world?

"Not exactly," Benedetta said. "He stays near her most of the time."

"Because he's the way she is?" I asked. "He's phobic, too?"

"No," Benedetta said. "Because he's her husband. He doesn't like to leave her alone. Anyway, he works downstairs in the same palazzo. He has a studio there, he's a jeweler. Come on." And taking me firmly by the hand, past the smiling fishmonger and the smiling cheese man, who had heard her voice and had come out on the sidewalk to salute us, she steered me in the direction of the secondhand shop.

3

Falling Palace

W ell, I guess I'll be packing my bags," I said to Donna Concetta on her balcony, once the elegant gentleman had left the courtyard. He was buying my *basso* out from under me, and doubtless it would suit his purposes. Though in a questionable district, it was only a few minutes' walk from Via Roma. It had a discreet, scarcely noticable entry. It was hidden from the world, and could probably be made cozy for a little money. And, most important, ladies from prosperous neighborhoods like the Vomero, where he lived, had no reason to come anywhere near here. Concetta gaily agreed with me: this was one place his wife would never find him.

If Concetta would not be grieved to see me go, that was because Benedetta seldom passed through the courtyard without a minor dustup with the rotund concierge. Concetta's comments provoked Benedetta, but Benedetta's salvos were also a way of venting her unconfessed frustration, I thought. For Benedetta resented my living in the Quartieri, and she visited me most unwillingly. Convinced that I was "doing research" there, she did not realize that in America people like me usually lived in low-rent areas at least as run-down as this one. That there was no condescension in my choice of address was something she could not imagine.

In that sense, the loss of the *basso* was no disaster. Benedetta's sensibilities deserved to be taken into account, and besides, the place was too tiny to serve as a workplace. I really did need a larger flat. And so, with little regret, I signed up with a real estate agency, one of the few representing landlords who deigned to rent out small apartments or studios.

Every day the agency gave me several new addresses, and every day I tried to imagine living in the places I saw. The trouble with the old city was darkness—deep shadows brooded in the stairways and welled up out of the corners of the rooms, and many flats, not only the *bassi,* had no windows at all. In the windowless rooms the tiled floors mirrored the energy-saving blue bulbs that glowed in the wall sconces, and in some flats hundreds of infernal blue lights seemed to burn underfoot. Into these same rooms, some six or eight decades earlier, the peasants of Campania had crowded for months or years before immigrating to America.

Day after day, roaming in and out of dilapidated palazzi, I came to infer, from the local way of arranging entrances and passage-ways, a conception of the human body at odds with the one I was used to. I would contemplate the minuscule hatches, the size of small children, cut into the locked double doors of many old build-ings. These hatches, sometimes called "pedestrian doors," were common elsewhere in Italy but seemed particularly Lilliputian in Naples. Such a door instantly diminished you, and if by chance you were tall, or carrying something bulky, to creep through them was to contort your whole body. The humiliation of such maneu-vers was not relieved by your generally being obliged, a moment later, to enter a tiny elevator, which wouldn't budge until you'd inserted a one-hundred-lire coin in a slotted metal box. Not that all buildings had elevators—most, in districts like the Quartieri, did not. In that case, once inside the courtyard, you often found yourself before a doorway, freakishly tall and narrow, that gave abruptly on a flight of stone steps leading almost vertically upward, like a ladder.

My trouble finding suitable lodgings had to do not only with my lack of funds but also with my being an American. Several landlords suspected my motives, as did one patrician lady who haughtily broke our appointment on the apparent assumption that CIA agents roved about town looking for rentals. Preposterous though the charge seemed in my case, Naples was tailor-made for spooks, being situated near the NATO base at Bagnoli and two hours from Rome. Besides, it was easy to hide in—indeed, its involuted layout and vast subterranean labyrinth tempted people to commit the sort of crimes that subsequently entail hiding. And in Naples criminals could easily acquire artfully counterfeited identity papers. When a cat burglar, a young girl, was arrested several blocks from my *basso,* the rumor circulated that she had already availed herself of seventy-nine different identities.

One night I had a dream that made me wake and sit bolt upright in bed, laughing. In my dream I stood outside the portico of a palace, tall and stately but covered in scaffolding. As I hesitated there, wondering at the reason for so many struts and braces, a young black woman appeared, veiled and regally clad, and graciously led me inside. She invited me to choose a bedchamber, and to regard the palace as home. We went from room to room—all were vacant—admiring the sculptured fireplaces, the way the light played over damask curtains and across marble floors. Finally we went back outside and walked some distance away, and as I glanced back at the edifice I saw for the first time how unstable it was, how spindly, and I knew that it would fall. And then, like so many real buildings in Naples—you pass their rubble all the time—it did fall, almost imperceptibly at first, loosening at the joints and undulating in the air until suddenly it lay in a mass of wreckage. And we stood there laughing, the black princess and I.

I not infrequently wake up laughing from a dream, but so do many people. What struck me about this dream was the element of surprise, which had roused me and made me sit up. The dream felt revelatory, it held some mirthful portent, and I wondered whether it could be interpreted and acted upon. I was (and am) very superstitious; at this time I was beginning to understand that we spend our days trying to enact what we have dreamed about at night, and that our paths through life are formed not by character but by coincidence. Though Benedetta was not black, I wondered whether the black princess did not stand for her, or for some part of my mind that strove to be in steady communion with her. Above all, I was keen to know which lotto numbers I should derive from my dream. Now, I would deny that I was addicted, in any real sense, to the lottery—for instance, I wasn't about to place more than fifteen thousand lire on a pair of tickets. But being perenially short of funds, I did secretly hope that I could turn my dream into a deposit on a larger flat.

I could wager not only on the Neapolitan Wheel of Fortune but also on the wheels of nine other Italian cities, all spun simultaneously twice a week, the Wheel of Bari being especially receptive to dreams. To use my dream effectively, though, I had first to transmute it into numbers with the help of an ancient Neapolitan dream-book called the *smorfia,* which contained an alphabetical inventory of everything you could possibly dream about, along with its numerical equivalent. (For instance, the first dream-category in my *smorfia* was "abbé," an "abbé in disguise" yielding 89 and a "scandalous abbé" yielding 80.) But dreams were not the only events worth a riffle through the *smorfia:* surprises in daily life were hot tickets, too. Earth tremors were hot, landslides were hot, and so were other typically Neapolitan events like storm-drain floods, washed-out boulevards, camorra killings, bank robberies, racketeering indictments, and pharmaceutical scams. Say I was thinking about Benedetta and suddenly she called me—that sort of thing had a numerical match-up, too. (To be precise, it was 76.)

From my friends I had learned to consider dreams as telegrams from the *buon' anime,* the "good souls," as the shades of the dead were known in these parts. The *buon' anime* foresaw the future, consequently also the results of the next lottery drawing, which they sometimes conveyed to the living in dreams. The dead could play some naughty tricks, however. They seldom simply stated a number, but enlisted hackneyed symbols instead. And sometimes they deliberately misled the dreamer, or floated out-and-out lies, as some of them had been inclined to do when alive. Benedetta, who sneered at the lottery with rationalist contempt and regarded the *smorfia* as colorful folklore, allowed as how deceased Neapolitan relatives might not be so different from living ones when it came to selfishness and duplicity.

I myself could have looked up the numbers for the falling palace dream in my *smorfia,* but I didn't really know how to do it. Deriving the appropriate numbers required a certain mystical knack, which tended to be the province of women. So I decided to consult the two ladies in my local *ricevitoria,* or betting parlor, who were known to be eerily intuitive. Their recommendations were as good as any I was likely to find, and I was really rather desperate for a windfall.

One evening, on a tip from the rental agency, I went to look at a studio in a building on Viale Elena, an east-west avenue running parallel to the shoreline. Though only a block from the seaside promenade, with its cafés and ferry slips and pleasure parties bound for Capri, the Viale seemed unreal at that hour, cast mysteriously adrift from the waterfront and the rest of the city. Flanked by tall palazzi and alleys of graceful palms, the boulevard stood for a fictitious, grand bourgeois Naples, a city of monocled flâneurs as reimagined by the Francophiles of the Belle Epoque. It was provincial and conventional and not truly beautiful, but that evening it looked beautiful and a desirable place of residence. I wondered if I might soon be living there.

I had made an appointment with a Signor Bettucci, carefully jotting the time and address on a slip of paper. But when I pressed his button on the intercom no answer came. Suspecting that he might be asleep, I tried several more times at regular intervals, until fifteen minutes had passed and I began to worry. Meanwhile various people pulled up in cars or on scooters, and each time I hoped that one of them would turn out to be Bettucci. But they all ignored me, and finally I went into an adjacent café and dialed his number on a pay telephone. An old lady answered and told me that he was away on business. Dismayed, I stepped back out into the street; twilight, an hour I loved, had by now stolen over the boulevard, and its rows of tall palazzi receded into the dusk in the washy manner of a Victorian watercolor, creating dramatic prospects. Standing there feeling lost, I grew aware that a man in a dark suit and tie was loitering nearby, eyeing me. He had been on the block the whole time, I realized, apparently occupied with something in the trunk of a car.

I glanced reproachfully at Bettucci's nameplate on the intercom and turned to go. Seeing this, the man in the suit came over and gave me a distastefully familiar glance, as if he knew me.

"Are you looking for Signor Bettucci?" he asked.

"Yes," I said, unsettled. "I had an appointment."

"Well, he's not here!" said the man, with a flip of his hand. He must have been about sixty, with a deeply creased face and inkwell eyes, but his hair was still youthfully black and glossy, combed back and zigzagged with highlights. In that suit, I thought, he was too well dressed—why was he dressed so formally while fooling around with his car?

Was this Bettucci himself? Over the phone he had sounded like a much younger man, but voices are often deceptive: had he been hovering on the street the whole time, with the aim of vetting me on the sly? That was possible: Bettucci was one of those landlords who had asked me point-blank whether I worked for the CIA. On the other hand, in any Neapolitan neighborhood, even one as atypical as Viale Elena, everyone noses into everyone else's business, and it was perfectly conceivable that this man merely knew that Bettucci had a studio to rent, probably to a foreigner. As he stood beside me, staring at me with a hyperalert expression, beads of sweat stood out on his brow.

"I tell you, Bettucci's out!" he said, irritably. "Why don't you come back another day?" He made the gesture denoting "later," a finger circling like a clock hand in front of his face. "Come back on Monday or Tuesday, why don't you?"

I stood considering this.

"By the way, sir"—he bent forward, lowering his voice—"would you like a suede sports coat? Look, it's by Valentino!" In a twinkling he had removed the jacket from his trunk and was showing me the label. "You can have it for only two hundred thousand lire, a giveaway."

"Thanks, I'm not interested," I said.

"Porca madonna!" he exclaimed under his breath. "At that price! How can you refuse?"

"I just don't need a suede jacket," I said, walking away and trying not to look too unsympathetic. But already he'd hopped into his car and was driving along beside me, wooing me through the window.

"One hundred fifty?" he hissed. As I hurried back up the Viale he tagged alongside me, and people began to gape at this strange pair, the foreigner on the sidewalk and the hissing man in the car.

"One hundred?"

"No."

"Eighty?"

"No."

"Porca madonna!"

Two days later the agency told me that an apartment had become available near Piazza Montesanto, one of my favorite spots in Naples. A piazza in name only, Montesanto is where Via Tarsia, bending away from Piazza Dante, hangs a sharp left and turns into the Pignasecca market, one of the liveliest and cheapest food marts in the city. Here, too, a funicular station adjoins the station for the Ferrovia Cumana, so that crowds of commuters mingle with the shoppers at regular intervals. Opposite the station there's a café and a popular pizzeria, and I liked to sit in the café and watch the teenagers gobbling their slices. Planting themselves under the big green sidewalk clock, which rose on its tall stalk like a dandelion, they would hunch far out over their feet to avoid slobbering tomato sauce on their fancy footwear. Over in front of the church of Montesanto, fifteen or twenty gents with foraging looks on their faces would half recline on their scooters, discoursing loudly and waiting for something promising to turn up. Now, hearing of the available flat, I pictured myself sipping coffee in the café every morning, reading the *Corriere della Sera* and masquerading as a man of leisure. I would look up occasionally to enjoy the rambunctious goings-on in the street, or to watch the sun's first rays tinge the heights of the Vomero behind the station.

The woman who met me at lunchtime in front of the station had described herself to the agency as a tall brunette. She was a brunette, but she wasn't tall. Sleek and plumpish, crowned by a rearward ripple of hair, she held herself straight as a plumb bob and cut a resolute course through the crowd. Her name, she said, was Assunta: as we hurried to the rental flat, her stride grew remarkably agile. Chin up, proud bust thrust forward like a breastplate, she marched with fastidious indifference past the smoking panzarotti stands and heaped-up vegetable stalls. Her brow caught the pallor of the sky: a sort of suppressed vehemence about her eyes, a tension in her hands, disquieted and fascinated me.

"This apartment," she said, as she gracefully glided up three flights of unlit stairs partly supported by post-earthquake scaffolding, "was my mother's for thirty years. I have just finished remodeling it."

The little flat had a separate kitchen, all white. It had tall french windows with internal shutters and tiny, marble-paved balconies. It occupied an airy corner perch, and looked across at the dentelated cornices of a seventeenth-century palazzo. Craning out of one window, I could see the prow-shaped bastions of the Castel Sant'Elmo, up on the Vomero; down below, on the other side, clustered the stalls of the Pignasecca market. I heard the hawkers' singsong, peals of girlish laughter, a passing loudspeaker touting a sale; from the stalls rose the aroma of sizzling panzarotti, and with it, so I felt, the fragrance of perpetual gaiety. Of course the rent was more than I could afford.

"I'll take it," I said to Assunta.

We shook.

Now, as it happened, most of my Neapolitan friends had rented apartments at one time or another, and some of Benedetta's pals even worked in real estate. All had warned me about easy deals. They had warned me about hidden costs, and phony contracts, and swindlers changing the lock on you. Naples was a very big city, they said, and such things were to be expected. What they hadn't warned me about was innocence.

Assunta told me that she was a schoolteacher, which should have worried me from the start. Like most Italian teachers, who have to pass a demanding series of qualifying examinations, she was inadequately paid. She had knocked herself out fixing up this little flat, which would serve, I gathered, as a rental property for herself and her husband. She professed relief to have found a tenant so quickly—I was the first applicant—but today she had to get back to school, as her workday was far from over. She looked weary, and anxious; when I pressed her about closing the deal, she shied away in a gesture of mild alarm. She noted only that the flat already had a telephone, over by the window, which she would leave for me, and that all the debris from remodeling—some fragments of tile and plaster dust—would shortly be removed. She said I should call her husband, Arnaldo, whom I could reach that evening at a number she gave me.

That same afternoon, prayerful yet pessimistic like most lotto players, I walked through the rain to the betting shop I patronized. Outside the shop, bedraggled customers were waiting in two long lines to present themselves at the ticket windows inside. Next door, people wandered in and out of a *baccaleria,* a salt cod store, in whose entryway great hunks of fish were draining over a marble counter. A pair of Senegalese peddlers scuttled by, shouldering enormous tote bags full of cheap merchandise, rain droplets beading in their hair. *"Ohè, capo!"* they called to the shopkeepers. Out of kindness, the shopkeepers darted out to buy butane lighters and packets of plastic combs.

Like most such places, the betting parlor consisted of a small room with a terrazzo floor; behind the barred windows two women, like prophesying birds, dispensed lotto tickets and numerical advice. The floor overflowed with discarded pieces of scratch paper, which were starting to work their way outdoors and swirl about in the rain, and the walls and outer windows were plastered with dozens of tip cards, each scrawled with numbers— for the Virgin, for saints' days, for a warship that had just set sail from Taranto, and a host of recent events. For a moment, Naples dematerialized under my scrutiny, dissolving into a primal ooze of integers, a sort of Pythagorean lava.

"Tell us your dream, we'll pick out the essential things," the two women told me as I came up to their window. Since I came here often I knew Tania and Silvana; sometimes they spoke in unison, like twins in an old movie.

I told them about the falling palace and how I'd woken up laughing. I told them I'd already selected a few numbers that I thought might hit.

"Those numbers are wrong," they said.

"Wrong? How so?"

Tania smiled a little sooner than Silvana, so the same smile sailed across their faces like a boat in high wind. Tania said, "You're a man. You dream a woman. So she's got to be the most important thing. Doesn't she?"

The black princess—how right they were! I'd forgotten to pick a number for the princess. I felt gooseflesh creep along the nape of my neck.

"Okay, let's put in the number for woman," I said.

"Twenty-one, seventy, eighty-eight, seventy-two," they recited together. *"Woman, palace, collapse, amazement."*

"Amazement? Why *amazement?"*

"Caro signore! If you don't like our numbers, you can go buy them from the gypsies."

"The gypsies—?"

"Listen," said Silvana, "Tania dreams every night, and we recommend numbers based on her dreams."

"Especially my warning dreams," said Tania.

"And they're good numbers, too," said Silvana. "They hit remarkably often. What I mean is, you can trust us."

I bought a ticket for Naples and another for Bari.

"Now then," said Tania, "about that princess of yours. I have to advise you that women in dreams are often deceitful."

"They're a bad omen," said Silvana.

"So watch out," said Tania.

Tania and Silvana peered over my shoulder and exchanged glances. Looking around, I saw that the shutter was half pulled down now, and the parlor lay deep in shadow. I said good-bye to the two women and crept under the shutter and walked through the rainy piazza toward my *basso.*

On the telephone, Assunta's husband, Arnaldo, sounded elderly and distracted. Indeed he scarcely touched (and with obvious repugnance) on the matter that chiefly concerned me—the lease.

His voice would halt and presently rise again, touching on all manner of topics, moseying along, then dwindle into a hoarse, unintelligible whisper. Whenever I slipped a question about the lease into this trickle of speech, he would fall instantly silent—out of some strange deference to me, it seemed—and then shuffle on to something else. Having heard that I wrote, he wanted to talk about Faulkner, Steinbeck, and, inevitably, Edgar Lee Masters, venerated by many educated Italians as our national bard. Was Arnaldo interested in the lease at all? Over and over I tried to pin him down, and at last, with well-bred reluctance, he came to this trifling matter. He wanted a registered lease, he said, and for that I would need a residence permit.

This surprised me. Ideally, in Italy, even the most honest landlord wants to sign an unregistered, informal contract with a permitless foreigner. In this way he pays no taxes on his rental income and remains protected against tenants who refuse to vacate the premises at the appointed time, since residents without permits have no domiciliary rights. As it happened, I did not have a permit—for various reasons, I didn't yet need one—but Arnaldo suggested in a barely audible voice that I could easily procure one at the police commissariat. Two days hence, at 5 p.m., when I had obtained this document, he would meet me in front of the Museo Filangieri, in Via Duomo. He pronounced Prince Filangieri's mellifluous name with evident relief; it allowed him to drop all talk of our vulgar transaction and dwell instead on that nobleman's collection of Neapolitan paintings. He asked me whether I knew Mattia Preti's *Meeting of Saints Peter and Paul.* I told him that I did, and together we bestowed our facile praise upon it, which apparently soothed him.

At the commissariat, a smiling officer in a uniform worthy of a field marshal told me that I was ineligible for a permit. Inexplicably, my passport had no entry stamp: who knew when I had stolen into the country? Silently I cursed the quaint Italian reverence for *carta bollata*—stamps, seals, signatures, letterheads; but later, when I explained my predicament to Arnaldo over the phone, he amiably dropped his requirement that I obtain a residence permit. We would still meet, as arranged, in front of the Museo Filangieri.

❧

Meanwhile Tania and Silvana's lotto combination had not come up, either on the Wheel of Naples or that of Bari, on both of which I'd wagered twice. I felt depressed; and also I began to think, in complicity with Benedetta, that the Neapolitans were basically stupid. God, what a stupid city! Why, I now asked myself, did so many people in this antique, ornate, bejeweled civilization, with its opera and university and theaters and museums, waste such a phenomenal amount of money on . . . lotto! But the answer, when I considered it, was obvious. They wasted it for the same reason that I did: lotto-playing represented a vestigial belief in divination, or, at the very least, a refusal to dismiss it with finality. Like hundreds of thousands of Neapolitans, I was often highly suggestible, startled by life's coincidences. These were by no means uncommon in the news, and an especially dramatic one happened at just this time. It revolved around the murder of a so-called *centauro,* that is, a boy on a motorcycle.

The boy was eighteen and had no criminal record, but he was briefly detained at a police roadblock before venturing, whether mistakenly or willfully, into the restricted zone of the Piazza Trieste e Trento. There people were milling around as usual in front of the Gambrinus, yet in full view of the crowd the boy was shot five times by an unknown assailant, and died almost instantly.

Why had he been killed, and who had killed him? For what reason had he wanted to enter the restricted zone, and if he hadn't, could he have saved himself? These were the questions people asked, in part because the boy's death distressed them terribly but also because the answers might help them select the right numbers from the *smorfia* for the next turn of the Wheel of

Naples. The crime had horrified the whole city, so the whole city was abuzz with arithmetical speculation.

It happened at once. Numbers fluttered like bats down the streets and through the alleys, across clotheslines, from driver to driver. Only hours after the killing, passing by the betting shop in Via Nardones, I noticed that the owner, Signora Antonella, had taped inside her window a large tip card recommending a "tern," or triple, based on the sinister event. This meant that she had already consulted and interpreted the *smorfia,* and many local players would surely heed her advice. As for myself, I was not—despite my sore need for money—tempted to bet. Repelled by the thought of profiting by someone's death, I walked on by.

And of course Antonella's combination hit the jackpot. And not only did that particular combination win—the extraordinary thing was how many people had won at least *something:* hundreds of thousands had won. Amazed, and annoyed with myself, I mulled over the fact that if I'd staked only ten thousand lire on Antonella's triumphant tern—that means about five dollars on her pick of three numbers—I'd have pulled in 42.5 million lire, or roughly twenty-five thousand dollars.

Rent! Who would have worried about paying the rent?

Arnaldo and I met as planned in front of the Museo Filangieri, in Via Duomo. As his face poked through the late afternoon mist, I saw that he wasn't old at all, at most forty-five, and I put his speech mannerisms down to some quirk of his temperament. They went along with his tweed jacket, which was worn and antiquated and yet, with its English cut, perennially acceptable to a certain genteel Italian taste. We walked over to the rental flat through the student quarter, and he told me in his wavering, wistful way that he had corresponded with various luminaries at the Massachusetts Institute of Technology, of which he had formed an exact mental picture, though he had never actually been there.

"Arnaldo," I asked him as we crossed Via Paladino, "what sort of engineering do you do?"

"Oh, that," he said, screwing up his face. "You know, I don't practice engineering. I've taught it, but I don't, well, *do* it." The subject apparently pained him, and he told me instead about his late father, who had been badly wounded in Cyrenaica during the war and had been mustered out of the Italian army. He had had a great affection for his father, he said.

In the failing light, the shadows in the street blended with the melancholy circles around Arnaldo's eyes. I couldn't see him clearly, but every time he finished speaking he squinted at me quizzically, I suppose to judge the effect of what he had just said. This diffidence continued until we arrived at Montesanto, at the ground floor of the rental flat. There, without warning, he let loose a stream of vicious insults.

Not at me: a third person had materialized beside us. He was half hidden by the cagelike scaffolding that webbed through the building's ground-floor landing, which effectively masked his features, but Arnaldo's face, so meek a moment ago, was now distorted with rage, eyes red, teeth bared. Like rabid dogs the two barked and snapped at each other, howling in dialect—I gathered that they both belonged to the building's co-op committee—and I made out something about a custodian who had been forced to leave and other quarrels among the shareholders. On the way up the stairs Arnaldo stopped every few steps to hunch over the railing and scream down at his detested neighbor, who obligingly (so it seemed) screamed back. It was almost as if the pair were playing a scene.

Once we were inside the flat, Arnaldo's alarmingly protean features settled back into their natural bewildered expression. Assunta was sitting, regally tranquil, on a convertible sofa, sewing tabs on curtains that cascaded about her in dignified folds. But she seemed to have changed somehow. Her hair had grown violently black, almost sorceress-like, and her lips intensely, tropically red. Or had I simply not noticed her colors before?

The flat had been carefully swept and cleaned—gone was the debris of remodeling. The fridge had yet to be delivered, but was expected within the hour.

"Whom do you know in Naples?" Assunta asked me, in halting, carefully enunciated English. English, apparently, was her subject at school.

"I know quite a few people," I said.

"Good people, bad people, clever, stupid?"

"All sorts," I said. I thought of mentioning Benedetta, but thought better of it. Then I added, in Italian, "I seem to meet a lot of eccentrics. Not that I mind. But I didn't set out to collect them."

"Naples is full of eccentrics," she replied, in Italian. "In a way, we are encouraged, even as children, to become eccentrics."

"So maybe," I said, sportively, "you are an eccentric yourself?"

Her eyes widened, and she drew herself up, straight in the back, statuesque. "No, I am not an eccentric," she said. "But I can be very strange."

Arnaldo nodded and flashed me a man-to-man conspiratorial smile. For a moment no one found anything to say. Then Assunta announced, "Here is the contract. Would you like to read it, please?"

It was brief and straightforward. I signed and dated it, and so did she.

I said, "Now let's do my copy."

"There is only this copy," said Assunta.

I suggested that we go outside and photocopy it, but Assunta shook her head. "Fabio didn't say anything about you getting a copy," she said.

"Who's Fabio?" I asked.

"I don't do a thing without Fabio," she said, sidestepping my question. "I'm not a businesswoman. I'm a schoolteacher."

Arnaldo said nothing—he was studying the lease.

"Well, I'm sure Fabio wouldn't mind," I said. "After all, if this is a contract, then both parties have to have a copy, that's obvious. Is Fabio your lawyer?"

"No."

"Your father?"

"No."

"Your brother?"

"No."

"I'm sure that Fabio would agree, darling," said Arnaldo. "It seems only reasonable."

Assunta went over to the window and dialed someone on the telephone whom I took to be Fabio. As she waited, I heard an ambulance screech by, doubtless en route to the nearby Ospedale dei Pellegrini.

"No answer," she said. "Look, why don't the two of you go out and get a pizza or something at Ventidue? By the time you get back, I'll have talked to Fabio. I'll have finished these curtains and the fridge will be here."

"Oh, darling, do come with us," Arnaldo pleaded. "It will be so much more jolly."

"No," Assunta said.

"But darling—"

She wasn't hungry, she said. She'd had a long day at school and felt too tired to go out. "You two go," she insisted.

Downstairs, we heard the bells of Montesanto toll eight-fifteen. The market had started to break up. Tripe still hung dripping over the tripe altars, but in the shops some lights were blinking off. We walked past a cat scrabbling on a mound of discarded produce, past cavernous, half-darkened *salumerie* where hams hung like sloths in long rows.

"I'll take a *margherita*," I said over the television noise to the waiter in the pizzeria.

After long deliberation, Arnaldo said, "I'll have the same."

When the pizzas were placed before us, he devoured his almost instantly. Finished, he gazed at me with a hangdog expression.

"My wife is a beautiful woman," he said, grimacing, "but sometimes . . ."—he broke off, and with praying hands made the gesture of sorely tried patience. "That apartment belonged to her mother, you know. It stood empty for years, and it cost Assunta the moon to fix up. These Neapolitan tradesmen! She doesn't know a thing about money, and she relies absolutely on Fabio's advice. But I'm sure she'll come around when she's spoken to him." Again he flashed me his conspiratorial smile. "Let's give the old girl a little time, eh? By the way, what's this we're drinking?"

"It's just Aglianico," I said. "One of your light local wines."

"*Mamma mía,* it's going to my head! Listen, there's something I wanted to tell you. About what you asked earlier . . . about engineering. It's like this, you see—the day after I got my diploma I suddenly admitted something to myself." His voice had dwindled to a confessional murmur, and I leaned over the table to hear him. "I should never have studied engineering," he said sadly. "It wasn't right for me, not really. What really interests me is literature, art— human beings!" He drew his hand across his forehead and stared at me feverishly. "*Mamma mía,* this wine!"

Arnaldo screwed up his face: together his dark hair and dark eyes and knit brows made a sort of sign, a hieroglyph of anguish. "Do you remember what Nietzsche said about the Greek gods," he asked, "about why the gods act like men?"

I confessed that I did not remember.

"He said that the gods act like men in order to make us happy with our lives."

The sense of this eluded me. "That sounds lovely," I said, "but what does it mean?"

"I believe it means that all our desires, our follies, our suffering would be unbearable if we didn't see that the gods themselves, in their Olympian glory, are misbehaving and suffering just as we do. The gods justify the life of men by living it themselves. They reconcile us to nature—to *our* nature."

"That reminds me," I said, "of Uccello's battle paintings. Those paintings have so many overlapping figures that the bodies turn into fragments, like body parts on the battlefield. But that's also what makes them beautiful. The pain creates geometry."

"Geometry! Too much of my life has been geometry," Arnaldo

groaned, slumping forward so that his forehead almost touched the table. "Italy is a country of great engineers, we're a very geometrical people. But Nietzsche tells us that geometry is not enough. Mankind also needs intoxication, inebriation, self-loss—the Bacchic principle!"

I refilled his wineglass.

"No!" he exclaimed, pushing the glass away in horror. He scratched his head impulsively and peered up at me out of a rich writhing nest of black tendrils. Nothing, I saw now, would stop the words from welling out of him; and as they began to pour forth, and then grow ever more erudite, I recognized him as belonging to a class of Neapolitans I had some experience of—the permanently unemployed prodigies. The prodigies spent their lives in drafty, high-ceilinged apartments, making the best of chipped china and threadbare linens; they struggled with Fermat's last theorem or worked on a new translation of Chekhov's plays or a biography of Cimarosa, and waited for a job to come through, and talked and talked. And so Arnaldo also talked, till the pizzeria had grown empty and the market had closed completely and the streets outside were silent.

"While we're at it," he said, calmer at last, leaning back, "there's something else I wanted to ask you about. This business of giving so much of oneself, I mean, giving one's energy, one's care, one's time, for so little in the way of appreciation after so many years—well, what do you make of it? Is it right to resign oneself to such a situation? Or should one make a fuss and insist on something better?"

What was he referring to, exactly? This way that some Neapolitans had of electing me their involuntary confidant—it made me squirm inside. There was Benedetta always telling me more than I wanted to know, Loredana trying to exact from me more trust than seemed warranted, and now this Arnaldo... Well, perhaps it *was* flattering... but no, he had placed me in an impossible position.

"In work situations," I began, steering toward a safe conversational haven, "I believe I have noticed . . ."—and I trotted out some serviceable nonsense.

But now something else intruded on my mind, something tied to my own dreams and wishes—why hadn't it occurred to me before? After my first attempts to parlay my falling-palace dream into success in the lottery, I had gone back several times to various betting parlors, and I had listened to various ladies work out various combinations. There were differences of intuition about different words: about palace versus home, about falling versus collapse, about princess versus woman, about surprise versus laughter. And in response to the ladies' questioning, I'd tried to remember my dream and to guess which distinctions applied. What I hadn't seen, though, was that this dream might be a premonition that didn't bear on the lottery at all. Maybe the princess was only trying to forewarn me, for instance, or maybe she was simply a deceiver, or maybe . . . but I was tired, and slightly tipsy, and my brain was too stupefied to function.

Back upstairs, we saw that Assunta had finished the curtains. She tiptoed on a chair and began to drape them over the french windows, her ample, amphora-like figure cut out against the backdrop of the night. When she was done, she climbed down and closed the internal shutters and shot the bolt. A diminutive fridge had arrived, and Arnaldo and I jockeyed it into its corner beside the sink.

"Now then, about Fabio—" I said.

"I haven't reached him yet," said Assunta. "I'll try again."

Going over to the telephone stand, she dialed a number. She waited, lips pursed; in a moment her eyes grew large and she began to nod, slowly at first, then more emphatically.

"Yes, Fabio . . . Certainly, Fabio . . . Fabio, I do understand."

Firmly she faced me. "Fabio says I can't possibly let you have a copy of the lease," she said. "It would be too dangerous for me."

For a moment the silence was absolute. Nothing is so quiet as a market that has just shut down, and in my mind's eye I saw the deserted streets outside, the shuttered shops, the garbage-strewn shadows.

"Darling," Arnaldo said, in a supplicating tone, "I think you're making too much of this. A contract is something that both parties share, and anyway this lease isn't really—"

"I don't care what you think," Assunta shot back, "I'm going to do as Fabio says. I can't take any chances." Her colors had grown ferocious, almost incandescent in the whiteness of the empty kitchen, and I sensed her magnificence, her tragic power. She was a great tragic actress at the moment when the play first calls for a note of fervor, a note of inspired hysteria.

But now Arnaldo, too, raised his voice, and I recalled uneasily that his voice also had two registers, one whispery and mild, the other savage and explosive. "Darling!" he said, almost shouting, "I don't think you're being quite fair. After all, this is *una persona seria,* you shook his hand, we have an agreement that we ought to honor. He has been waiting for almost a week to take possession of the flat."

"That's fine," she said, "he can have the flat. He just can't have a copy of the lease." She was no longer looking at me but appeared to be gazing far out, into another world. "Anyway, I can't bear any more of this, I just can't bear it! I slaved away for twelve hours at school today and then I had to do these curtains. Let's go!"

It was then, at last, that I saw what I should have seen from the outset. I had imagined I was part of this drama, when in fact it was they, and they alone, who were onstage. Like a spectator in a darkened theater, I was invisible to the true players, who stood there glowering at each other.

"Assunta dear, I think you ought to reconsider—"

"No! Let's go!" she shrieked. "Let's get out of this place! I'm tired, tired, tired!"

Stanca, stanca, stanca! The words seemed to expand, to fill up the whole room, and then suddenly the room went pitch-black.

Staring into nothingness, I realized that Assunta had switched off the lights.

Stanca, stanca, stanca! Her voice rose to a tremendous volume as my hand scuttled across the wall, searching for a way out of the palace that was to have been mine.

4

Signora Perna and the Other World

The place I eventually found was a large corner studio on the fourth floor of a seventeenth-century palazzo near the Galleria Umberto I. The ceiling was almost twenty feet high, and the french windows were lofty enough to afford a view of the sky and to allow, for much of the day, patches of sunshine to dawdle about the floor. My landlady, a semiretired architect, lived across the hall from me. She told me that the building had once formed part of the headquarters of the Spanish garrison, my studio being a subdivision of a former reception parlor. I believed her. I had no trouble imagining mustachioed officers in bouffant pantaloons arranging themselves about the place, ready to belt out a drinking song.

My room had virtually no heating. The glacial vastness chilled my bones, yet when I crossed the passage to my landlady's room I discovered that it was even chillier than mine. Unperturbed by the cold, she did worry about some artisans who, she suspected, were enlarging a tunnel under the house and perhaps corrupting its foundations. Frequently out, she wore a rakish bonnet and on weekend evenings sat in the Caffè Gambrinus at what she called the *tavolo dei vecchi,* the old people's table. She was by her own report a lone wolf, but she had two sons in Avellino, a small city east of Naples much damaged by recent earthquakes, and whenever one of them came to visit her cheeks flushed and her eyes glistened.

The palazzo enclosed a courtyard with the standard Neapolitan open-air stairway, resembling a stack of loggias. Often, leaning over the balustrade of one of these loggias, a matriarch in a chemise or unbuttoned blouse would vociferously remind somebody who was leaving to mail a letter or to call on *nonna.* The otherwise aristocratic courtyard was also crisscrossed by about a dozen clotheslines. Sheets and pillowcases, nightgowns and underpants floated there like a riotous display of signal flags. Sometimes, entering by the front portal, I was stopped short by a cascade of long white linens draped from on high and edged by a silvery, celestial light.

Slowly, as the weather warmed, I grew fond of my lodgings—I liked their airiness and brightness, their curious views down into a lively intersection where pushcart men hawked shellfish and tiny, tasty vegetables. From my corner perch, I could look across at other windows similar to my own pair, each with its pediment of gray *piperno* stone and wrought-iron balcony. Some windows stayed permanently, queerly shuttered, but most were encumbered with clothes racks holding underwear ranged according to size: papa bear, mamma bear, baby bear . . . I could almost deduce the composition of the family that lived inside. Canopy-like plants sprouted from some of the balconies, and in the afternoons, during the postprandial siesta, slanting shadows stole across the walls and the balconies and the plants and the rows of drying laundry. Then the sunlight so sharply defined the windows that the scenes they framed—a housewife cleaning, an old lady watching a military parade on television, a child sitting on the pot—seemed to hover just outside my room. Naples, usually so noisy, grew quiet at this hour, and as the light waned I heard women singing to themselves or ghosts of accordion music or a band would march by, trumpets blaring hosannas to the Virgin, then rapidly recede into silence. Toward nightfall I heard the horns of the ships in the harbor, and maternal voices calling from balconies to children in the streets.

My landlady, whose name was Nunzia Perna, was plumpish and comely and wore spectacles on a cord. Her eyebrows formed high, patrician arches over eyes ever primed for conversation. Whenever she put on her spectacles, lassoing me into focus, her lips parted with incipient speech and a smile hovered at the corners of her mouth. But she was slightly hard of hearing, and every now and then she turned up her television set very loud to hear the news or the weather report.

Sometimes we met by chance in the spacious corridor that separated our rooms. Then, using her title, as was proper, I would ask her typical lodger's questions.

"*Architetto,* can you recommend a greengrocer?"

"*Architetto,* where can I get my laundry done?"

"*Architetto,* what should I do with the trash?"

And she, too, had questions for me. One afternoon, looking vaguely distressed, she said, "Signore, do you hear drilling or something? Perhaps with a masonry drill?"

"I think it's downstairs," I said. "They're doing some sort of shop-fitting on the ground floor, behind all that plywood sheeting."

"It's not underground?"

"It could be, I suppose."

"I hope they know what they're up to . . ."

Nunzia believed that her cavernous quarters, which she had bought ten years earlier and subdivided, had gone up in value, and that pleased her. The people in the neighborhood did not please her, however. Once she stepped outside and a man reached for her throat. Terrified, she took him for a strangler, perhaps a drug addict, and to save herself she thwacked him with an architect's ruler she happened to be carrying. Actually he was lunging for her gold chain; luckily, the ruler was of iron. "I gave him great saber cuts," she told me, grinning mischievously and smiting the air with the side of her hand. But she went down under the strength of his arm, and as she did so the shutters of the shops along the street went down with her. He loped off sullenly, without the chain, and as she picked herself up, the shutters, too, went up, and the shopkeepers dashed out to help her. Nobody had seen anything, but gazing in horror at the welt on her throat, they advised her to hang up an ex-voto to the Virgin.

"If they had said what they'd seen, their shops would have been burned," Nunzia told me. "I don't blame them. All the shopkeepers are paying the *pizzo*. But I don't—I refuse to pay the *pizzo*. That's why I don't have a brass nameplate with 'Architetto' on the portal downstairs, even though I still get a fair number of commissions."

Sometimes I joined Nunzia at the "old people's table" in the Gambrinus. There she would chat about art with the painter Arturo Assante, a noble old gentleman who sat leaning forward on the handle of his cane, or she would listen to Pasquale Converso—"Don Pasquale," they called him—talk about the Neapolitan popular song; a retired actor, he had been a member of a famous troupe. The café's pianist, a round-faced Russian émigré girl who had once played keyboard in the streets of Naples, chose half-forgotten airs to entertain the patrons, and Don Pasquale would sing along from the table in his wavering voice, always specifying the name and date of the tune. Don Pasquale also liked to hold forth in learned fashion about Pulcinella, the Neapolitan *maschera,* or comic figure, and once he had words with another patron who failed to grasp Pulcinella's true nature, which was, Don Pasquale insisted, at once beneficent and malicious. Nunzia herself rarely spoke, but sometimes, quietly at work in their midst on a watercolor of the Gambrinus's mirrored interior, she would listen with a half smile to her companions' tales of the *monacielli,* the sprites who infest the houses of Naples. Once, when somebody jocularly proposed a murder, she made, with a wink at me, the *mano cornuta*—the "horn hand" that wards off the evil eye—under the tea table.

Nunzia kept a properly outfitted studio in Avellino, where she had several projects going and where, as I have mentioned, her two sons lived. Though her room in Naples contained a drafting table, she used it mostly for working up her watercolor studies of the Gambrinus, whose pier glasses and chandeliers and Belle Epoque nymphs would gradually bloom upon the page. The room was also furnished with an iron camp bed, imposingly spartan, and a utilitarian rocking chair. Beside the rocking chair glowed a portable electric fire.

One afternoon, encountering me in the hallway, Nunzia invited me into her room and motioned me to sit down by her desk. She resumed her place in her chair, and drew her sweater about her, bathed in the orange light of the heater. "Do you hear it?" she asked me. The muted sound of drilling rose from somewhere beneath us.

"Maybe it's the *monacielli,*" I suggested, to put her at ease. "Maybe they're engaged in home improvement."

She looked away pensively. "My mother," she said, after a moment, "had a vexing problem with a *monaciello.* It was really terribly distressing—indeed, I believe that sprite got the better of her."

Before her birth, Nunzia told me, her family had lived in a part of the Chiaia district previously occupied by a monastery. The monastic buildings had long ago been torn down, perhaps during the suppression of the conventual orders, and this destruction had upset the balance of things. For the monks' chapel must have stood over many ancient tombs, and in and around these tombs, she supposed, the *monacielli* had made their dwellings. The dislocation had left them homeless, and also provoked their resentment.

"My mother was then a young wife," she said, "intelligent, artistic, something of a feminist at a time when such ideas had no currency in Italy. She would eventually have four children, of whom I was the fourth, but only two, both boys, had yet been born. Mamma was very level-headed, I should add, and not given to dabbling in the occult. She was also a strict disciplinarian—we children called her 'the Field Marshal.'

"Well, the trouble with the sprite started when Mamma found money here and there, little coins lying scattered among the bed linens, in places the children couldn't have reached. At first this merely bewildered her—then she began to grow afraid. And one day, all at once, she sensed something especially frightening—that the sprite had taken offense at her very fear of him, and now aimed to wreak serious mischief.

"She was right. The second baby's high chair began to walk around the house. At night, whenever her husband, my father, was away, the high chair would grow restless and march noisily from room to room, ending up in strange places. This went on for several weeks, and then the sprite took a fancy to the baby himself. Mamma would watch in horror as the baby's tiny hands floated upward as if lifted by an invisible playmate, and she would pull him down into her bed with her, deep under the covers, and press his body to her own. At other times the baby would giggle and reach for an invisible bauble in the air, only to burst into tears of despair the next moment, as though it had been mischievously withdrawn."

Nunzia's smile, as she recounted these events, suggested that the *monaciello* was not beyond the reach of her sympathy: perhaps she herself had remodeled a building or two hereabouts, evicting some pitiable sprite. Generally disruptions amused her (as long as they didn't tamper with load-bearing walls). One morning over freshly made coffee from her *caffettiera* she informed me, suppressing laughter, that a certain film star from Rome, hard-pressed to find lodgings in Naples, had stayed over for the night and "made pipi on the floor." The star, she revealed in due course, was a Labrador much used in Cinecittà.

Nunzia said that her father had been an official in the municipal tram company, and that lacking his wife's feminine intuition and artistic temperament he perceived nothing of what was going on in the house. Though much in love, the young couple often quarreled at this time. The wife would look on with a jaundiced eye as the husband donned his hat and gloves to frequent the city's cafés chantants, where women performed half naked. She asked him to stop; he wouldn't; and so it went, Nunzia told me, week after week.

"One night," she said, "during their regular quarrel about this diversion of his, the exasperated husband left the marriage bed to sleep on the divan in the sitting room. He had just fallen asleep when he felt that he was being boxed on the head, on the shoulders, all over his body. He sat up with a jolt, thinking his wife had had an access of spontaneous rage, but saw no one at all in the room. So he rejoined her in bed, and there fell peacefully asleep. Yet their woes continued until Mamma, who had fallen into a decline, insisted on moving house. Which was not so difficult, because that place was only a rented apartment. And when the family moved, the story came to an end."

I noticed now that the drilling sound from below had also come to an end, but I wondered about the cafés chantants. Had that issue, too, been amicably resolved? I decided it was best not to ask.

As I got my bearings in my new neighborhood, my life changed in several minor but pleasant ways. Benedetta felt more comfortable visiting me here, and several times, in the early morning, she bought fish from a skiff docked in Mergellina—including, once, I recall, a *pezzogna,* caught in the depths of the Gulf—which she later cooked on my range. I also spent more time at the Gambrinus, where I got to know Arturo Assante, the elderly painter, who gave me a strange figurine he had made in his youth—a wounded sylph in terra-cotta, wearing a Regency riding topper; the figurine came to dominate my room and also had a tonic effect on my moods.

At this time I also began to dream even more vividly and uncannily. I often dreamt of a parallel world, of a city that resembled Naples but was not and of a room that resembled mine but was not and where strangers slept under the worktable and out on the balconies. I wondered why I was having such dreams, and even devised a little theory to explain them. Generally I drank a glass of light Campanian wine before going to bed, and it occurred to me now that these wines might be affecting my brain. If I drank Taurasi, which was violet and velvety, would I have a violet, velvety dream? If I drank Falanghina, which the ancient Romans had developed and which went well with prawns, would I have a Roman dream, gladiatorial, enfevered by crustaceans? And if I drank the effervescent Asprinio, would I have a fizzy dream with a sudden "finish," a total evaporation of memory? When I put this theory to the test, however, the findings were inconclusive; so I dropped the experimentation but continued my vinous routine.

It was also around this time that I got into the habit of listening to the radio as I lay in my darkened room. My favorite show aired on Radio Camaldoli Stereo—in fact, I don't think RCS had any other show—and was hosted by a fortune-teller named Gennaro D'Auria. Gennaro billed himself as a clairvoyant and a card reader, but the commercials for his practice—based in Torre del Greco, in the Vesuvian zone just outside Naples—also vaunted his skills with crystals and ashes. He was clever and jocular, and, as far as I could make out, free of the usual spiritualistic venality. Unlike the TV mediums who crowded the Campanian airwaves every night toward eleven-thirty, Gennaro didn't charge his callers for waiting on hold or even for talking with him—sometimes he indulged them for ten or fifteen minutes at a stretch. After all, the program promoted his psychic services, and besides, he obviously loved being on the air. He loved the sociability of it, the vast circle of devotees, the voices calling out to him from the wide volcanic landscape of Campania—from Somma Vesuviana and Pianura by the smoke-exhaling Phlegraean Fields, from the lava-filled byways of San Sebastiano and the lawless backstreets of Torre Annunziata, from Pompeii and Boscotrecase and salt-smelling Portici. He was a modern Tiresias, and he gloried in it.

Elderly spinsters called in, and lonely widows, and childless women entering menopause. Jilted fiancées called in, and young girls forsaken by their lovers, with plangent voices. Young men called in who couldn't find brides, and young men who'd been passed over when everyone else was getting promoted. Few middle-aged or older men called in, but some did who'd recently lost a loved one and wanted to contact the departed soul before it drifted out of range. All these people called in, and all of them Gennaro tried to help or console.

Gennaro also put them on guard against the TV mediums, the ones who charged while you were queued up and waiting. "Some of you may not know," he would say darkly, "that I have grave reservations about the TV mediums." These clairvoyants were wildly popular all over Italy; they tended to work in partnerships, like law or accounting firms, offering a range of consultants, including, say, a card reader, an astrologist, a *sensitivo,* or seer, and a *lottologo,* or lottery specialist. It was illegal to sell lotto combinations, but a famous psychic up in Lombardy was making billions of lire doing just that, among other things. "As many of you know," Gennaro D'Auria sometimes said, "I have often worked with the Law."

Gennaro gave every appearance of being reasonably considerate, yet peculiar conditions had to be satisfied before he could say what was in the cards. "Turn off your lights!" he might bark out to a caller—he could sense bright lights at the caller's end of the line.

"But Gennaro, my lights are all off!"

"That's a lie, signorina, there's a red glow in your room. Oh why for the love of heaven must you lie to me? Do you think I can't see it, signorina?"

"*Mamma mia,* you're right, Gennaro! But it's not my light, it's the sign outside, the sign over the *salumeria.*"

"Very well then, dear, please close your shutters. When you've done that, we can begin . . ."

Gennaro, like many priests, seemed ageless when heard and not seen. He had a curiously nasal voice, as if afflicted with chronic sinusitis, and an unmistakable regional accent, which only made him sound more folksy, more avuncular. He had the Neapolitan kindness, the Neapolitan fellow feeling, and often he would break off a session to direct a caller to a medical specialist.

"Signora," he would say, "a psychiatrist is what you need—not me."

Or: "Signorina, have you ever heard the word 'gynecologist'?"

Eventually, as I lay listening in the dark, I realized how well Gennaro used the resources of radio. On the line his callers not only unburdened themselves of their troubles, a recognized therapeutic act in Campania, they also hoped to get their complaints addressed by one endowed with supernatural powers. Gennaro was in no sense a saint, yet he reminded me of those saints who are constantly plied with written requests in the churches of Brooklyn or the Bronx. Like Saint Jude, for instance, he was a community figure with a proven track record; to call him on the phone was to partake in a far broader association than that fleetingly established between two people—it was like joining a street procession. Gennaro D'Auria's show temporarily banished people's sense of isolation; it brought the loneliest voices of Naples up out of the streets and fused them in a chorus in my skull, and I would listen to his program and feel strangely at peace. I was soothed by the sound of so many voices, gravelly voices, smokers' voices, gamblers' voices, the voices of those who talked through their teeth, but all so candid, so human in their sore affliction: to my ear they had a family resemblance. For most of the night the voices streamed in, the voices of the lovelorn, the chronically ill, the lonely, the despairing, the credulous, the incredulous, and after a while I no longer heard them, except as voices in my dreams.

Nunzia Perna's husband, I knew from our conversations, had been, like his wife, a licensed architect. He had also worked as professor of life drawing at the Faculty of Architecture, which was housed in the dourly majestic Palazzo Gravina, in Via Medina. He had been eight years older than she and had died long before my arrival; an accomplished artist, not yet fifty. His name was Ettore Guerriero dei Conti—the Guerrieros were a noble family with a large estate near Avellino. They had served as notaries to the Bourbon monarchy, and, amateurs of the chase, had turned their domain into a game preserve.

In Palazzo Gravina, Nunzia told me, Ettore Guerriero began his fifth year of study as she was beginning her first. Like the other male students, most of them recently demobilized soldiers whose schooling had been interrupted by four years of war, he was fascinated by the presence, then quite novel, of several young female students. "I was rather on the prim side," Nunzia said, "but he saw me and asked who I was." By chance one of her brothers was a classmate of Ettore's—they were working together on a design for a new municipal aquarium—and he grew aware of Ettore's interest in Nunzia. One day this brother came and told her to look into the common room, because there was a student there, he said, who resembled Basil Rathbone, the actor. But when Nunzia looked she couldn't find anyone in the common room who fitted that description remotely, and she left feeling cheated. Still Ettore did not give up. Knowing that she enjoyed painting still lifes of flowers which she sold at the school, he approached her one day and asked whether he couldn't look them over to select one. And this Nunzia recognized as a pretext to meet her.

In time Ettore began visiting her family's apartment, in Via Mezzocannone, next to the university. She thought him gentle and cultivated, and she found that she enjoyed his company. Before long he was spending most of his free time there, especially on weekends, when he would linger until late Sunday evening. This perplexed and irritated her father. "What's going on here?" he said to his daughter. "After all, Ettore isn't your fiancé."

They married when she was twenty-two and he thirty. She had set down one condition—that she be able to devote herself to her architectural studies—which he accepted. She continued, slowly

but steadily, to pass thirty-five out of the forty required examinations. Later, when he was appointed director of an art school in
Ancona, on the Adriatic, she enrolled in the Faculty of Architecture in Florence. By this time the couple had two sons, of eight
and four years, but she was still determined to pass the final five
exams. This meant rising at two every weekday morning in order
to catch a westbound train, but she acquired the remaining credits
and received her degree. Until Florence Nunzia had led a totally
protected life, but there she found herself suddenly and disconcertingly on her own. The first time a young man pestered her for
a date she was profoundly shocked. "Don't you see that I'm wearing a wedding ring?" she sputtered, and rushed off to telephone
Ettore. "Calm down, calm down," he said. "These things do happen, you know."

By the time Nunzia told me all this I had already formed a
pretty good idea of what the pair looked like in their youth, since
Nunzia had shown me a photograph of herself and her husband
taken during the first year of their marriage. In the picture they
are standing in Piazza Plebiscito: he is sketching something, presumably Laperuta's neoclassical colonnade, and with his short,
trim beard, he looks self-possessed and authoritative. She, obviously much younger, with tenderly molded cheeks and gleaming
eyes, still has something of the well-bred filly about her.

Nunzia told me that she spent nine or ten years with her husband at Ancona. He scrupulously declined to hire her at the
school he directed, but "destiny," as she told me, "intervened." She
had found a teaching post at nearby Fano, and together the couple
entered a competition for the redesign of that city's Piazza Mala-
testiana. Their project won second prize, attracting the attention
of a government educational inspector who had grown up in
Naples. Coincidentally, Nunzia at this time had just finished
designing a piece of furniture, a mobile home bar, modeled after a
copper container then used by Neapolitan deliverymen to keep
pizzas warm. The lids of these containers had a unique, dome-like

shape, which the inspector recognized in Nunzia's drawings. Beguiled by this witty allusion, he arranged a position for her at Ettore's school without having to call in any favors.

Yet after a while Nunzia began to lose heart at Ancona, finding it socially cool and insular. Still closely tied to her siblings, she missed the gaiety and warmth of Naples, the ceaseless clamor, the sound of housemaids singing in the courtyards. She had episodes of a mysterious illness and pined away for her people in the south. She also had a foreboding that something terrible was going to happen. And soon afterward, perhaps because of the good offices of a former professor of hers, she and Ettore were transferred to his hometown of Avellino, he to serve as rector of another state art academy, whose teaching faculty she would join. There they bought the top floor of a building under construction and turned it into a beautiful loft.

"One day," Nunzia told me, as she was making us coffee in her kitchen, "a day I'll never forget, while Ettore was sitting on the sofa and our younger son, Bruno, was playing on the rug, Ettore said to me, 'Now I'm even happier than before. I really am a very happy man.' I gave a sort of start, you know—I was overcome by a terrifying premonition—and I said to him, 'Don't talk like that!' And soon afterward a lump was discovered under his armpit . . . Well, the doctors kept him alive for a year."

As Nunzia Perna's lodger I was no longer truly inside the Quartieri Spagnoli—Via Roma cast its commercial pall on my immediate surroundings—but I did most of my shopping and other domestic errands in the web of narrow streets known to me from my previous flat. And as I made my rounds, chatting with shopkeepers, crossing paths with friends and acquaintances, I grew aware of something I hadn't noticed before.

This was the profusion in the district of generic shelter images, like a child's basic drawing of a house. Such symbols of home were everywhere, and chief among them were the portals of the quarter's many small churches, which on warmer nights stood ajar. Softly lighted, richly colored, and crammed with hangings and gilt-framed altarpieces, their naves reminded me of Neapolitan sitting rooms—"oversize *bassi* for the pious" was how I described them to Benedetta. Echoing the church portals were the *edicoli,* or wall shrines, which, capped by their own tiny pediments, also resembled little houses, in this case houses for the statuettes inside. Every thirty yards or so such a shrine stood forth from the wall, tenanted by a plaster Madonna and filled with votive knickknacks. Electric candles, silk flowers, donor photographs, swags of lace, pendant lamps, festoons of grosgrain ribbon . . . the more clutter the better, the shrines seemed to say, as though the sheer density of objects proved religious fervor. I began to take an obsessive interest in these shrines, and sometimes, as I finished my shopping circuit, I would stand almost mesmerized before some particularly crowded and barbarous specimen. Only by a conscious exercise of the will could I tear myself away, but then, climbing to my flat, I would encounter the same motif, the same little house shape, as soon as I entered my room. It was caused by a trick of the light: as day was fading outside, the glowing windows across from mine shone with ever-greater brilliance, and one in particular, with its pediment and supporting pilasters and framing draperies, began to masquerade as another wall shrine. But this one was crowded with gesticulating figures, nightmarish credenzas, and armoires like confessional booths.

⟡

"Listen, signorina," Gennaro D'Auria was saying, "I'm getting a very funny vibe here. It's getting clearer, something's coming into my vision . . ."

My light was out, and I lay in bed listening to Radio Camaldoli Stereo. I'd had a hard day and I was exhausted, but I wasn't relaxed. My attempts to locate a certain press officer in the

Municipio, the city hall, had led to my being directed to the Castel Nuovo, where the city council sits, and back again to the Municipio. I had negotiated meandering stairways, circumambulated a courtyard on a quaking catwalk, tried to use a derelict men's room, and finally, following a custodian's directions, come up face-to-face with a marble bust behind a grille. Mostly I'd waited around for hours. In the end, no one knew where the press officer was, or indeed whether he really existed.

"My God!" Gennaro exclaimed. "Your tummy and thighs are all red, aren't they, signorina?"

"Yes, Gennaro."

"You . . . you spilled boiling pasta water all over your front, didn't you? Twice in one week!"

"Yes, Gennaro."

"Please, please, my dear, *per l'amor del cielo,* be careful around the stove! And I beg you, *ti prego di tutto cuore,* stay off the phone while you're cooking, okay?"

"Okay, Gennaro."

"Promise?"

"I promise, Gennà. *Ti giuro.*"

For a few moments Gennaro's signature melody played. Then a young male voice came on the line. A boy had telephoned Gennaro in anguish because he had dreamed his father's death and that death had come to pass; now his father returned to haunt him in dreams, offering unsolicited guidance. The boy said, "My father told me to go downstairs and look at my car, and I did, and the windshield was smashed"; and he said, "My father told me what numbers to play in the lottery, and I played them, and I won." The boy's voice quavered with fear. He loved and missed his father, he said, but the visitations were endangering his sanity.

Gennaro suggested that the father's death had come too suddenly for the boy to come to terms with a great many unresolved questions. It was a case of arrested mourning, Gennaro said, perhaps best addressed through prayer; but his impromptu paternosters clouded my mind, and I sank softly and swiftly into slumber.

I was awakened some time later by the voice of a different youth, very circumspect this time, almost defiant. "I don't know, Gennaro," the young man drawled. "I'm kind of skeptical about the powers you claim to have."

"Okay, okay, you're a skeptic"—curtly—"but there's obviously something you want to know about. Is it love, family, or work?"

"It's love," said the boy.

"Okay, then here's what I have to say." Gennaro's voice grew more than usually nasal. "You're a disaster in the love department. No woman is ever interested in you. Am I right?"

"Maybe. I guess so."

"Still skeptical?"

"No, Gennaro."

"Well then . . ."

I'd report the rest of this exchange if I remembered it. But once again I slipped into sleep, from which I did not awake until morning.

Nunzia Perna, as it turned out, had a reputation in the neighborhood. She dressed artistically, sometimes in a cloak and that dramatic bonnet of hers, but sometimes, too, in painted jeans, like a teenager on her way to a rock concert. She was also regarded as having what folk called a *caratterino*—a stubborn, difficult will. Once she went to Donato to have her picture taken, then denounced the results. ("What did she expect?" Donato asked me, nonplussed. "She wanted *passport* photos!") But in my view Nunzia was determination personified: she had come of age during the wartime bombardment, struggled for more than a decade to become an architect, and kept her practice afloat after her husband's death. In brief, she had shown just the sort of tenacity that Benedetta, for all her taste and charm, did not appear to possess.

"Several years after the death of my husband," Nunzia told me during one of our chats, "when I was working as headmistress of the art academy in Torre del Greco, I was approached by one of my teachers. 'Why are you so sad?' she asked me. 'I'm not sad,' I answered. 'Yes you are,' she insisted. 'Listen. I am in communication with a spirit guide. He can be very helpful—let me show you.' And to prove that it was true, she took me out into the country, where we sat down under some trees and heard faraway voices, voices that were not of this world. Mind you, this teacher was perfectly rational. She taught science at the school and worked as a pharmacist in Torre. She knew nothing about me, nothing about my life or my husband's death. I thought about her offer, hesitating for a while, and at last I confessed my secret wish: 'I want so much'—oh, you can guess what I wanted! I couldn't accept my husband's death, I just couldn't. Every day I asked myself: Why?

"We decided to hold a séance, with her as medium. We held it in my office in the academy. And she summoned her invisible spirit guide. The guide communicated by writing, using the teacher's hand, not mine. The teacher's hand held the pen but it moved by itself, in the oddest way, free of her volition—her muscles did nothing at all—and the handwriting wasn't hers either, it was awkward and strange." Nunzia let her hand dangle to illustrate this motion. "Using the teacher's hand, the spirit guide wrote: *'Why have you called me? Are you ill?'*

"'No, not I,' the teacher answered aloud. 'But there is one here who is—my headmistress.'

"*'She is not ill,'* wrote the spirit guide. *'It is only sadness. And she is worried about a son.'*

"This was true—I *was* worried about one of my sons. It was Carlo—the shock of his father's death had upset him terribly, and he wasn't applying himself at school. Well, for a while the spirit guide said nothing. But then the hand started writing again, and it spelled out *'She must not worry about her son. He will get his university degree.'* Which turned out to be true, I might add, because Carlo recovered and did get a degree, though much later on. But at the time I was weeping uncontrollably. I was totally overcome."

Nunzia fell silent for a moment, as if a little confused. "A while later," she went on, "we held a second séance. That time I knew my husband himself was in the room, and I knew that he wasn't alone. Other spirits crowded around, other family members who'd passed on to the next world. The hand wrote *'I want so much to speak with my beautiful wife.'* And then the hand wrote a wonderful phrase, courtly and poetic: *'She is my rock, and I am her precious stone.'* It wrote many other things besides, which I have kept somewhere among my papers—perhaps one day I'll show them to you." Nunzia as she told me these things sat in her rocker with her hands clasped in her lap, tranquil, rocking gently. There was no sign of sorrow in her face.

"Sometime later," she said, "I went to a séance in Salerno. None of the people there knew me. We were all sitting around a big circular board with the letters of the alphabet written on it, and a glass, an ordinary wineglass, was floating in the air by itself, hovering over the letters, spelling out messages. And it spelled out the words *'Who is this man?'* which caused a commotion in the room. I sensed that my husband was present, and I said to the others, 'It's all right, it's all right, don't be frightened.' Then the glass spelled out the words *'I want to speak with my beautiful wife.'* I wept, and the people cried out in alarm, 'Who is here? Who are you? Who's writing this?' But I knew who it was."

◆

One afternoon Nunzia's older son, Bruno, now married with two children, came from Avellino to visit Nunzia, and the two fell into a good-natured argument about the Neapolitan perception of death. The son claimed that the Neapolitans were terrified of death, which explained why they spared no expense in propitiating the gods of the underworld. The mother claimed that they had made their peace with it, and so could acknowledge it with solemn and pleasant festivities.

I missed most of this argument as my mind drifted back several months. I recalled that I myself, one autumn morning, had witnessed the celebration of the day of the dead. Out walking, I'd found myself caught up in a dense crowd of pedestrians heading eastward, toward the edge of the city. The crowd surged forward as if pulled by gravity, compact as lava and so single-minded that I felt no urge to resist its momentum. Thousands of families, many dressed in black, some carrying flowers, were marching cheerfully together. I supposed they were accompanying a funeral cortege until I remembered that the date was November 1, Ognissanti, or All Souls' Day. Arriving at the great cemetery of Poggioreale, the people bought bouquets of chrysanthemums, marigolds, and lilies from street vendors, then trooped into the fantastic walled necropolis, which, rising on a terraced hillside, receded like a succession of stage flats into the early morning mist. I felt, as I entered it, that I was vanishing into a sheet on a set designer's drawing table.

The crowd followed a steep skyward path between rows of temples surmounted by scaly cupolas and overarched by cypresses. I knew only the sort of Italian cemetery that consists of small tombs enclosing tiers of drawerlike stone *loculi,* or burial niches, leaving you with the impression that the dead are much like the living, only smaller—with the stature of, let us say, elves. But at Poggioreale the tombs were huge, with lawns, backyards, and, occasionally, picture windows, proclaiming a settled faith in the resurrection of the body at life size. The people stood patiently in line, waiting their turn to enter their family tombs, then reemerged with heads bowed in meditation, and the endless replication of these groups of figures across the monument-studded terraces suggested an entire tribe in rapt communion with its ancestors.

By the time my silent recollection of the day of the dead had passed, the argument between Nunzia and Bruno was flagging. But I could tell that it had followed the course of many such discussions, in which Neapolitans reviewed their customs with a certain defensiveness. In the seventeenth century the city had re-draped churches, avenues, squares, even emotions in the Baroque style, so that everything became theatrical, even death. On the surface, death today still meant towering funeral carriages, plumed horses dyed black, cemeteries like draftsmen's render-ings—the burial rite, critics said, was overdramatized. But Nun-zia's reticent smile argued otherwise. There was nothing false in this people's acceptance of mortality, she quietly insisted; death, here, had always been too visible for that. And wasn't there such a thing as a failure of truth to the dead, just as there can be a failure of truth to the moment, or to a friend? If so, it was something to be guarded against; and what then was the harm in addressing the dead with ritual regularity, or even in throwing them a party—a citywide bash—as one did once a year, on Ognissanti?

"When my husband died," Nunzia told me, a few days later, "I was forty years old. I had to reeducate myself. In my girlhood I was totally protected by my family, and then I passed under Ettore's protection. After his death I would leave the house without my keys, I would walk out of cafés without asking for the check, because Ettore had always paid. The waiters would run after me—'Signora!'

"Before his death we had been working on a project together. It was an urban renewal plan for the town of Irpinia, and he was so much more experienced than I that I always followed his lead. He was so talented, I really don't know which he was better at, the artistic or the technical side of his profession. And then, suddenly, I was working on the project all alone. It was daunting, and some-times dismaying. At each step I asked myself: What would Ettore do? How would Ettore solve this problem? It was as though he were still alive, still helping me out. I had not really accepted his death, and I could not have continued to work except for the feel-ing that he was there, guiding my thoughts."

5

Benedetta in Springtime

May, and the end of rain—of puddled streets and fouled stone stairways—both cheered and troubled me, for my long history of visiting Naples had entered a confusing phase. On the one hand there was Benedetta, and my flat, and my growing rootedness here; on the other the paucity of writing assignments, for at present my prospects did not look good. In fact my prospects appeared to lie behind me, while a checkered future lay ahead. It was more than likely that I would be leaving Italy within a month or two.

I was meditating on this predicament one morning on my way back from the San Paolo stadium, in Pozzuoli, where I had gone to buy soccer tickets, when I saw a face, momentarily unplaceable, smiling at me from the doorway of a bar in Via Galeota. It was an oddly puffy face, merrily disenchanted and creased like an old wallet under the eyes.

Then I recalled that the scalpers, the *bagarini,* hung out across from the box seats at the stadium, waiting to pounce on groups of desirable tickets. "Luca Corsaro," I said.

I hadn't seen Luca in more than six months, but after I'd first met him, at Donato's, I'd joined him a few times at a gaming room in Pozzuoli. The place had a bar and a television and a big electric fire, and Luca and his cronies would sit there in comfort under the benign gaze of Padre Pio and Totò and play *scala,* Naples's answer to rummy. Four players, a double deck, twelve-card hands—that was the usual setup in *scala.* You aimed to close first, with poker-type combinations, but there wasn't any bluffing, it wasn't a blood-on-the-floor kind of game. The men, cordial and heavyset, wore sagging tweed jackets and breezy shoes with woven uppers. Stakes were one or two thousand lire a hand. "They think they've got old Luca," Luca would say after a few bad rounds, "but Luca's just lulling them into a false sense of security." Whenever I played, I lost.

Now Luca embraced me, with a cuff on the cheek for my not having called him in so long. In the bar, his *bagarini* friends stood sipping coffee and trading tips. They smacked him fondly and chucked his jowls, and one caught my eye and jerked his chin slyly toward Luca, making the money gesture, the friction of thumb against pointer. After coffee we all went back outside and drank in the breeze off the Gulf, watching the youngbloods gun their bikes down Via Galeota. Then Luca, who was feeling expansive, revealed to me the secret of the scalper's trade. Why would anybody buy a soccer ticket for five times the price stamped on its face? It was a way of saying "I love you." Luca sold most of the tickets in pairs, to old gents with mistresses, and the price told the girl how much she was valued.

Defying his paunch, Luca leapt agilely on his Vespa, and offered me a ride back downtown. So mounted, with his black Napoleonic curls and feathery eyelashes, he cut a dashing figure. But we didn't go downtown, we tore over to the university hospital— he changed his mind midway. Luca explained that he worked as a nurse in maxillofacial surgery and had a bit of business in the ward; but the business had nothing to do with nursing, I discovered. In a storeroom he pinched the cheek of Maria, an elderly cleaning lady in black work clothes and sandal clogs with brass-tinted hair. Her storeroom smelled of wool and was piled high with bolts of wool and woolen garments, which she apparently hawked on the side; but Luca hadn't come to discuss her sweater sets either. He chided her in dialect about a certain precarious mortgage of hers, shaking his joined hands at her in the prayer gesture, as though he were her big brother, while she gazed glumly at the floor.

Later, in the hospital lunchroom, we jumped the line of personnel leading up to the counter, because Luca knew all the cooks. "*Ohè* Giggino, *ohè* Gennarì!" he called to them as they overloaded our plates. We paid with a wink, and I ended up spending the afternoon with him, on and off the Vespa. From a porcelain atelier he commissioned a set of biscuit-china lamps for his on-the-side lamp business, and from a lumberyard he bought some moldings for his on-the-side frame business, and as he boldly swerved through the streets people waved and called out his name.

"*Ohè*, Luca!" they shouted. "*Ciao*, Luca!"

"You'd think," he murmured in my ear as we shot past Piazza Dante, "that I was the *puttana di Napoli* . . ."

I saw a lot of Luca for a while; and in fact, it was people like him, indulgent, accommodating, who almost convinced me that I could hang out in Naples forever, that I could go native and never say good-bye. And Luca, I saw, feared nothing, which I admired, up to a point. He had said that his forte was sidewalk-ology, but to get around he drove, and drove intrepidly. Once, in his Fiat, on the way to drop me off at the Cumana railway station after one of our nightly card games, he cut off a city bus with a very naughty left turn. The traffic in the intersection froze—there was a moment of unearthly silence—and then the bus driver came flying at us, fists clenched, screaming.

"*Omm' è merda! Scurnacchiat'!*"

In a trice fearless Luca charged out of the car at his assailant, whereupon another uniformed personage, a low, powerfully built, man-faced woman, rushed out of the bus as well. Luca heaved his bulk back inside and began to rummage furiously in the glove compartment. He rummaged and rummaged, but by the time he'd given up looking for his knife the two bus drivers had vanished.

He sank back in his seat and stared at me, appalled. "Did you see that? Tough guys! They thought they could frighten old Luca! And that woman, *Dío mío*—a mastiff, a boar!"

≈

If Luca's driving sometimes rattled my nerves, I found the antidote that spring in Sandro Scudellaro. Sandro, and Sandro's convertible, gave Benedetta and me our happiest times together, the balmy times I really want to remember, though I'm a little vague now on how it all got started.

I do seem to recall that Sandro had telephoned to tell Benedetta about a hypnotherapist he'd found for Tina's smoking addiction; casting about for help in kicking a habit of his, he had heard that the man worked wonders. I also recall that the wonder-worker flopped—he had started, with his somniferous baritone, to put Tina "under" when he unguardedly used an off-color dialect word and she broke into a giggle—and Sandro apologized to Benedetta for recommending the wretched quack. So it may have been partly his contrition that led him to offer to take us for a spin in that new pearl-gray Mercedes of his; but I also think Sandro liked to play chauffeur simply because he had been a chauffeur, and a prize one, in an earlier life. He had been none other than Achille Lauro's driver for a while during Lauro's long reign as mayor. The stories Sandro told about Lauro—how he'd received delegations in the buff, while rising dripping from his bath, and how he'd trotted around the stadium after soccer matches waving a handkerchief at the fans—were offered reverentially. Sandro felt that Naples had gone downhill after Lauro's fall because the people needed "a strong hand" (though not necessarily a monarchist one like Lauro's). The reign of Lauro had been a golden age for Sandro; apparently he had not held a steady job since, and as for the convertible, we hadn't an inkling how he'd come by it. We had no intention of asking.

When I think of Sandro now, I see a powerful projection of nose, a mask of wraparound sunglasses, arched cheekbones, a toro neck, glove-sized hands, a prizefighter's stance: Sandro had the *guappo*'s way of looking sculptural in all lights. I mean that he was physically of the *guappo* type; I had no idea what he really did for a living. He was, in age, one of Benedetta's older friends—I realize only now that a lot of her friends were older—and almost certainly she had met him through her father. He had in the past performed some service for Beppe, possibly connected with distribution. Sandro's marital circumstances were unusual. Though separated, he and his wife had remained on good terms, being equally attached to their two teenage children, and they spent a lot of time together. Currently Sandro was working his way through a succession of women, and though some were charming, others, according to Benedetta, were louche and conniving. One of Sandro's weaknesses, she claimed, was his antiquated sense of honor, wherein he again resembled a *guappo* of lineage, one of those *guappi* who no longer existed except perhaps in the Rione della Sanità, that perennial camorra stronghold. Sandro was overprotective of women, Benedetta said; he'd do better to protect himself against them. When I asked her whether she found Sandro attractive, she replied, "Alessandro? *Puh.* I've known him since I was a kid. He'd lay down his life for his friends, but he's got problems. He's really had to struggle with his problems." For her, that meant drugs.

Be that as it may, Sandro's sports jackets were beautifully cut, he wore the best Marinella ties, he never talked out of the side of his face, and he was perfectly *disponibile,* as they said in these parts—he always knew what you needed (a cigar? another grappa?) before you'd thought of it yourself. Sandro seldom spoke at any length, and whenever Benedetta did, drawing those fine distinctions of hers, describing exactly how a certain palazzo or piazza ought to be restored, he would gaze at her with quiet admiration. Once Sandro invited us out to his beach house for lunch together with his girlfriend of the month, a tanned, smiling creature in a pale sundress; though the house turned out to be a sort of stage flat a half mile from the sea, and the meal little more than spaghetti with garlic and oil, he carried it all off with such panache that I still remember that afternoon as the most delightful of my life. The fragrant oil, the volcanic wine, the sun, the couple's kindness—all bestowed a sort of lazy benediction. So when Sandro honked to us from the Mercedes one evening by the monument with the carved lions in Piazza dei Martiri, we were only too happy to hop in the back and sit as close together as we decently could. Settled behind Sandro's square shoulders and grizzled head, we rolled westward toward the first shy stars that gleamed over the Tyrrhenian Sea.

I recall sneaking sidelong glances at Benedetta, trying to memorize her profile, losing and finding it again against the masses of foliage and stonework that flew by on the Riviera di Chiaia. Soon it would be a year since I had met her: so much had changed since then. A lot of that time I had spent in Naples—even when away I had daydreamed of the place, and she was never long absent from my thoughts. Yet I naturally supposed that whatever we had was temporary, unless she would be willing to share in my precarious, nomadic existence. Now, as summer approached, a little sadness seeped into most of our times together, tingeing them with longing and regret.

I had begun to suspect that my fascination with Naples served largely as an alibi for my fascination with Benedetta. Whatever was involuted, self-enwrapped, calyxlike about the city sufficed to account for the mystery of the woman. In this way her unrelenting coquetry could be interpreted as a feature of the southern female's famous commitment to sex, a particular instance of a general behavior; the likelihood that this seductiveness expressed a specific tropism toward (and demand upon) myself I consid-

ered with a certain unease. Unease, because of my misgivings about
the terms of our attachment, which I knew she had sedulously if
silently considered.

But hadn't I also formulated terms, equally implicit and hypo-
thetical? As I contemplated, dreamily, what those terms might
entail (such as bearing her bodily out of this city, like a Roman
with a Sabine on his shoulder!), I began to see it all the other way
around. Maybe Benedetta attracted me primarily as a Neapolitan,
and if one were to subtract her ethnic identity. . . . But of course
that was impossible, it was meaningless. The only reality was this:
her terms and mine, however vague or wordless, were surely at
variance and perhaps irreconcilable.

Twilight falls rapidly over Naples, and as we headed into
Mergellina a sort of opalescence washed over the boulevards, as if
all light had passed through milk glass and was equally diffused
over the colonnades and the storefronts and the streetcars sliding
forward with a muffled sound. A tremulous sky was mirrored in
the windows of the ornate office buildings, and the faces of the
people looked vitreous too, spun of glass charged with traces of
the sun's final radiance. Little seemed left now of the clamor of
the day, as if the sea beside us had engulfed it, and for a spell the
city seemed almost immaterial, a reflection of our own wish that
everything stay the same.

Sandro drove confidently but not self-importantly, lulling us,
for five or six glorious and almost identical evenings, into a state
of wistful calm; then he got himself a girl, I mean one he cared
about enough to bring along on our outings. It was touching how
much he respected Benedetta's judgment: he mentioned the girl
once to test the waters, again two days later with growing warmth,
and then one evening there she was, climbing out of the convertible's passenger seat in Piazza dei Martiri to greet us, with plenty
of thigh showing and her streaky-blond hair coiled up on her head
and her lip gloss picking up the setting sun. Around her neck she
wore a fichu of palest yellow, giving her a jeune fille air, and when
with a smile she extended her hand to me she narrowed her eyes,

as though I were a dangerous customer. Her name, she huskily announced, was Imma. Seating herself in the back with Benedetta, as Italian form prescribed, she at once lit a cigarette and started chattering so rapidly in Neapolitan that I could scarcely make anything out. Understanding so little, I at first didn't bother to listen, exchanging a few words with the laconic Sandro, but after a while both the cadence of her speech and certain common expressions conveyed that she was gossiping about some locally notorious people. For her part Benedetta seemed to have heard of them, indeed she had clearly met Imma somewhere before—which wasn't surprising, because she seemed to know almost every Neapolitan in her age group. But she barely put in a word, she who was so voluble, and then with the utmost reluctance.

As we climbed higher on the road toward Marechiaro, Imma occasionally bent forward to tap my shoulder and address me, in Italian. Whenever we passed a point of interest, some villa overlooking the sea, for instance, she would offer a racy chronicle of the social careers of its various owners, and tell me with which film star or ex–prime minister's mistress it was currently associated. At the same time, she lost no occasion to touch, however tangentially, on her enthusiasm for various Hollywood movies and television series, which she naturally assumed I had seen; such irrelevancies, I supposed, being her way of welcoming me to her homeland.

"That woman!" Benedetta said under her breath, when Sandro had stopped for gas and cigarettes; the two of us had ambled a little way along the road.

"Oh, she's just trying to be friendly," I said.

"*Eh eh, ma tu non capisci.*" Benedetta faced me, squaring her shoulders in a posture of defiance, as if to badmouth Imma were to stand up for free speech.

A flight of stone steps trodden into scallop shapes led down to an overgrown orchard. We followed it for a few paces to a sheltered spot where Benedetta took me by the hand. There was, she declared, a whole syntax of vulgarity that I seemed unable to grasp. Take that ridiculous fichu with which Imma tried to assign herself, quite falsely, to Benedetta's generation; or that hoarse voice and those chain-smoker's crepey lips; or that keep-off way of looking at men, practically inviting a pounce. Not to mention that battery of Neapolitan clichés and doubles entendres, whose stupidity I couldn't appreciate.

"Verbally," she said, patting my cheek, "you'll always be an outsider here." I was, she said, like somebody walking around with a suitcase full of nouns and verbs and idioms, Italian words I'd laid plausible claim to. But that suitcase had another compartment to which I had no key, full of Neapolitan words I would never decipher—"It's a compartment that could easily explode in your face. Whenever you spend time with people who talk dialect, you're unable to figure out what they're saying. And, well, Neapolitans smirk, they simper, they try to oblige, as they've done for a thousand years. But only to curry favor. And what I say is, Don't trust them."

"Okay, so I shouldn't trust you," I laughed.

"That's hardly what I meant to say."

"Oh—so you're protecting me from Imma."

"Of course not. I only wish you were more . . . discriminating. You and Sandro both. More able to see what any of our Marias or Rosarias could see in an instant. That this Imma is —" She left off, seeing the look in my eye.

When the car was tanked up Sandro suggested that we dine somewhere in Marechiaro, overlooking the sea, which made sense, given the hour. But as he now had to fight his way through a congested nightlife quarter, he was forced at times to drive off the road or to back rapidly up one-way streets. At length, however, he gained speed on a serpentine thoroughfare separated from a plunging escarpment by a masonry parapet. Low structures, cafés, and restaurants rushed by, then patchy vineyards, warehouses, loading docks; we raced along unobstructed for a while, allowing Imma to praise the brilliance of the moon and to resume her gossipy tale. Then a row of flares loomed up, causing Sandro to brake abruptly. A patrol car sat broadside across our lane, while beyond it four or five carabinieri gesticulated under a tow truck's headlights: as we got out of the convertible I felt Benedetta's hand searching for mine. A little farther on, a Cinquecento stood rammed against the parapet, unharmed save for a crumpled fender, and behind it an Alfa Montreal with its hood up, pouring out steam. Sandro pointed to where a small section of the roadbed had buckled, opening a pothole about two feet in diameter. Barring our way, a carabiniere told us that it had caused a minor accident—one or two motorists had perhaps been slightly hurt—but in any case traffic had backed up behind us. We would have to wait here until given leave to turn around and depart.

Sandro at once drew the carabiniere into a technical discussion of the mishap; with a shrug Benedetta sauntered over to the parapet. Nudging off her suede mules, she sat down with her legs dangling over the far edge, and glancing at me she patted the coping beside her; but I declined the offer, being subject to vertigo. The rounded coping slanted unevenly, and beneath her was a long dizzying drop to a stand of laurels and holm oaks, beyond which the sea beat against an outcropping of rock. She wore nothing but a light cotton dress and a cardigan, and to see her perched above the chasm, so exposed in the suddenly opaquer darkness, gave my stomach the jitters. I was about to plead with her to come away from the edge when Imma straddled the parapet beside her, lit a cigarette, and resumed chatting.

Doubtless Imma's palaver was intended to be merely chummy, but if so her technique was all wrong. Through the haze of her dialect I heard that she was mentioning several people over and over by name, and Benedetta's expression soon revealed that they were people she knew. As Imma went on, Benedetta began to interrupt with displeasure, deploying her usual gestures, and as their voices grew shrill and their hands assailed the air I began to fear that at least one of the pair would end up losing her balance. This image, of the two women quarreling in dialect by the precipice, lives on as a dumb show in my memory: and as I replay that memory now, studying Imma's face, I grow aware that despite her conspicuous prettiness, she is used to not being liked, and that Benedetta does not see this, or seeing it, does not pity it. More striking than that, though, is what I see in Benedetta's features: that Imma's story has broadened to include her, that she is now one of its characters, and that she is both chagrined and afraid. But that, unhappily, is not all. For how strange it seems to me today, that afterward I never questioned her as to the meaning of that story, that I was so amazingly, so culpably inattentive. But of course I could not have known then how things would turn out later.

The altercation was cut short by the sudden appearance of Sandro, impassive in the convertible. *"Va buo, iammuncenne,"* he said. That's enough, let's go.

Now in the city each evening was more fragrant, more intoxicating than the last, but Benedetta and I could only shudderingly imagine our next outing with Sandro and Imma. Knowing how he valued Benedetta's friendship, what, we wondered, could we say to him? *We don't feel like going on any more drives? We'll come if your girl-friend keeps her comments to herself?* Obviously we couldn't simply make ourselves scarce, so we decided to follow the established routine. We would meet him, smiling, at Piazza dei Martiri, and for the whole time, as far as conversation went, Benedetta would restrict herself to a few words of sociable assent. This final jaunt would allow us all to play down our disharmony, and after that Benedetta would stay clear of Imma.

When we arrived at the piazza, however, we found Sandro standing by the car, alone. His nose looked even more sculptural than usual, and he wore a debonair smile. His face betrayed no sign of regret over what had happened last time.

He tossed me the keys.

"Meet me here at midnight," he said. "And take care of the little *bellezza.*" He turned on his heel.

The *bellezza* was smiling, but I wasn't. In addition to the obvious reasons for embarrassment, I had a bad driving record in Naples. I misread the signage, got traffic tickets, and fell afoul of the wild-eyed characters who ruled over the parking lots and answered to no one but the camorra. But Benedetta, who had a taste for luxury, had instantly made herself comfortable in the car, so I got in, too, and turned on the ignition. We kissed. And as we sped along the Riviera di Chiaia, still kissing, I had already lost my embarrassment.

Benedetta put her head on my shoulder and her hand on my thigh. It was that enchanted time of day when the city swam together in a grayish, opalescent hush, and everything, even the facades, looked translucent. Suddenly impassioned, I found that I could not go slow in this car. When I had to brake briefly for a bottleneck a few teenage boys drifted toward me, waving their arms, wanting, I knew, to ask about "cylinders" and "horsepower," but I stepped on the gas and sped past them. I sped past the corner where the man had said *porca madonna,* past the quay where Benedetta had bought us freshly caught fish, past Palazzo Donn'Anna, a dark blur lapped by white waves, and as I sped faster and faster still, I couldn't imagine ever being without her.

6

Melisurgo's Well

On some evenings I could not tempt Benedetta to come out with me, because she planned to visit friends or prepare for an exam or help Tina with her homework: her sister had not yet mastered the art of sitting down and studying for two straight hours without getting distracted. On such evenings I might set out walking with no special goal, aware however that I was free to explore certain zones that Benedetta would have nixed had we been together. For in her mind more than a few streets, squares, and cafés, whole neighborhoods, were off-limits. Some were tainted with memories of childhood boredom, adolescent frustration, or scenes of distress that she didn't care to recall or to speak of; others had been rebuilt and brutally denatured, yet others claimed by tourists or slumming *cafoni*, louts from outlying towns, people who weren't real Neapolitans. One district that she never frequented, and that continued to attract me, was my former turf, the Quartieri Spagnoli.

Sometimes I would roam around in the upper end of the Quartieri, the part that backed into the Vomero. I roamed here because I liked how the dark settled over these steeply slanting streets, how they filled up with restless figures, silhouettes that called back and forth and often resorted to pantomime, like shapes in a magic lantern. I walked briskly, without tiring, and one evening, crossing Via Teresella, I saw a tiny garage slotted between a row of *bassi,* and in the garage a man reading at a desk, immersed in a pool of light. This scene was new to me: I was used to peeking into *bassi* and seeing all sorts of things, but I'd never seen a garage converted into a study, least of all one like this, whose walls were decorated with yellowed street maps and architectural photographs. I couldn't resist stopping for a moment, at which he glanced up and, in typical Neapolitan fashion, motioned for me to come in.

Michele Quaranta, I soon learned, was known in the quarter by the dialect moniker *chillo d' o' sottosuolo,* meaning "He of the Underground." He was trim and wiry and limber as a ferret, with a trick of jabbing the air with his chin to nail down an argument, yet he also exuded an indefinable air of melancholy. He told me that evening that he had pursued a self-invented career as a speleologist, and that he had intimate knowledge of the subterranean world beneath the city. Michele was often joined by his younger brother Salvatore, who was stocky and ruddy-faced and as naturally explosive as his brother was pensive and scholarly. Salvatore didn't so much speak as pop his words off his lips, often sharing tidbits of local gossip or folklore. The pair fascinated me, and so did the garage-workshop. On the wall behind Michele's desk hung a picture of his grandfather in the prewar uniform of the *bersaglieri,* a crack infantry corps of the Italian army. A history book on a stand lay perpetually open to an engraving of Ferdinand II on horseback. And on a nearby bookshelf stood a statuette representing a knife-sharpener at his grinding wheel, looking just like one of the itinerant Italian knife-sharpeners of my childhood in New York.

I spent many hours chatting with Michele, and it was he who told me the following story.

One day, in the late 1970s, a fire had broken out in a cabinetmaker's workshop in a street called the Gradoni di Chiaia, in the Quartieri Spagnoli. It started when one of the carpenters dropped a lighted piece of paper into a basement well shaft to see how deep it was. Smoke billowed out of the well and then out of the workshop's doors and windows, as if a petroleum tank had been ignited, and the streets filled up with onlookers, whose astonishment mounted steadily, since the fire, which nobody could see, burned unquenchably, like a sacred flame. Many local families had to be evacuated for fear of smoke inhalation, and despite a relentless dousing, the conflagration raged on for days, for weeks, until the brothers, who had grown up in the neighborhood and knew the tunnels that honeycombed its bedrock foundation, discovered why. The secret of that fire, they later realized, was also the secret of Naples's construction, of its inner life for more than two thousand years.

Before the reign of Achille Lauro, the Gradoni di Chiaia had consisted of a great flight of steps fashioned of volcanic stone. Old-timers in the neighborhood told me that provisions had to be brought up by donkeys laden with packs or panniers, while larger loads, such as the huge casks of the new wine that people here loved, were pulled up laboriously in carts: mules would be hitched up on both sides of the traces to help the donkeys heave the cartwheels over the massive stone risers. In those days fruit vendors patrolled the streets, extolling their peaches and pears with cries like love songs which some people could still imitate, and costumed touts called *pazzarielli* performed skits on behalf of restaurants or shops. The "Spanish church" in Via Santa Teresella, now bolted shut, was still used for worship, and children whispered among themselves that a "sacred land"—their term for a crypt—lay beneath it. The children also knew that under many of the quarter's houses broad passages burrowed deep into the earth.

Achille Lauro removed the flights of stone steps in the sixties, opening the district to motorized traffic and defacing its already derelict beauty; but even before that people had grown oblivious of the passages beneath their dwellings, filling them with the rubble of the war bombardment and eventually sealing them off. During the Allied bombing of Naples, in 1942–43, the tunnels had served as corridors to shelters, and afterward nobody wanted to remember the experience of huddling underground for hours, waiting for the all-clear. In time the tunnels were almost forgotten, like the donkey carts and the singing fruit vendors and the sacred land beneath the church. But they were not forgotten by boys like Michele and Salvatore.

The Quaranta brothers' obsession with the underworld had begun with that fire beneath the woodworking shop next to the "Spanish church." What had happened, Michele told me, was this. As the hidden blaze persisted and even intensified, a dense pall of smoke veiled the streets and seeped into shops and apartments. The firemen grew more and more worried, but the locals, with their disenchanted humor, made a joke of it. "The Vesuvius doesn't smoke anymore," they cracked, "but now it's smoking under Naples." And this very idea—that something was literally *smoking under Naples*—gave Michele and Salvatore an idea. During their boyhood, in the fifties, they had played hide-and-seek in the underground passages with their father, who knew a little about the netherworld and found nothing frightening or even especially interesting about it. Later, by themselves, they engaged in amateur spelunking, stealing down the back stairways of the *bassi,* squirming into the maze of half-obstructed passageways that lay beneath the part of the Quartieri nearest the Via Chiaia, and they discovered that many of them led to cavernous, vaulted cisterns, which communicated laterally with other cisterns. Crawling like inchworms from one chamber to the next, they found that they could also climb up abandoned wells until they neared people's flats at street level. Coming closer, they could hear the voices of women and girls and maybe smell a family's long-simmering ragù. One time they pushed through a partition and into a *basso* and scared the wits out of a woman; another time they had to hide in an armoire for fear of being caught. Later, while deep underground, they discovered an intermittent torrent which seemed to be leaking from a building in Via Nardones. They realized that this leak, if left unrepaired, could erode the structure's foundation, and they decided to warn the tenants about it. Climbing back up to the street, they identified the imperiled house and knocked on the door. A "pretty, plump signora" appeared—so Salvatore (with suitable gestures) described her—and they told her about what they'd discovered. She invited them in, and they rooted around in her *basso* until, at the back, they came on an old-fashioned hip bath whose drain leaked badly and was clearly the source of the torrent they'd seen down below. The brothers then determined that the flooring under the little tub had decayed all the way through, and that just beneath it a forgotten well shaft plunged straight into a cistern. They stood there aghast. "I pictured that tub going right through the floor," Salvatore told me, "and the pretty, plump signora going right down with it."

The fire on the Gradoni di Chiaia broke out more than twenty years after these youthful escapades, but the brothers had never forgotten the underground tunnels: the map of the labyrinth lay imprinted on their memory, and it occurred to them now that the smoke might not be coming from the cabinet shop at all, or even its cellar, but rather from a fire burning deeper underground. It just might be that by climbing down a nearby well shaft they could reach the fire from the side, through one of the passages they knew from their boyhood. They decided to contact Clemente Esposito, a civil engineer who headed a local speleological society and had studied the Neapolitan subterrane, and together, in Via Conte di Mola, the three climbed down a disused shaft, a former well outfitted during the war as a stairway to a bomb shelter. "You might not believe it," Michele told me, "but we found that there's no such thing as a blind alley down there. The Neapolitan underground goes on forever. Oh, it can be blocked by refuse, or wreckage, or piles of rock fragments, but there's nothing you can't get over or through, and eventually we found a vantage post right under the fire. There it was comfortably cool, because all the heat was rising, and there we figured out why the workshop continued to pour out smoke."

It was a matter of simple deduction. They knew how the fire had started, with that lighted scrap of paper tossed into a well, and they realized now that the flame had fallen through to a cistern that was probably filled with decades' worth of sawdust and wood shavings from the shop. The flame had ignited this detritus, and the underground fire had then spread sideways, into refuse-choked cavities that no water from above could reach. They concluded that the blaze had to be attacked not from above, but from the side, which was how, in the end, the firemen put it out.

The Quarantas' background was purely Neapolitan: their parents had kept a café in Santa Lucia, the seaside district of the grand hotels, and they themselves had made their living doing mechanical and electronic repairs. Grayish and wan, Michele gave the impression of being the more solitary of the pair, while the playful, peppery Salvatore could be seen at all hours trudging about the quarter or halting to chat with one of his many friends. He generally carried a briefcase and wore, except in summer, a half-length raincoat; he was known to be making his rounds in the service of his two daughters and their children, dutifully performing a daily list of favors, and people still talked about the pains he had taken to arrange one daughter's wedding. It was he who told me that the street called the Vico Lungo del Gelso had derived its name (*gelso* means mulberry in Italian) from a now-vanished grove where the Spanish soldiery had stained their uniforms by lying with harlots on the drupe-strewn ground.

Michele had a way of making me feel that I was in grade school again, that time had somehow stood still. He would welcome me in with a wave, reminding me poignantly of my high school Latin teacher, Emilio Calvacca, who always returned my erratic translations splotched with red wine, an act of pedagogical bravado I admired. Often, while he answered a telephone call, I would examine one of his puzzling machines or scrutinize an archaeological pamphlet or a chart of the city's subterranean galleries. Then, as he hung up, I would turn back to him and he would smile at me amiably and, I thought, rather wistfully, before launching into one of his erudite discourses.

Whenever I mentioned the Quarantas, the locals grew wide-eyed. Clemente Esposito, the engineer, told me a story. He said that once, when he had driven over to see them, he had been obliged to park his car where it obstructed a shop entry. A man came out to ask him how long he would be, and when Clemente explained that he would be calling on Michele Quaranta for five minutes the man retreated into his doorway; he said with a bow that Clemente could block the whole street for the rest of the day for all he cared. The Quaranta family, local rumor had it, were "people of respect." But not Michele and Salvatore; not the brothers personally. They were *pulitissimi*—"totally clean," though apparently some older relatives were not to be trifled with.

Since I frequented Michele's garage-study, I met a fair number of people there, and I came to see that the brothers had an eye on the doings of the quarter; like Donato, they formed part of its brain, its central nervous system. I remember that late one afternoon, a young man with a strange, asymmetrical head came limping into Michele's study. His affliction looked severe, and it saddened me. His name, he said, was Tancredi—a knightly name, a name out of Tasso—and he lived in a house a few paces away.

Tancredi spoke in a halting manner that suggested brain damage. The effort of speaking contorted his facial muscles, but his words came out lucid enough. He asked me, "Are you from England?" and when I answered, "No, from America," he said, "I love peanut butter," and "I love America."

"He loves America," Salvatore echoed, shooting me a mischievous glance. "Hey, why don't you take him with you?"

"Take him—take him off our hands," said Michele.

"Take him and *leave him* in America!" exclaimed Salvatore, grabbing Tancredi's lopsided head with one hand and fondly slapping his cheek with the other.

As Salvatore teased Tancredi his own face reddened, and a black stipple of beard stood out on his cheeks. I suppose he might have seemed coarse, but his jesting was just the old-school southern Italian way of responding to a handicapped person. People like Salvatore didn't pretend not to see the disability, they turned it into a joke.

"This one," he said, fraternally punching the young man's shoulder, "is already thirty, and he still doesn't have a woman." Tancredi smirked as Salvatore made saucer eyes at him. "Wake up, *baccalà*, wake up!" cried Salvatore, using the word for salt cod, which is also slang for "softie."

"You," Salvatore said, turning to me, "you who live down by Via Roma, why don't you find him a woman? Maybe one of those little misses in Piazza Carità. Or maybe that girl of yours has a friend?"

Tancredi broke into a face-cracking smile—he was thrilled by the attention—and suddenly I saw what I hadn't seen before. This exchange was a comic routine. Tancredi came in all the time, I was sure of it now. The brothers were *always* ribbing him. They were *always* telling him to wake up.

It was like a Pompeiian wall painting of a farcical scene, and as I followed the ritualized dialogue I noticed that the blue glow coming through the garage door had faded. The twilight had dwindled, it was night now, and the place felt like a grotto overcrowded with shadows. I saw that Salvatore was trying, in his archaic way, to get through to Tancredi, as he had tried many times before.

"Listen," he was saying to Tancredi, "you say you love America, you say you want to travel, but you're letting your sister gobble up your sick pension. Aren't you? Aren't you, Tancredi? . . . What? Why are you smirking at me? You've got to hang onto that money, Tancredi. For your travel expenses, for your women, for yourself!"

Tancredi's face was twisted with glee, but Salvatore leaned forward and grabbed his misshapen head. "Wake up!" he shouted with tender ferocity, slapping Tancredi's cheek.

Tancredi shook with laughter.

"Wake up, wake up, *baccalà!*"

The more I thought about the fire on the Gradoni di Chiaia, the more it fascinated me. When I asked around, I discovered that many in the quarter remembered it well, and remembered being frightened by it. Apparently it had set off a sort of alarm throughout the city of Naples. It seemed that not everyone had repressed the memory of the underworld—some residents knew quite a lot about it. The Quaranta brothers of course knew about it, and Clemente Esposito knew about it, and the municipality possessed detailed charts of the sublevel maze; not long before, another friend of mine, the muckraking journalist Eleonora Puntillo, had begun a series of carefully researched articles about the area's many lethal potholes and landslides and structural collapses, tracing them to shifting rubble in the neglected subterrane. But now the underground emerged into the general urban consciousness. It figured partly as a sort of monster from the deep and partly as something more positive—a basic element of the city's patrimony, a historic labyrinth worth unblocking and restoring. Two and a half thousand years of expert engineering had gone into that vast network, leaving hundreds of miles of aqueducts, sewers, storm drains, and transport tunnels, and more than five thousand major cavities, including wells, crypts, catacombs, and cisterns. Much of this had an eerie beauty, for the void under the city was a city unto itself, a parallel metropolis with its own burial grounds and frescoed chapels, its streets, shops, and marketplaces. It even had its own denizens, modern counterparts of the prehistoric troglodytes, because the camorra used the maze to store weapons and contraband cigarettes, and burglars tunneled up from the maze into jewelry stores, post offices, and banks. (One morning, I recall, in Piazza Carolina, a young man in a green jacket materialized inside a branch of the Banco di Roma and vanished back underground with a hundred thousand dollars.)

At the time of the fire, the Quaranta brothers were working as *flipper* repairmen. A *flipper,* in Italian, is a pinball machine, but the brothers, masters of occupational improvisation, had had and would have many other jobs, since they could fix just about anything. They had not ventured into the underworld for years, but once the fire had been vanquished they felt a growing desire to reclaim it, or at least a part of it. Their interest lay in the extensive system of chambers and galleries that meandered beneath their neighborhood, near the Via Chiaia, and now they began exploring the maze, which included the enormous, trapezoidal cisterns used as bomb shelters during the war. And almost at once an idea came to them: why not turn the underworld into a paying scenic attraction? The idea was ingenious, and classically Neapolitan: here a collection of cavities—emptiness itself—could be turned into a source of hard cash.

The pair got hold of a set designer at the San Carlo Opera House named Ettore Massarese, with whose help they mounted an underground show called *Dea Demeter,* after the Greek goddess of the earth. The audience was conducted along a trail lighted by torches and marked out by imitation Greek statues, and the spectacle was such a success that the brothers decided to open up a much larger section of the labyrinth. They had confirmed that the spelunking itself offered no great difficulties, since the network was never completely occluded. Yet one big problem remained: they desperately needed to rid the cavities of refuse, most of it inorganic junk.

For this they hit on a piece of trickery that was like something out of a farce by Eduardo de Filippo. Michele began to make publicity visits to the Italian army district headquarters, to the American officers' Archeo-Club, to the university, to the city's schools. He talked up the underworld venture to anyone who cared to listen, and soon curious people began to book tours. The visitors, including entire classes of schoolchildren, would descend into the pair's underworld domain, where they were escorted around and then cajoled into carrying big bags of detritus, two per person, back up to street level. "In this way, over several years," Michele told me, "we got the system cleared out. And for this we never received any public money whatever. Not one lira."

During years of visiting Naples, before I met Michele and Salvatore, before I even heard them mentioned by name, I had enthusiastically followed the rediscovery of the Neapolitan underground. I tried to enter it whenever I could, and found sporadic opportunities all over the city. For the Quaranta brothers were not alone—others, above all an enterprising speleologist named Enzo Albertini, who opened a huge system under Piazza San Gaetano, were engrossed in the same adventure. In the newspapers every now and then I would read that this or that catacomb or network of passages or archaeological excavation had been opened to the public (though often, for technical reasons, these offers would be hastily retracted). I would promptly call a telephone number and book an appointment with a technician or guide, and gradually I came to realize that if I'd been able to obtain permission I could have walked most of the way across Naples without surfacing. The netherworld was as labyrinthine as an owl's ear, an endless succession of plutonian chambers, some dank and dripping, others powdery and airless, some black as pitch, others illuminated by clerestories pierced at street level in the tufaceous vault overhead. When in the end I emerged into the daylight, rubbing my dazzled eyes, I might discover that I'd poked out from beneath the undulant stairway of a Baroque facade, or into a shop or café (though never, as it happened, a bank). The city seemed to want to tell me that every chamber communicated by some secret corridor to every other chamber, that every business meddled in every other business, that nobody stood on truly solid ground.

The multiplicity of hidden cavities boggled the mind. There were five systems of catacombs, one of which, the Catacomba di San Gennaro, notable for its fourth-century mosaics and frescoes, Benedetta had been required to study, on the assumption she'd be leading school groups there. There were extensive ancient transportation tunnels; three aqueducts; and an early-modern sewer system, as well as the innumerable cisterns and well shafts. There were the ever-expanding excavations under the church of San Lorenzo Maggiore, which were uncovering the Roman Forum; there were at least three ossuaries, in one of which, the crypt of Santa Maria delle Anime in Purgatorio ad Arco, the cult of the bones of the dead was still furtively observed; and there was even a fossilized Roman theater off Piazza San Gaetano, which Albertini allowed me to enter through a trapdoor under a table in a private home.

My descents also evoked memories. When as a teenager I'd first visited Naples, shreds of storybook fantasies floated in my brain, awaiting coloration by the actual ancient city. I recalled that somewhere hereabouts, according to Roman mythology, was the passage leading down to the underworld, the way perhaps taken by Orpheus and certainly by Aeneas; and I saw so many squat portals and barred, sublevel windows fronting on the city's steeply descending alleys that I began to fantasize that any one of them might lead directly to Tartarus. What I couldn't have known (having been assigned the second book of the *Aeneid,* rather than the sixth, in my high school Latin class) was that the Campanian corridor to Tartarus was situated not in Naples proper but by the Lake of Avernus, about a half hour to the west, closer to Cumae. The day came when I saw that lake (already a tame suburban pond), but by then what did it matter? Over the years, my daydream, nourished by tangible facts, grew steadily more vivid. Many Neapolitan *bassi,* cantinas, cafés, and shops—especially, for some reason, poulterers' shops—had rear access to the world below, so that the underground came to seem a vast, meandering river, like the Styx of legend, with numberless backwaters and tributaries; and I can say, only half jokingly, that I began, like many of her citizens, to conceive of Naples as a place with easy access to the next world and those who dwell there.

From Michele I learned that the local bedrock is yellow tufa, a porous, elastic stone that can support tremendous weight. I learned that it can easily be hewn and hefted, a fact already known to the prehistoric Cimmerians, who lived in Campania in caverns and underground chambers of their own devising. I learned that Greek colonists arrived in the seventh century B.C., and as their settlement grew they built a subterranean aqueduct, about six miles long, running from springs near the Vesuvius to the outskirts of Naples; and I also learned that the Romans, who took over the city in 326 B.C., constructed a longer aqueduct, also subterranean, that originated farther to the west. Meanwhile, reservoirs, sewers, transport tunnels, and burial chambers proliferated in the relatively unresistant substrate; Spanish conquerors, who arrived in 1503 A.D., hollowed yet another aqueduct out of the bedrock in 1629, and a fourth, outfitted with pressurized tubing, was added in the late nineteenth century.

In 537 A.D., exactly five hundred years after the aqueduct's construction and ten years after the Goths had occupied the city, Belisarius, Emperor Justinian's fabled general, besieged Naples and cut off the water supply. He wanted to parch the barbarians into surrendering, but when this failed—the municipal wells brimmed with water—he marched his troops through the empty aqueduct and took the city by surprise. Nine hundred years later, Alphonse of Aragon followed the same strategy, wresting Naples from its dumbfounded Angevin rulers.

One of the oddest aspects of Neapolitan history is the impression it sometimes gives of unfolding like a poem, a work of man, rather than the usual play of arbitrary forces. Perhaps the most arresting example is offered by some Spanish legislation of the sixteenth century. As Michele explained it to me, Don Pedro di

Toledo, the Spanish viceroy, promulgated seven edicts which for-
bade the building of any new, nonecclesiastical buildings both
within and immediately outside the city walls. Construction sites
were abandoned, and oxcarts laden with stone blocks vanished
from the streets, but behind the facades of the buildings, in their
basements and inner courtyards, the nobles and burghers of
Naples began to burrow deeper, quarrying the soft yet resilient
tufa. The way the Neapolitans circumvented Don Pedro's edicts
was a source of personal pride to the Quaranta brothers (Salvatore, grinning: "See how wily we Neapolitans are!"), and it sometimes seemed as if the whole business had happened yesterday,
and to them personally. Many buildings were seen to shoot
upward, like mushrooms after a rainstorm, under the very nose of
the viceregal authorities (who, I later learned, may well have taken
bribes to permit the infringement of their own edicts). Until this
legislation was repealed, in 1718, interior pits, some reaching a
depth of eighty yards, multiplied throughout Naples; for reasons
of fluid dynamics, many wells were linked laterally to others or to
one of the aqueducts, giving the city's substrate a spongiform
quality.

So the stones of Naples continued to be excavated out of the
city's bedrock and then hoisted higher, ever higher. The cavity
beneath a palazzo became its material source, its mother or womb,
so that as a building climbed upward its basement expanded
downward and also outward, by means of multiple passageways.
Soon the city had no real base but rose out of a sepulchral void, an
inert version of the Campi Flegrei, or "Flaming Fields," at Pozzuoli, to the west, where the hollow earth still shifts and heaves
and belches out sulfurous smoke. The mass of the city, considered
as a whole, emerged from its own approximate negative.

It was, of course, the endless lateral ramification of the subterrane, begun by the Greeks and continued until modern times, that
allowed the city to drink and so to survive: the netherworld functioned as the vascular system of the urban body. It was equally this
hollowing-out in all directions that explained the fire on the

Gradoni di Chiaia, why for so long it had raged on unquenched. For the city beneath the city had its own streets, its avenues and alleys, and along these the fire, like a jaunty boulevardier, had gone for a sort of blazing promenade. And it might have continued indefinitely, finding ever more fuel to consume, if the Quaranta brothers and Clemente Esposito hadn't figured out how to stop it.

In time I discovered that Michele and Salvatore upheld a veritable tradition of descent into the netherworld, a tradition established by illustrious precursors. I was to learn, for instance, about an engineer named Guglielmo Melisurgo, who had died, in his nineties, in 1943, and who, mesmerized by the depths, had rechristened himself the Underground Man. Melisurgo was the scion of a family tracing its lineage back to the Byzantine era; regarded as a prodigy when still a student, he would eventually originate hundreds of projects in and around Naples. Among his other contributions, he designed a hydroelectric plant on the river Lete, in the nearby province of Caserta, and helped organize the electrification of the city. During the cholera epidemic of 1884, which at its height claimed a thousand victims a day, Melisurgo became convinced that the commingling of waters from the municipal aquifers and effluents from the sewer system was spreading the contagion, and he resolved to see the two networks mutually sealed off. To achieve this he had to map the underworld, and for two years, carrying a huge tallow candle, he worked his way through the city's circulatory system, emerging each evening to return home for the night. It was a heroic exploit, reminiscent of Victor Hugo or Jules Verne, and when it was finished, Melisurgo had his map.

To me, more than a century later, the Underground Man seemed more legend than history. In his *Napoli sotterranea,* a cult classic of 1889, Melisurgo talked in tones of wonderment about a

fantastically deep well shaft somewhere in the hill of Pizzofalcone, one of the earliest zones of Greek settlement. He claimed
that this shaft, long since dry, was so perfectly shielded from sunlight that you could stand at its bottom and "look up at the firma-
ment," even at noon. You could, in other words, see something
like the night sky at midday. As it happens, Pizzofalcone is a mysterious quarter veined with wandering flights of stone steps and
narrow streets threading their way under tenebrous arches. In the
seventeenth century, the Hispano-Neapolitan nobility built themselves huge palaces here, sometimes surrounding smaller palaces,
and over these edifices rose the dome of a church, Santa Maria
Egiziaca degli Angeli, whose stone membranes conceal the tomb
of many a Spanish hidalgo. Likewise the palazzi of Pizzofalcone
jealously enfold their back gardens and orangeries, their stands of
ilexes, palms, and araucarias, their crow's-nest *garconnières* and
miniature villas, and I was never able to find the well shaft in
question, though I inquired and poked about. But secretly I
thought Melisurgo's contention preposterous on its face. Granted,
you might be able to rig up a sort of camera obscura at the bottom
of a dry well, with lenses and a "black glass" to mirror the sky, and
so see every wisp and crevice of the cloud canyons as they sailed
together and unraveled; certainly you could see Venus, toward
nightfall. But that obviously wasn't what Melisurgo meant.

In Homer, in Virgil, in Dante, the protagonist undertakes an
underworld passage in order to discover his destiny. Encouraged
by a sorceress, or a sibyl, or a virtuous bard, he descends into the
depths, in Dante's words, to "see the stars again." I thought chiefly
of Virgil when I read Melisurgo. I remembered the drowned Mi-
senus, left sacrilegiously unburied, and the Cumaean Sybil's fierce
remonstrance; I remembered the Golden Bough, which assured
Aeneas's safety; I remembered Aeneas quitting Elysium through
the Ivory Gate, which is the portal of false dreams as the Gate of
Horn is the portal of true dreams. These things perplexed me no
less than they ever had, yet I recognized the themes of pollution
and purification in Melisurgo's personal epic, just as I recognized

the theme of the glowing wand and the leading of the tribe to salvation. As for Melisurgo's well in Pizzofalcone, that, too, had to be a metaphor.

But it wasn't. One evening, as I was heading toward Uncle Ippolito's, I ran into Salvatore. He was carrying his trademark briefcase and wearing his usual blustery look and had obviously been huffing and puffing up and down the neighborhood, running errands, I supposed, for his daughters. He told me where to find Melisurgo's well.

"It isn't in what we now call Pizzofalcone, but down below, in Santa Lucia," he said with his percussive diction, rapping out his consonants. "Do you know those big blind arches at the foot of the cliff? Those arches were open once—not walled up as they are today—and beneath them was a shaft, about one yard wide and fifty yards deep. It must still be there, of course, but you can't get at it now. Anyway, it had iron rings driven into the side, going all the way down, but I didn't trust them, so I went and got a rope."

"You climbed down that well shaft?" I said.

"As a boy I climbed down that shaft—the one Melisurgo talks about. And I looked up at the sky and I saw the stars at noon, just as he did—I saw them, sure as I'm standing here."

I would never get to see Melisurgo's well, or the stars at noon—that was obvious. But I was pleased to learn that the shaft still existed, since his map of the underworld, for which he'd labored so hard, had long ago disappeared.

7

Treasure Hunt on a Hot Afternoon

Aggio pregat' a tutte 'e sante!"* Benedetta said, veering into dialect. I have prayed to every saint . . .

She didn't mean it literally, it was an outpouring of frustration. But tears were almost flowing, there in Via San Biagio, in front of the statue of the Nile, where we had agreed an hour earlier to meet. Approaching its reclining form, she looked tormented and haggard, and several strands of her hair had escaped and clung to her face. She lay her head against my shoulder like a child trying to calm herself. It was thoroughly out of character, this loss of poise, this lapse into the vernacular.

Any strong emotion of hers, or anything untoward that happened to her, tended to excite divergent responses in me. This time, too, though alarmed to see her distraught, I was gratified by her loss of composure. The suggestion that something had flustered her, or even put her in jeopardy, sparked my protective instinct and made me feel needed.

I have already said that Benedetta had for a long while given signs of some secret distress. Often she fell into moody silences, and her caresses at times felt distracted; on many evenings she rang up Loredana for a long conversation. Most worrisome was her waning desire to improve her English, which she now claimed she might never have need of: she would no longer ask me to pronounce a strangely spelled word or to explain one of our ludicrous idioms. My questions about her studies and her future as an art history teacher met with stubborn silence or evasive phrases. "I don't know yet," she would say, or "I've told you already"—when actually she had told me nothing.

I had lingered many months in Naples, and now, with my freelance work finished, the time for my departure approached. Soon I would have very little money left. For a while I took a spartan satisfaction in sheer hardship (no lotto, card games, cigars, or theater tickets), and contented myself with the town's more elemental pleasures. I loved the keen taste of the tiny local molluscs—*fasolari, maruzielli, telline,* and the like—which itinerant fishmongers hawked in the streets, and the bitter greens, called *friarielli,* which the greengrocer at the corner sold for a pittance in luxuriant quantities. Poverty in Naples, I decided, could be like a near-death experience—it heightened your energy and sensuality—but as a quarter of the native population could gladly have informed me, it also ruined your relations with your landlord and your lover. I had no intention of going begging, and despite Benedetta's suggestions that I seek local employment, I couldn't see how I could possibly find work in a place where several hundred thousand people were forced to improvise new jobs for themselves every month, often on the black market. And so, as her mood sank, my own was hardly improving. I felt powerless to stem this decline.

Benedetta kept a diary. I never saw more than one volume, though others doubtless existed, to judge by the hours she spent writing. It measured about five and a half by eight inches, with a hand-sewn spine and a hard cover pasted over with Tuscan cockerel paper. The book had a clasp but no lock, and fitted snugly into a box of inlaid wood furnished with a tiny brass padlock. Yet this box, which Benedetta had found in one of her curio shops, served no real purpose, because she carried the diary around in her purse or pocket almost everywhere she went. Having a daybook to write in forestalled boredom during the many interminable waits Naples obliged one to endure, and she also liked to sketch things she saw in the city: bits of architecture, boys playing soccer, shopkeepers in their doorways, and so forth. The diary was, in that sense, an illustrated journal. This diary-keeping tended to put Benedetta at a distance from active companionship, and to the degree that she was devoting more time to it lately, she withdrew a little from me. She did not encourage me to read what she wrote or look at what she drew, but neither did she forbid me to glance at it.

Her diary, she explained once, had these qualities: it was composed, first and foremost, of random thoughts that hung together only as she wrote them. "I don't want to be like a bad actress," she said, "an actress whose every gesture says 'I'm playing a virtuous person, or a vain person, or a fool.' I want to surprise myself." So she did not edit her entries, as that would have defeated their spontaneity. She might write down her dreams—she dreamed no less vividly than the rest of the city—but only so long as they seemed to tell a story. She wrote to solve problems, to cope with fears, to come to terms with bad habits, to make resolutions. But primarily she wrote to "understand the past," to uncover what she called "buried truths." What "past" did she mean, and what "truths" had required interment? I didn't know—I wasn't brave enough to ask—but when I did inquire whether it wouldn't make her anxious, all this raking up of the past, she told me it produced the opposite effect. "It gives me peace of mind," she said, "like eating a chocolate truffle."

Once, too, she had written love poetry in her diary, but no longer. "Anyway, not to you," she said, with a teasing look. In high school, a boy had found such poems and mistaken himself as their object, which had caused an imbroglio. So she had abandoned this schoolgirlish practice. Instead, she took to making amorous drawings of footwear. In fact Benedetta had tiny feet, and many shoes. She bought them for their erotic allure, always at sales, especially the end-of-January sales along the Rettifilo and in Via Roma, and when I came to see her she would hold up the new pairs by their heels, toes pointing down, like a pair of theatrical masks, comic or tragic. Many freehand sketches of shoes skipped through the pages of her diary, and it was amazing, how economically she could render the curve of a strap, a seam, a crocodile's hide.

Benedetta was so visually alert that her journal often broke into drawing, as the players in a musical comedy break into song. Her drawings were executed with the same calligraphic pen she used for writing, but unlike her entries were sometimes heavily reworked. As the revisions and hatchings piled up, the ink seeped through to the other side of the page, plugging up the writing there and leaving it molten, inchoate. Yet amid this laboring the lighter doodles turned into sibylline faces that spewed out comic-strip balloons. These bore big chunks of illegible text, always ending with fat exclamation points.

As we sat together at Uncle Ippolito's or in a café in Piazza Bellini or the balcony of the Teatro Diana before the curtain rose, my glance might fall on a page or two she was working on, but I was seldom able to read it at length. And I was not, to my surprise, especially eager to do so. This reticence did not represent any delicacy on my part, but rather my misgivings about what I might read. I was afraid of finding thoughts too queer to interpret—memories of a recessive, unreachable past, projections of a future without me. It occurred to me, of course, that Benedetta positively wanted me to invade her diary, as she had beckoned to me as a sexual trespasser. At times I was almost certain that she did; but not, I believe, very often.

Meanwhile, however, she betrayed a relentless curiosity about me and my habits. Once, after a stay of some hours in my flat,

Benedetta as we were leaving said, "You don't have very many clothes, do you?"

"What do you mean?" I said, taken aback. It had never occurred to me that anyone would try to tabulate the contents of my armoire.

"Trousers, for instance," she said. "How many?"

"Well, I have plenty of underwear," I said.

"Yes, but trousers, how many have you got?"

"Four," I said. "Okay, three, now that that black pair has had it."

"*Un ragazzo ben messo come te,*" she said, flatteringly, "you need more. We have to get you some clothes. That jacket of yours . . ." —she made a gesture of disdain. This conversation led us to visit a haberdashery, from which I undoubtedly emerged a more suitable, if also a more impoverished, escort for my style-conscious friend.

So much is perhaps not unusual. But casual conversation revealed that she had gone through my case of toiletries, my desk drawers, my nightstand. She unblushingly asked me about several names in my address book, which I wasn't even aware that she'd looked at, and once, when my wallet was sitting on my worktable, she "reorganized" it without asking me.

If she was going to know so much about me, I felt, shouldn't I know a little more about her? I began to peek into her diary, rapidly and infrequently, on the occasions when she ran out on a hasty errand. I still remember a little of what she wrote, since one never forgets phrases that offer a verdict, whether pleasing or chilling, on one's own character. I recall one entry objecting to my fondness for Eduardo de Filippo's plays, which she deemed dated and depressing. Another said something about her being "a little stoned on *spinello*"—*spinello* is reefer, which I had thought that she disdained—a comfort she took when "after four days Uncle's electricity has been turned back on and I can live like a human being again." I clearly remember a few entries beginning "Last evening you were so . . ." followed by some adjective (sad, gentle, silly, etc.). "When I think of you missing your train," one entry went (more or less), "or of you talking a mile a minute in your abstracted way, it seems I play no part in your life, and then I almost have trouble recalling your face . . ." Coming on such words, I deliberately left off reading and put the diary back where I'd found it. The awareness that I was being watched over gave me an unwelcome sense of vulnerability.

Wherever Benedetta went, her diary usually came along—in her handbag, in her Vespa's storage compartment, or poking out of a side pocket of the little fitted jacket she often wore. I came to conceive of that book as a sentient being, attending her like a handmaid in a classical tragedy, with silent vigilance.

Though sometimes mislaying her diary, she appeared sanguine about the risk of losing it altogether. Often, on entering Ippolito's flat, she would rummage in her bag, look up in puzzlement, then pat her pockets and discover that she had it. Leaving a café in the Galleria, she would tip the gaunt violinist who with the air of a chimneysweep dragged himself about the place, begin to step away, then absently turn to retrieve it from our table. I recall her vanishing back into the underground cinema beneath Palazzo Cellammare to look for it under her seat. After witnessing many such casually sustained misplacements, I grew confident that she would never actually lose it. And, in fact, she never did, until that time she met me by the statue of the Nile, disheveled and stricken-looking, saying she had prayed to all the saints, she didn't know which saint to turn to.

Benedetta did not at first believe in this loss. It was like discovering that her nose or her navel was missing, something that couldn't be true. And initially, she told me, she had stayed calm. She had searched Ippolito's flat and all the other obvious places, but found nothing, and then the situation began to unnerve her. With increasing desperation, and convinced, as in a nightmare, that the very air impeded her, she revisited her haunts in the quarter, friends' houses, cafés, and shops, feverishly asking various cloakroom attendants to search the lost-and-found. But each place was fatally barren, and all the benign, familiar faces—the hall porter at the university, the librarian, her favorite barista on Via Mezzocannone—seemed, this time, to be smirking at her. It was as if they'd all read her diary without letting on.

In this way hours passed, and after a while, she told me, she nearly despaired. But then she girded herself to continue looking, farther afield. She telephoned her sister, who volunteered to help, then arranged to meet me; Tina would join us shortly, she said, and together we would set off on a hunt, stopping first to check at my little flat. I'd never seen her so upset.

When my flat yielded not a clue, Benedetta resolved to remember every single place she had visited since the last time—perhaps three days earlier—she had written in her diary. She jotted them all down on my spiral notepad.

By now it was midafternoon. The siesta hour was ending, and the air rose shimmering over the broiling streets—it was the first really hot day of early summer. We dispensed with the Vespa in short order, partly because there were three of us and partly because Benedetta seemed too jittery to cope with the traffic. So like waifs we trooped along, retracing her circuitous route around the city's older quarters, stopping repeatedly to question shopkeepers, concierges, tobacconists, and elderly ladies who sat on the sidewalk fanning themselves. None of them quite understood what we wanted; none could grasp why we would so value, of all things, a book. With little hope, Benedetta insisted that we poke around in two or three dumpsters, but they overflowed with an impenetrable tangle of trash.

Benedetta failed to notice Sandro Scudellaro's eyebrow acrobatics as we entered the gleaming café where he worked. Two men in uniform told us to kindly stand by the bar and refrain from addressing him. This was, they announced, a "sanitary inspection," at which Sandro's left hand twitched sardonically. An interminable interrogation followed. The owners of the place, of which Sandro had only recently become the manager, were universally presumed to be laundering money, and I saw that for the two officers Benedetta's arrival as one "looking for something" and Tina's outfit, a provocative miniskirt and a little cotton blouse, appeared highly equivocal. The pair offhandedly sneered at me as "this Milanese" until I produced my passport. Their insinuations outraged us all, and I was afraid that Benedetta might make a scene; but Sandro quietly stood his ground in our defense, and at length we were let go.

We came to Via Costantinopoli, in the quarter of the *rigattieri*— this word means something like secondhand or curio dealer, but any *rigattiere* worth his salt could also restore antique furniture and even cleverly confect it. Benedetta knew them all, so we had to inquire in practically every one of their musty and oppressively crowded dens. The rather scruffy dealers fawned on Benedetta and Tina, but they snubbed me roundly, so I took to standing outside on the sidewalk in the stifling heat as the sisters went from door to door. The pair stayed a long time in the last *rigattiere*'s lair, and I watched them through the vitrine as they described the diary with their small, pretty hands.

I suppose I looked noticeably disgruntled by the time the sisters emerged from this shop, because Benedetta asked me whether I wanted something to drink.

"Isn't there a point at which we ought to give up?" I asked. I felt sure that our mission was doomed and she was simply punishing herself. "It seems this is making you miserable without accomplishing anything."

"But I know we'll find it in the end," she said.

"Dear Diary, Today I lost you," I said, clumsily trying to lighten her mood.

"Oh, shut up," she said.

We trudged through the sluggish bath of heat. I was sweating freely, continually mopped my forehead. When we did sit down at a bar for fresh-squeezed lemonades, Benedetta asked me, "Suppose people could see right into your brain—I mean, right through your skull. Would you like that? Would you want them to know what you were thinking?"

"It all depends on *what* I was thinking."

"I mean all the time, every day."

"I guess not."

"I wouldn't necessarily mind," put in Tina. "Then I'd really get through to people."

"You can't see into your *own* brain," said Benedetta, reaching for Tina's chin. Giggling, Tina swatted Benedetta's hand away.

With the first taste of lemonade the two sisters brightened. "Hey," Benedetta said to me, "don't you want to know what I was writing about?"

"Should I?" I said, cautiously.

"Well, don't you?"

"If you want me to," I said.

"Okay, I'll tell you one thing," she said. "You know that painting called *The Flaying of Marsyas* that I showed you, in the museum? By Ribera?"

"Of course, the one where Marsyas gets his hide stripped off. For claiming to be a better musician than Apollo."

"Well, I wrote down my interpretation of the picture."

"And?"

"Well, I totally disagreed with your view." Slowly sipping, she peered at me over her straw in flirtatious defiance. "You said it showed the cruelty of nature, the unfairness of talent—how some people have it and some people don't, and there's no way to even the score. Well, I don't agree. I think Marsyas *wants* to be flayed. Hearing beautiful music is like having your protective shell removed, and in that way we're all a little like Marsyas. To really love music or art or a person entails some suffering, but sensitive people accept that. They want to be able to feel as much as they can."

"I think she's right," said Tina, with conviction.

"You," Benedetta snorted, "you've never even seen the picture."
She made a gesture of annoyance at Tina. "When was the last time
you went to a museum? Eh?"

Tina laughed her tinkling-chandelier laugh.

As we walked on toward Via Roma, Benedetta and Tina linked
arms. Tina relieved her boredom by counting the late-model
sports cars she saw passing by—so many Alfas, so many
Maseratis . . .

Meanwhile Benedetta disclosed more and more things she'd
written in the diary, as if trying to reconstruct the lost narrative. It
was all to do with discussions we'd had, and how I'd been wrong in
every one of them. I was wrong about that movie, that painting,
that person. Wrong, wrong, wrong. At first her taunts were amusing, but then I began to get sick of them, and finally, exasperated,
I put my foot in my mouth.

"Oh, right," I cut her off, as we reached Via Roma, "what
should I say about someone who thinks Eduardo is second-rate
and depressing? He's the greatest Neapolitan writer and everyone
knows it."

"But I've never said anything to you about Eduardo," she protested, looking down. I sensed that we'd arrived at the point
where she wanted us, and we shuffled on in silence, both remem-
bering, I think, the time we'd seen Eduardo's *Napoli milionaria!*
together.

"Are you angry I looked in your diary?" I said, contrite.

"No—and not pleased, either," she replied. "But you don't
often ask me questions about myself, you know. About what I'm
thinking. Or what I've been through."

"Maybe I'm afraid of the answers."

"Well, the upshot is that you don't really know me. Or that's
how it feels sometimes."

Hearing this, Tina left Benedetta's side and moved a few paces
away.

"What do you mean, I don't know you?"

"Well, you talk vaguely about me coming to New York, but how can I? Use your head. Leave my poor father? He gets crazier every year, and Mamma doesn't see it. And what about my English? I'll never learn English, no matter what you say. I'm just no good at it. And I can't live in an apartment with two doors, one door for us and one door for who knows who."

"God, you two are boring," Tina said, with self-satisfied superiority. Lingering discreetly out of earshot, she gazed into a shop-window full of lingerie.

I half agreed with Tina, and in my irritation I leaned up against a wall. By now it was rush hour: crowds hurried by and Vespas buzzed in the street. I tried to stare down the passersby who were watching us quarrel but only felt ridiculous, especially as the women looked on with disconcerting sympathy.

"So what else did you read in my diary?" Benedetta said accusingly.

"Nothing," I said. "Really, nothing."

"Hmmm. Did you read what I wrote about you?"

"No . . . Well, every once in a while my eye fell on a line or two, but that's about it. Actually I didn't *want* to read your goddamn diary."

"You didn't? Why not?"

"I just didn't. But I liked your drawings."

"And my words—my feelings? They're too silly to read?" she said, frowning.

"Of course they weren't silly," I said. "It's just that . . ." I stopped short, suddenly aware of what I didn't want to say. I didn't want to say that the little I'd read made me feel obligated to her emotionally, and that I didn't want to feel that way.

"It's just that what?" she pursued. "You're not going to say?"

I couldn't find the right words.

"Okay, okay, you're not going to tell me." Her voice dropped. "Well, that's your male prerogative." She drew a lock of her hair over her upper lip in mockery of my mustache. "But you have to keep on helping me look. Don't give up. My most cherished thoughts are in that little book. Lots of stuff about you, too." She pinched my cheek, holding the flesh between thumb and forefinger. "Intimate stuff."

This coquettish blackmail was more than I could take; I leaned against the wall again and closed my eyes. By now it was early evening, the sultriest time of day. For a moment I felt dizzy: in my mind's eye I saw the entire city as if from above, with its pockmarked palazzi casting their slanting shadows, its littered streets and shabby public gardens. Somewhere in that infinite maze, those passages and chambers beyond number, lay Benedetta's lost diary. I thought—unkindly—of how oddly appropriate it was to lose a diary in a city of such easy expansiveness, where everyone was always blurting out confessions.

I stood there bewildered, wishing that this day would be over and blaming myself for our argument. Yet strangely, as my eyes blinked open I became aware that Benedetta was smiling at me. It was as if she'd been reading my mind—"seeing through my skull," as she might have put it. She looked serene, and sweet, and slightly amused, and the whites of her eyes had a silvery glint I'd never seen before.

"Did you read the part about your mother?" she asked.

Across the street was a sign saying TRIPPA COTTA. Beneath the sign, tripe was dripping water on a pyramid of lemons, and I marked each braided trickle.

"My mother?" I repeated, returning to the here and now. "Benedetta, what are you talking about?"

"The page I wrote about your mother. With the picture I drew of her, the imaginary bust."

"Benedetta," I said. "You never knew my mother. I never really knew her. What are you talking about?"

With that her irrepressible right eyebrow arched upward, and she said, "I do sort of know her. I do. Did you look at what I wrote? Or at the picture?"

"Oh God, Benedetta," I said, reaching the limit of my patience, "how can you start on this now? It's always mamma, mamma, first yours and now mine . . ."

My sourness had grown insufferable (I see this in retrospect), but fortunately Tina came over. *"Ragazzi,"* she said, tilting her lovely head, "shouldn't we hurry up? The shops are going to close soon, you know."

She looked beseechingly at Benedetta, the elder sister she was always trying to shock; and I knew from that look that she would have followed her to the ends of the earth.

One thing Benedetta had said was true—I had not known her till then, and I had not known Tina either, nor the wound of love that united them. But touched to be included in the treasure hunt, I scarcely registered the feeling, being too upset by the certainty that we would fail, and at the same time too plagued by an intense desire for Benedetta.

"Of course we're going to keep on looking," I said, pulling myself upright. "We haven't even tried the Galleria yet."

When a school chum of Tina's named Marisa made plans for her wedding, I was disappointed that Donato wasn't chosen for the photographs. Marisa's mother had picked a much older and fancier photographer. But at least Beppe was enlisted to provide the wedding pastries, big trays of sfogliatelle, bignè, babà, and other confections. The morning of the wedding, one of his casual helpers was sick (or maybe in detox—I didn't want to ask), so Benedetta and I had to come to the shop at five o'clock to help out with the baking. I have no love of pastry, much less a feel for raw dough, but Beppe had enlisted me every now and then to fill cartons or load the delivery van. Today I was to work a mixing machine.

Benedetta, loving and loyal daughter that she was, could make excellent sfogliatelle; I was fit only for the babà detail. The pasta sfoglia for flake pastry had to be rolled out to the thickness of butterfly wings and then folded neatly into shapes, but anybody could make babà just by mixing up a savarin dough of flour, eggs, sugar, salt, and yeast. The job was easy, and I'd done it before. As the arms of the big mixer spiraled around each other, I had to add several dozen eggs to the mix, two by two, taking care that the stuff never lost its elasticity: it should stiffen a bit, but never stick to the walls of the mixer. Next I filled an array of cylindrical molds, and when the babà rose, doubling in volume, I stuck them in the oven at about 180 degrees centigrade for rather less than an hour, keeping an eye on them. When they had cooled, I added Beppe's sugar-and-rum syrup and then eased them, golden and unctuous, out of their molds.

Toward seven, lots of local tradespeople dropped in for coffee and a cornetto and to say hi to Beppe, but he scarcely cracked a smile—he seemed almost vain of his glumness. Every now and then he inspected my work or shared an offhand observation. ("The babà was invented in a monastery," he muttered, *"perchè non avevano un cazzo da fare"*—because the monks didn't have a damn thing to do.) Aware of my plans to return to America in a few days, Beppe to my relief seemed totally unconcerned about my relations with his daughter. He was certainly preoccupied with the many financial gazettes stacked around the back of the shop, the latest of which he would occasionally peruse for a moment or two. When one patron addressed him, courteously, as Don Giuseppe, he wryly answered, *"Levame 'o don e aumentame 'a semana,"* which means, in dialect, Drop the honorific and raise my wages.

Toward ten o'clock, Benedetta and I delivered a couple of big flat pastry boxes to Marisa's family home. There chaos reigned. In the kitchen, surrounded by chattering bridesmaids, including Tina, Marisa was having her hair dressed. She was a dark little girl, eighteen perhaps, of the so-called *saracena* type, with huge eyes, a thick chestnut mane, and feminine forms that fairly burst out of her bridal gown. Around her fidgeted the coiffeur, a short, stout, oily man who commented freely on her "fine head of hair" and what he cheekily termed her *bella fisica*. ("You see what boors these Neapolitans are," Benedetta murmured in my ear.)

In the apartment Marisa's parents rushed about, greeting well-wishers, paying the florist, putting the flowers in water, cleaning ricotta off the flower girl's face and lace collar; Marisa's mother changed earrings three times. Then a crowd of photographers' assistants arrived, including a young man with a camcorder to shoot the wedding video. He directed Marisa to pose fetchingly by various windows and mirrors, then to bounce up and down on her parents' bed together with the flower girl. *"Ma so' tutta sudata,"* protested Marisa—her underarms were visibly wet, from stress—but the video man ordered her to bounce anyway. "It'll look lovely," he said. "Always does."

Benedetta took veiled offense at the photographer, fuming from the moment he arrived. A local celebrity, he moved with the grace of a refrigerator and wore his shirt untucked; he hadn't shaved that morning and smoked as he worked. For an hour he treated Marisa like a department-store mannequin, maneuvering her about the apartment, throwing pink and mauve lighting on her uptilted face, bobbing and weaving with his Hasselblad. ("There's no question who's the star here," Benedetta muttered to me.) Leading with his lantern jaw, he bullied his helpers cease-lessly and addressed Marisa, whose name he had forgotten, as *tu* or *la sposa*. The flower girl he called *bimba,* meaning "kid." Once, when I mistakenly blocked the glow from his white umbrella, he barked at me, *"Muoviti tu, l'americano, Joe!"*

At this Benedetta smothered a scornful giggle, dragging me back into the kitchen.

"You see what kind of people we are, Joe?" she said. "You see what kind of city you're leaving, Joe?"

Benedetta and I scarcely knew Marisa and hadn't planned to attend the wedding. But when it came time to walk to the church, Tina implored us to join her, and we could hardly say no. The ceremony was to be held at Santa Maria dei Sette Dolori, which, cresting the western rise of Spaccanapoli, once a Roman road, gave us a view straight through the city: from here, under a lowering sky, we could see buildings a mile away. But despite the church's austere dignity, the wedding merely restaged and amplified the pandemonium we had witnessed at the home of the bride. In the murky, humid nave, half-deaf elderly relatives nattered and traded places. The photographer lumbered pontifically by the altar.

As Marisa marched up the aisle, Benedetta whispered, "Those shoes."

The priest began reciting the sacrament.

"Marisa's pretty," Benedetta whispered during the vow, "but those darts on the bodice are all wrong."

She had a catch in her throat, and by the time we joined Tina outside on the grand stairway overlooking Spaccanapoli, her nose was running. Benedetta always cried if she saw Tina crying.

"What a crummy wedding," she said.

Raindrops freckled the stairway's stone parapet. The photographer and his crew were hurrying down the steps toward a bright yellow van.

Benedetta had once threatened to "walk away first" if it came to good-bye, but actually neither of us walked away from the other. The evening before my departure, we went out walking together. As we were leaving Uncle Ippolito's flat, I tried desperately to fix her image in my mind—the expressive arms, the vividly veined, marble-like wrists, the dark hair that so often smelled of café— and as I did so the corner of my eye caught her diary, peeking out from under the bolster of Ippolito's bed.

We walked for a long time in the deepening twilight, up beyond the hairdressers and transvestites of the Quartieri, beyond the last of the newsstands and clandestine betting shops and *circoli sociali,* until we had climbed to the Corso Vittorio Emanuele. And there, standing by the parapet, surveying the city, we listened to its innumerable sounds, which seemed to merge at this hour into one huge sigh of frustration. We gazed out at the scrabble of rooftops beneath us, at the clotheslines and church domes and TV antennas, at the pink clouds boiling up in the distance like a parody of a painted ceiling.

The spectacle brought a smile of derision to her lips. She asked me what had kept me so long in such a place, where time itself stagnated, where all the people were thieves, where everything was turned on its head. Hearing this, I realized for the first time that she adored her city and would never leave it; and I told her about the Native American belief that everything is upside down in the afterlife. Maybe we'd gone to heaven, I said.

"But in that heaven we'd be walking around on our hands," she replied, "hating each other." She blushed so deeply that I could see it even in the dusk. Then she took me by both shoulders and commanded, "Say it."

"Say what?" I asked.

"Say *mirror*."

I said it; she gasped with delight; the next day I got a flight out of town.

As for that diary, I did not for a second believe that Benedetta had deliberately hidden the thing and then dragged us all over town on a wild-goose chase. She was too forthright for that, and too truthful. But I do believe that some part of her knew that it wasn't really lost. Some part of her knew that the treasure lay close at hand, even as some other part was so full of foreboding that it canceled out that knowledge. No doubt the diary had turned up, and she was too mortified to admit it. I was leaving anyway.

You could say, I suppose, that there were some things Benedetta didn't know that she knew. But there were some things I didn't know that I knew either, and they were far more important.

PART TWO

8

The Letter

Frankly? Frankly I cannot offer a plausible explanation of how I wound up in Naples again, because the way it happened is not at all plausible, it is merely true.

One day, in New York, I received a letter from Benedetta. It bore an anonymous poste restante return address, and was not, to my admitted disappointment, a love letter, but a fond remembrance of our time together, drenched in nostalgia and regret. We had not corresponded in almost three years, and at first her words touched me deeply. She wrote of our evenings in Uncle Ippolito's apartment, our walks up those stone stairways to the heights of the Vomero, our drives with Sandro, our visits to museums and churches and antique fairs. Dwelling on our happiest moments, she charitably passed over my wariness of Loredana, and candidly confessed that she had rediscovered her diary in—wouldn't you know it?—the most obvious place. She also recalled with a certain pleasure my fondness for Neapolitan painting, especially Jusepe de Ribera, and my strong leftist sympathies. Actually the last item was somewhat curious, because I had no particular leftist sympathies. Benedetta did, and I respected her opinions, but I knew little about the Italian Left and on that basis had no wish to learn more. Politics bored me, and Italian politics especially.

I read her letter many times, and each time it seemed odder. Her memory of our walking hand in hand through the antique fairs at the Villa Comunale—well, really she had always walked there *alone,* probably clutching her bag, while I waited nearby, at a nice café in the Riviera di Chiaia, sipping espresso and grappa, perusing my *Corriere.* Nor, knowing Benedetta's power to repress all episodes of embarrassment, could I fathom her jauntily revisiting the diary fiasco. Above all, the writing was devoid of her singular charm and playfulness. She had not used her broad-nibbed pen, and even her usual hand, with its whimsical up- and downstrokes, seemed to have yielded to a more inhibited style. At length I came to the unsettling conclusion that the document was a forgery.

Now my musings took a suspicious turn. Wasn't this missive just the kind of thing an unscrupulous private investigator would confect for some sordid purpose? After all, the right response from me would be welcome evidence for a divorce suit based on infidelity. The thought caused an icy tingling to rush through my veins.

But what was I imagining? Of course it was conceivable, indeed eminently so, that Benedetta had married in the intervening period, a possibility I found remarkably disagreeable: even the haziest mental image of her conjoined to somebody else I drove from my brain. But she had been single when I knew her, and so no such legal tangles could possibly involve me. One thing was certain: whoever had written and signed the letter, while possessed of quite a few facts, didn't really know me. But what, I wondered, could be the point of such fakery? I couldn't explain it, nor could my most imaginative friends in New York.

The strange communication had excited something akin to jealousy in me, but it had also confirmed my growing belief in the mystic power of fate. I cannot remember whether I had yet become convinced of the rule of coincidence over human life—that was one of the effects Naples would eventually have on me. But whatever the depth of this conviction then, the letter arrived at a moment of susceptibility. For the truth is that I had recently begun to dream very often about Benedetta.

These dreams were of a vividness to rival wakeful reality, as my dreams at Naples had been. I dreamed that I saw Benedetta passing softly through my room, that she sat on my bed watching me, and, once, that she said my name aloud, the whites of her eyes burning with the molten-silver brilliance they had had on our last evening together. Roused from this dream and sitting bolt upright, I began to miss her terribly, with a raging sense of longing. I missed the feel of her skin, her cotton underwear, her overlong sweaters, her eye shadow, a certain pleated woolen skirt, the clear sweet sound of her vowels; I missed her café-smelling hair. It amazed me suddenly that anyone so desirable, so tender, actually existed somewhere in the world, and it felt unbearable that I had actually lost her or given her up.

I decided not to answer the spurious letter. But two weeks later I was standing in the Capodichino airport, dialing directory assistance for her number.

The operator told me that it was unlisted, at the subscriber's request.

I did not wish to talk to Benedetta immediately but only to discover where she lived. I could not have explained to her or even to myself what I wanted of her, and certainly had no right to expect anything. Many crosscurrents of feeling played together in my mind. A sense of gratitude and an inkling that we had a common destiny were held in check by the awareness that we had not seen each other in three years. Yet the letter itself, its appearance out of the blue, led me on with an almost mystical force. It was as if I had to bring her something precious, like the pilgrim in the fresco in San Rocco who has carried a bowl of milk across a continent without spilling a drop.

Having left my belongings at a friend's place, I walked over to Uncle Ippolito's, purely to honor the memory of the old days. His flat had been sold, as I might have expected—that was clear from the new brass nameplate for the third floor on the palazzo's portal; but, surprisingly, the nameplate for the second floor no longer bore Benedetta's family name, either.

I walked over to the bakery but met with a similar situation. I saw no familiar face there. The shop sign remained unchanged, but apparently the premises had been sold off entirely, along with Beppe's name. Inside, none of the people behind the counter could say what had become of Beppe himself—it was as though he had turned into a fairy-tale pastry chef, a figure of legend. It occurred to me that the whole family might have moved bag and baggage to another, nearby town, maybe Nola, where I seemed to recall that they had property, but for the moment I was stumped.

Of course I could have called Loredana, or some other friend of Benedetta's, but that seemed horribly embarrassing, and besides, it would have given my presence away. So I spent my first few days in the city just wandering around on foot, half hoping I would somehow run into her. I found myself unwittingly drawn to every place we'd spent time together, from the dingy café on Via San Biagio to the weathered statue of the Nile, and I felt deeply indebted to these mute objects merely for reminding me of her loveliness.

For about a week this situation continued. I had no leads as to Benedetta's whereabouts, nor the nerve to contact her friends. I drifted in a sort of limbo, directionless. And then, with nagging shame, I began to find relief by trailing after young women in the streets, women who looked as she might by now, a little older, a little more polished in bearing or manner. One afternoon, imagining I saw her in an alley not far from Piazza dei Girolamini, I began, at a discreet distance, to follow her. She was wearing her hair pinned up and a blue pullover with overlong sleeves, and she walked vigorously, without glancing back; I stayed with her around several bends and under two or three dark archways into a maze of narrow, pestilent byways in which I was at some pains to remain unseen. In one of these she turned aside and rang at an iron gate; a buzzer promptly responded; she pushed the gate open and entered a spacious court I had never seen before. She did not shut the gate firmly, and I pursued her into what turned out to be a garden enclosed by a cloister. The cloister was overgrown with fruit trees and straggling vines; beyond its mounting tiers of windows and overhanging cornice I could see the tops of other buildings—a dome clad in brightly colored tiles, the clockface of a campanile, and several crenellated walls. Though the city lay all around us, a near-silence reigned in this precinct, and only the sounds of masonry being chipped, and of schoolchildren calling in some unseen playground, punctuated the almost rustic serenity.

From the shadow of the portico I watched the woman I thought was Benedetta: she moved slowly and gracefully, as if lost in thought, stepping amid dense stands of lemon trees and orange trees, now and then pushing away a low-hanging branch, then disappearing behind a blossoming rosebush; I saw her figure half screened by tall cacti, and then she reemerged into clear view and approached a large marble fountain surmounted by a wrought-iron wellhead. She peered for a moment into the well, as if to see her reflection; then she vanished once more amid the sun-dappled shade of the portico. Wanting to approach her yet feeling somehow restrained, I marked her passage amid gelsemina and trailing bougainvillea and huge earthenware jars; and so it was, gradually, as I watched her, that I lost heart. Perhaps this person was not Benedetta after all, I told myself, and what a fool I'd seem if I tried to address her. I turned finally and walked out of the cloister; and this ridiculous pursuit of an unknown girl filled me with a self-loathing that only slowly dwindled away.

❧

Several days later, walking near the Accademia delle Belle Arti toward sundown, I did meet somebody I knew, though I had not expected to see him. Laden with parcels, he almost bumped into me as he emerged from an art supply store.

"*Come mai?*" Luca Corsaro exclaimed as we embraced. "Whatever brings you back to Naples?" He reeked of cigarette smoke and benzine.

I thought of inventing some pretext for my presence, but the easier dodge was to put the same question to him. What was he up to, I asked, in a color merchant's shop, where paints and inks and pastels were sold? As we sat down at the café facing the Accademia, he told me of his success in the frame-making business and how with several assistants he was producing huge carved frames, fake-Baroque, for mirrors, mantelpieces, and pier glasses; he had come here to replenish his supply of gold leaf for the water gilding of a new line of counterfeit moldings. Of course this was only a sideline, he assured me, like ticket-scalping or lamp-making; he had retained his featherbedding job at the hospital, and had also embarked on a magnificent new venture that was sure to make his fortune.

"There might even be a place for you in it," he said.

"For me?"

"Absolutely, *caro*. As Luca's American agent!" He ground his knuckle fondly into my cheek.

After coffee he took me on his Vespa to one of the heights overlooking the city—up beyond the Policlinico, I think it was, a district I'd never visited before. He parked in a street fronted by warehouses, mostly white-painted, and, opening a triple-bolted door, led me into a large workroom illuminated by a skylight. Many long sections of elaborately carved molding lay in a rack; most were not yet gessoed, but those that were gave no hint of the modern laminates beneath their artful finish. Luca saluted two cheerful men in overalls who were operating a huge table router.

"But of course our work is beautiful," he said to me, casually cutting off my exclamations of wonder; for the few completed frames ranged along the walls looked straight out of the seventeenth century. "This isn't what I brought you to see," he went on. "Come along now." He steered me into a smaller, darkened room off to one side. There he flipped on a light, and I saw about twenty bags of multicolored latex hanging in folds from a track on the ceiling. They looked like deflated balloons: some appeared to be printed with faces, others resembled collapsed houses or deboned animals.

"My God, what is all this?" I asked.

"It is my answer to the Neapolitan loneliness!" he replied. "It is Luca's answer to the great, devouring loneliness of all his brothers who have left this beautiful but devilish place to make money in Milan or Turin or in your city, Chicago—"

"New York—"

"Wherever. In all those sunless, heartless places."

"I wouldn't actually—"

"It doesn't matter, you know what I mean. I mean that we have here certain amenities that you can't find anywhere else. True? Aha! *Luntan' a Napule nun se ne pò sta'!* Now then, you, *caro,* have been here many times, I believe. You know a little about our city. What are the two most typical features of Neapolitan life?"

I thought for a moment, but I couldn't answer. There seemed to be so many "typical" features. I thought of pizza, but that could be found everywhere now. I thought of Sunday dinners with maccheroni al ragù, but that had become pan-Italian. I thought of Benedetta's mamma's house, where no shelf or tabletop had been left uncluttered by a forest of genteel bric-a-brac, but did people really miss such things?

"What if I told you," Corsaro said, "that the two most typical features are the *caffettiera* and the *presepio*? How do you say *presepio* in your language?"

"Let me see, that would be a Christmas 'crèche' or 'crib,'" I said, "depending on where you live."

"Cribb*eh*," he pronounced, Italianizing the word. His eyes glittered. "Luca hopes to sell many in America."

He removed a jumble of keys from his pants pocket and began to unlock one of the metal lockers that lined the room. Gesturing "Be patient" with palms extended broadside, he removed from the locker a medium-size aluminum suitcase and placed it flat on the floor. As he opened it, I saw that it held a little air-compressor and a mess of tightly wedged-in latex bags like the ones hanging from the ceiling. Then he began to explain his creation.

Neapolitans, he said, were frightfully lonely away from home. The only reason for leaving the city was to make money, but Neapolitans hated the mists of Milan and those other northern hellholes, and wished only to come back to the sunshine as soon as they'd saved up enough. In the meantime, they craved the southern way of life and loved anything that called it up. Chief among these mementos were good coffee and the Christmas crèche. Northern coffee was always inferior, Corsaro said, because it wasn't made with Neapolitan water. It was the water that gave coffee the right taste, and Corsaro proposed to sell Neapolitan water worldwide.

"Bottled?" I said, even more perplexed than before. "You're going to bottle the local tapwater?"

"Not exactly," he said, with a conjuror's smile. "That's where the *presepio* comes in."

Of course I knew about the Neapolitan custom of the Christmas crèche—you couldn't live in Naples and not know. The tradition went back hundreds of years, so that almost every Neapolitan family had one, and some I'd seen were fantastically elaborate. The crèche figures—the three wise men, for instance—were made of wooden armatures fitted out with embroidered robes and terra-cotta heads and hands, while the manger and the Bethlehem inn were of corkwood. Sculptors in the neighborhood of San Gregorio Armeno fashioned the figurines and settings, and every year a typical Neapolitan family would spend a few hundred thousand lire in the shops around the church buying additions to

their crèche, which might eventually have a cast of scores of figurines. They represented not only the Holy Family and the
manger animals and the wise men, but also shepherds playing
pipes, the innkeeper and his wife, camel drivers, servant girls, and
a crowd of assorted raggedy onlookers. For an extra fee, the sculptors could work in a statuette of the customer praying to the baby
Jesus, as in the altarpieces commissioned by the great Renaissance
families.

Corsaro flipped the compressor switch and things started to
happen. Air hissed, and in the open suitcase the latex bladders
started to rustle and swell. A smirking donkey sprang up, then a
black turbaned wise man, then two more wise men and a group of
genuflecting bedouin. A mob of little angels hoisted themselves
over the suitcase on a puckered tube vaguely resembling a
Corinthian column. Finally the Holy Family ballooned upward,
nestling inside a miniature stage set imprinted with an illustration
of a stable and a Positano-type inn. Three rubber peasant girls
bulged into shape, dancing the tarantella. The fully inflated creation stood a little under three feet high.

"Now—do you see?" Corsaro said triumphantly.

"I see a complete *presepio*," I said. "It's incredible."

"And will it remind people of home?"

"It will remind them beautifully."

"And will it serve real coffee made from real Neapolitan
water?"

"Will it?" I said, confused.

"Luca has thought of this also!" he said buoyantly. "I cannot
provide the correct water for every cup of coffee that my clients
drink, that would be impossible, but at least . . . at least . . .
watch!"

He knelt and fiddled with something inside the suitcase, shifting his considerable weight with agility. With that gibbous shape
of his, he almost belonged to the little world he had invented, the
world of the inflatable crèche. Corsaro presented himself as a man
with sidelines, in a way as a man with nothing but sidelines, but

spiritually he was pneumatic, even aerial. He might at any moment be aloft.

"There!" he said, turning a knob, and I saw that a tiny basin which I hadn't previously noticed, in front of the infant Jesus, was filling up with water from a spout hidden under the donkey: the basin was actually the bottom part of a tiny *caffettiera*. Onto it Corsaro screwed the rest of the apparatus, which he had meanwhile fished out of the suitcase. A heating element began to glow under the *caffettiera,* and in a minute it had brewed enough coffee for two thimble-sized cups.

"*Ecco,* authentic coffee!" said Corsaro. "The real thing, for the homesick Neapolitan. Ah, I can see in your eyes that you're impressed."

We drank.

"As you see, *caro,* my suitcase has everything. Selling my suitcase, you will be rich in America!"

Pinching my cheek, he flung an arm of partnership around my shoulder .

A few days later I took a short sublease on the flat where I was staying—my friend the owner had to fly to Argentina. Feeling rested, I fell into my old walking habit, and in the succeeding weeks, for some reason—perhaps because it was late spring by now and the weather stirred my blood—I began to favor the trek up to Capodimonte, the former royal palace and now a famous picture gallery. There, with Benedetta in mind, I repeatedly paid my respects to Ribera's masterpiece *Apollo and Marsyas,* then on loan from the Museo di San Martino. Each time, it took me a moment to locate Marsyas's inverted head, which seemed to fall out of the bottom of the canvas, and as I did so I could practically hear his scream. Over the vanquished satyr hovered an epicene Apollo, flaying him with a smile, and I would let my eye trail pleasurably over the pair's mushroom-like flesh tones and ash-gray halftones. Ribera had a way of dragging silvery impasto over a dark undercoat like viscous lightning over a thundercloud. His followers had said that he "tinted his brush with the blood of all the saints," and Marsyas seemed the saintliest to me—a martyr not to a credo but to beauty. Recalling Benedetta's interpretation of the picture and thinking of her bewitching eyes and expressive arms, I tried not to identify with the poor satyr's suffering; I thought instead about Ribera's implicit vision of Naples, his sense of the city's anguish and purgatorial expectancy. Ribera's cast of characters had subsisted, I felt, on a prescribed diet of wavering beliefs, residual loyalties, and half-forgotten promises, and I admired his feel for his pallid, hollow-cheeked models, with their forthright, chastened eyes; on my way back down from Capodimonte I saw their heirs moving about the streets.

I descended through neighborhoods sliced into wedges and triangles by the rays of the declining sun. Making visors of their palms, housewives in the greengrocers' markets picked through vegetables harvested on the volcanic slopes along the bay, testicle-shaped tomatoes and thorny purple artichokes and forests of bitter greens. Sometimes I stopped to buy lotto tickets or a cheap cigar, and always I halted on the overpass beside the mosquelike dome of Santa Maria della Sanità to peer down into the Sanità quarter. Below, the buildings sprawled along a sort of gulch or dried-up riverbed of the sort the Arabs call a "wadi"—this was the fiefdom of Giuseppe Misso, the only camorra chieftain with a regard for old allegiances and a taste for good wine, and at this hour the quarter looked benign, filled with rosy light and the bustle of shoppers.

It was on a descent from Capodimonte that I saw someone else from my earlier life. I had practically reached the Banco di Napoli on Via Roma, which was thick with the usual strollers, when I realized that a young woman was staring at me furtively from the doorway of a shop. At first I didn't recognize her. She had abundant, light chestnut hair, which fell in swaths of slightly varying tones, and wore a long narrow skirt, perfectly cut; her sunglasses hid her eyes. Scrutinizing me as though trying to confirm an identification, she turned away toward the door and back to glance at me. Then, looking uncertain, she slipped into the shop.

This was, I now noticed, one of the more tasteful and expensive women's boutiques in the avenue. Positioning myself in front of the vitrine, I peeked between two mannequins to see what the girl would do inside. I watched her remove her dark glasses and take up a stance behind the counter, alongside several shop assistants. She addressed them with an air of authority.

As I crossed the threshold, the noise of the avenue died instantly away. Swags of velvet gave the rear of the establishment the aura of an inner sanctum, in which only the rustling of tissue paper could be heard; a customer was having an item wrapped. Moving her long, tapered hands in and out of a beam of recessed lighting, the girl doing the wrapping seemed a priestess of some strange cult, and beside her, erect and even more priestess-like, stood the creature who had been spying on me. She was not only elegant, she also had, at least superficially, the bearing of a woman of the world. By now both of us were smiling.

"Hello, Tina," I said.

"Oh! I thought it was you!" She swung around the counter to greet me.

We chatted for a few minutes with what felt like remarkable ease, but the entrance of two talkative patrons, who wanted to discuss the new summer tops as well as try them on, cramped our conversation. I decided to put off asking Tina where her sister was living. She invited me to telephone her so we might arrange a get-together over the weekend.

When, several days later, Tina and I were able to talk unhindered, over pizza and wine, she filled me in a little about her family's circumstances. Her father had sold his business at a considerable profit and retired with Gemma to a propety he owned near Nola. He had left Naples and the *pasticceria* with no regrets: at last baking had brought him enough money to spend all his time speculating on the Milanese bourse. As always, he neither made nor lost any money to speak of.

"Our poor papà never took any particular pride in himself as a pastry chef," Tina said. "He told me once he'd be happy to make the worst pastry in Italy, if that's what his customers wanted. A lot of people here think he shouldn't have gone. They think it was a cultural disaster."

"And Gemma?"

"Oh, you know, Mamma's well. As always. But she's quit teaching now, and catechism, too. She spends all her time in her garden. Whenever I visit them she talks and talks about her favorite pupils—you know, the ones who've done well, the ones she's proud of. She gets out their letters and reads them to me. '*Gentile Professoressa,* If it weren't for you . . .'"—the heel of Tina's hand was at the corner of her eye. "So that's what she does, aside from criticizing me. She reads me her favorite pupils' letters."

Tina herself had been working in retail almost since my departure, she told me. She loved selling women's clothing, and had recently landed that job in Via Roma; she was indeed managing the boutique where I had greeted her. Our conversation shifted to the new fashions out of Milan, for me a tedious matter though Tina described them with verve; then it shifted to Tina's friends and what they were doing after high school. Tina exulted in telling me she had a wonderful boyfriend (a *fidanzato,* she called him) who proposed to her outright at least twice a month. She wasn't quite ready for marriage, she said, laughing her tinkling-chandelier laugh, but their finding each other was still *un colpo di fortuna.* Everything was not all right with her sister, however. Her sister was *una bella persona,* but *inguaiata*—troubled.

"Tina," I said, leaning forward, "why did you write me that letter?"

She covered her face with her hands. "I know it was a bad thing to do," she said, her voice dwindling to a whisper. "I was so ashamed of myself, when I actually saw that you'd come."

This did not move me, and I said nothing in response.

"Maybe I'm a liar," she went on, tilting her head to one side and setting her earrings atremble, "but I lied for a very good reason. I lied for somebody else."

"You're not a liar," I said, softening despite myself. I took her hand: her earrings, I now saw, were pearl drops set in gold. The boyfriend must be a catch.

"That letter—" I began, then stopped to consider for a moment. "Well, I thought at first some private investigator was trying to trick me into answering a love note. I thought that perhaps your sister had got married. Had perhaps been married even when I knew her. Can you see that?"

Tina started slightly, then froze. Lit by an unnatural gleam, her eyes slanted down, away from my own. She sat silent for a moment, her hand withdrawn from mine; both her wrists slipped from the table. "I just hoped you could help in some way," she said.

"But how were you to know if I did come back to Naples?" I asked. "How would you know if your trick worked? I didn't have your sister's address anymore. Or her phone number. How many people live in this city? A million?"

"Oh, I'd know if you came," she said brightly. "I'd see you. Didn't I see you?"

"*See* me? I don't get it. It was blind luck that you spotted me the other day in Via Roma."

"No it wasn't. It wasn't blind luck. I knew I'd see you. Or one of my friends would see you."

I stared at her, incredulous.

"Oh my, do you think you were hiding here, three years ago? Do you think that nobody knew you? Everybody, everybody knew you! You were the American! You were the *only* American!" She laughed her tinkling laugh again—and her remorse about the letter seemed to evaporate. Then, all at once, she stopped laughing. She said, solemnly, "My sister really cared about you."

"I know that," I said.

"No you don't," she said.

"Where is she? Where can I find her?"

She sighed, and looked away. "I can't tell you that," she said. "Not without asking her first. Call me in a couple of days."

"Is she teaching? Did she get the job she wanted?" I knew the answer.

"No," Tina said, "she didn't, and that's when the whole problem started. A little after you left."

An appointment as an art history *maestra* would have suited her sister perfectly, Tina said. She loved art, any good art, and she liked being with high school students, too. She enjoyed spending time with minds just starting to grasp what artists like Ribera or Luca Giordano or Cosimo Fanzago were trying to accomplish (Tina knew the names in her sister's pantheon if not the grounds for their selection). Though a somewhat erratic student, Benedetta had passed the extensive battery of qualifying examinations. But she could not, that year, find a position in Naples proper, only elsewhere in Campania or even farther afield, in places where she knew no one and had no wish to live. She would have languished far from her parents and her sister, far from Loredana and her other friends and the great churches and museums she adored. A more competitive woman, with a better academic record and better political skills, might have fought tooth and nail for a job at a good *liceo* in Naples, but Benedetta was not that woman. She was neither a bluestocking nor a climber.

"God, but it's ironic," Tina said, "how she struggled to keep me out of trouble when I was in high school. It's pretty easy to get in trouble around here, you know. And now . . ."—she threw up her hands.

A tremor of her earrings told me she was on the verge of tears again. And I wondered: was Tina another purgatorial soul, like those people in Ribera's paintings?

Tina . . . and her sister Benedetta?

9

Blood of My Veins

G igi driving on Via Nuova Marina, hair combed up into quills, eyes darting, was like a boy playing a car-racing game in a video arcade. He had turned on the radio, and as a tenor belted out a Neapolitan ballad, vehicles and pedestrians erupted without warning into our field of vision; police barriers and steamrollers and flea markets popped up out of nowhere, forcing him to swerve abruptly into an adjacent lane. A green van loomed up that had been abandoned, inexplicably, in the middle of the road, and Gigi swerved. A stray dog crossed the road, and Gigi swerved.

Though frightening, the traffic wasn't nearly as bad as the last time I'd been along this way, several years earlier, on Benedetta's Vespa. Then all the stoplights had been dead because the municipality hadn't paid its electric bill and the utility company had cut the juice. Taking advantage of the de facto freeway, the cars and trucks had raced along fiercely, bearing down on anyone who tried to cross the boulevard, aiming pitilessly at school groups and flocks of elderly nuns.

Gigi didn't remember Benedetta anymore, since she'd only

known him secondhand; I think it would have troubled me if he'd mentioned her. In a way, being out of touch with her allowed me to cultivate some of the other Neapolitans I'd known, and Gigi was one of them. Often, when I ran into him, he regaled me with another tale of Naples. In my heart of hearts, though, I always associated him with Abinotto, the hero of his screenplay, the concierge with the pistol and the seven hundred condoms purchased on the black market. I couldn't get over Abinotto's reckoning up the number of times he was likely to make love to his wife before he died, and then her dying first, and his being stuck with that pile of contraband rubbers—the perfect Neapolitan memento mori. I'd contacted Gigi after I'd noticed that he had a part in a dialect musical playing at the Teatro Cilea. It was closing soon, but I'd arranged to see it with his girlfriend, Graziella, having no way of even asking Benedetta. Frankly, I was intrigued by the idea of a stutterer in a musical, but the problem had been neatly disposed of. In the show, a satire of the camorra, Gigi played a hood whose tongue had been cut off by a gangster for speaking out of turn, so he had to create the character by means of gesture alone. Watching him onstage, I promised myself that I'd devote some thought to the relation between stuttering, comedy, and *l'omertà,* the mafia's conspiracy of silence, but I hadn't really got anywhere. All that had come of it was that Gigi had invited me to lunch the following Sunday.

Now, as we headed out toward Arzano, the outlying neighborhood where Gigi and Graziella lived, Naples looked less and less European. In fact this part of town had always reminded me of a Central American city. The streets broke up into mesas and arroyos, apartment blocks met at murderous angles, and disjointed shop signs and cables dangled precariously above the sidewalks. From tiers of identical balconies, dark-eyed women surveyed the men in the streets—men playing cards, selling black-market merchandise, vociferating in phone booths on the cusp of a deal—while in the meridians vendors grilled purple artichokes, lacing the air with a pungent aroma. As we rattled around Piazza

Enrico Caruso, near the great tenor's birthplace, I caught sight of his bust, mounted on a plinth in the square. Scarcely larger than a plaster bust you'd keep on your piano, it was dwarfed by the swirl of wheezing buses and howling flatbed rigs.

We stopped to pick up Graziella, who had floating dark hair and dimples and a little air of refinement. Then we raced off toward a restaurant Gigi liked.

"Punks!" Gigi snorted.

"Who's a punk?" said Graziella.

Gigi jerked his head in the direction of a Mercedes that was nearly crowding us off the road. It was white, with black leather seats, and was packed with young men in dark suits and wrap-around sunglasses. Then we turned up an alley, losing the Mercedes, and parked.

"I hate those baby punks," Gigi said, starting to stutter. "The camorristi just use them and throw them away. The only heavies I go for are the old-time *guappi*. Come on, let's sit out back in the garden."

In the restaurant we passed through a dining room filled with families into a vacant, gravelly courtyard half shaded by corrugated-iron sheeting. We sat down at a big wooden table. Graziella was thin, with huge eyes behind wire-framed glasses, and she shivered slightly in her black leather coat.

"Shouldn't we go inside?" I suggested.

"We're staying out here," Gigi said gruffly. "I don't like Sunday crowds—too bourgeois." He stared quizzically at Graziella. "What?" he said.

She said, "So you like the *guappi*. You love the *guappi*."

"Yes, I do," he replied, "and do you know why? If a *guappo* has to kill somebody, it's only to protect the neighborhood or the family. It's not in order to kiss some fat cat's goddamn ass." Gigi's porcupine hair looked especially bellicose as he praised the *guappi*.

"So it's okay to kill people for the right reasons?" Graziella said. She gave him a patient, exasperated little smile.

Gigi didn't answer. "Come on, let's order," he said.

The yard was full of tables and chairs, but no diners aside from ourselves. The proprietor came to take our orders, and as he was leaving a man emerged from inside, crunched his way across the gravel, and sat down alone, at a distance.

"Ruined," said Gigi.

"What's ruined?" said Graziella.

"Our meal, that's what," Gigi said.

"Because of that guy over there?"

"Yes, Graziella, because of that guy! It was so nice when we were here alone, just the three of us. Now it's totally ruined."

"But what in heaven's name is the matter with him?" said Graziella, in the tone you'd adopt with a fussing toddler. "He's sitting so far away."

"Just look at the way he's dressed," said Gigi, in his scornful *guappo* voice, eyeing the man. "And that watch he's got on! Tell me," he said, turning to me, "where did you get that coat you're wearing?"

I told him I'd got it at the old-clothes market in Fuorigrotta, and that I'd paid ten thousand lire for it—a little less than five dollars. My ancient suede jacket had disintegrated and I didn't have the leisure or funds to shop for a replacement. So I'd gone to the so-called old-clothes market, which actually purveyed new clothes with phony labels, and bought this five-dollar coat. The wool wasn't wool, the leather buttons weren't leather, and the coat wasn't really a coat, being rather too short, but otherwise it was quite well made, a commendable piece of Neapolitan fakery. It would certainly tide me over till I had some time and cash at my disposal.

"You see, Graziella? Our American friend is genuine, a real human being," Gigi said. "He doesn't bother about appearances. He's not like that creep over there!"

"Gigi dear," Graziella whispered. "The guy can hear you."

"As if I care," said Gigi, raising his voice. "Graziella, you don't know anything. Why don't you just shut up?"

Something odd had happened to him. His eyes gleamed with

animal ferocity, and his stubbly face seemed darker, more aggressive. As Graziella studied this suddenly irate Gigi, she half smiled and the dimples appeared in her cheeks. Beneath her intelligent, reticent gaze, another expression lurked which I couldn't quite decipher.

When our food and wine arrived, Graziella said there was a flea on her plate. She pushed the plate away. Then she picked up a cloth napkin and began cleaning out her wineglass with some mineral water.

"Graziella, that's my napkin," Gigi protested.

"Sorry," she said, "take mine."

"But I don't want yours, I want my own. And now you've gotten it dirty."

"Well, let's get you another one."

"No, Graziella, that's not the point. The point is that you just took my napkin, without asking, and got it all dirty."

He began a stammering denunciation of her table manners, and he might have waxed more and more orotund, might indeed have gone on forever if, without warning, she hadn't calmly reached across to the breadbasket and thrown a piece of bread at him.

Gigi burst out laughing and threw bread back at her. And as the food fight progressed, the man across the courtyard stared openly at us, not bothering to conceal his disgust at such barbarous behavior.

How odd it was to see Gigi laugh. His jerky, frustrated movements, which always made others laugh, generally seemed to impede his own laughter, and when he couldn't find enough work he tended to grow bitter. But his stuttering had some of the aural quality of laughter, the compulsion, the rapid repeats, and he played on this similarity. Watching him now, I remembered that he called his brand of humor *cacaglio,* the Neapolitan word for a stutter.

We ate, except for Graziella, who had lost her appetite. When we had finished Gigi said to me, "Listen, I want to tell you a story.

It's a true story about Naples. About a friend of mine, a photographer. And I want to see what it means to you, I want to see if you understand it."

"Are you going to smoke at the same time?" I asked, afraid he'd set himself on fire, as he almost had that time at Al Portico, when he'd bobbled the cigarette down his shirtfront.

"No," said Gigi, perplexed.

"Then shoot."

This Gigi tale belonged to the Italian genre of first communion stories. A boy had recently been confirmed, and a photographer, a friend of Gigi's, had been hired by the family to take his picture in his altar boy's robe. This sacrament is important in Naples, even to families who aren't devout, and the photographer, bored with the prospect of the assignment, had asked Gigi to keep him company.

"The family's house was in Poggioreale," Gigi told me, "and it wasn't really a house at all but a mean little concrete box with a tiny yard and a tiny ironwork fence and a tiny door, and in the tiny door stood a big fat lady."

Gigi took a mouthful of *paccheri*—big, tubular pasta. He was telling the story in his usual stuttery dialect, and the strain of following him would have exhausted me but for his gestures, on which my comprehension depended.

"So we squeezed into this tiny house," Gigi said, "and then we squeezed down a narrow hallway, and there was this twelve-year-old in his altar boy's robe. So the big fat lady started to slap his cheeks, okay?"—Gigi cuffed the air—"to flush them up for the photographer. She told us to keep very quiet, because the father, who worked a night shift, was asleep in another room, and she sent us out on the balcony to set up the shot. But the balcony was too narrow—there wasn't enough room for the boy and my friend and his camera and his brollies. So we had to take everything back into the kitchen. The lady thought for a moment and said, 'Let's do the photos in here!' But that house was so tiny, those people were so terribly poor, that there wasn't enough room for all of us to stand in the kitchen either. So—what to do?" Gigi took a swig of wine and made the quandary gesture, hands out, palms up.

"Well, after thinking the whole thing over," he went on, "the big fat lady—"

"The *big fat lady*," said Graziella. "Gigi, we know that she's big and fat by now."

"Thanks, Graziella. So the big fat lady decided that the best place for the shot was the bedroom. Where unfortunately her husband, Alfredo, was sleeping. But she decided we should go in there anyway. The room was so small that the double bed almost filled it, and in the bed, under a crucifix, we saw a disheveled, exhausted-looking man tossing and murmuring in his sleep.

"'*Ohè*, Alfrè!' the big fat lady shouted. 'Alfrè, wake up, the photographer's here!'

"'The who?' muttered Alfredo, turning over and hiding his head under a pillow.

"The woman bent over him. 'Alfrè!' she bellowed into the pillow. 'Alfrè, wake up, we need this room. For the photographer.'

"'The photographer?'

"'*Cretino,* for the first communion pictures!'

"'For the pictures?' said Alfredo, half asleep. 'But why are you bothering me? You have all the room in the world out there. In the kitchen, on the balcony, in the garden.'

"'ALFRÈ!' screamed the woman, beside herself now. 'Wake up! It's much too cramped in those places! We need the bedroom! We need you to move!'

"So she roused Alfredo," Gigi said, "and he stumbled out into the corridor, and we rolled up the mattress and folded up the bedspring and hauled it all out of the room. And—are you still with me?—my friend took the pictures of the kid in there, in his altar boy's robe, with his red cheeks, and then we packed up and left."

Gigi took a sip of his wine. "So," he asked, "what's the meaning of the story?"

"I'm sorry?" I gulped.

"What does the story mean to you?"

I could think of nothing diplomatic to say.

"Gigi," said Graziella, "he doesn't want to spoil your story. Don't you know it spoils a story to have it explained?"

But he silenced her objection with a peremptory wave. Eagerly his eyes engaged mine.

Gigi, I reasoned, was an actor, and for an actor the audience response was everything. And so, wincing with self-consciousness, I muttered a few phrases about Alfredo's dream. I told him that it seemed to me, from what Alfredo had said, that while his wife was shouting at him he was dreaming about another house, not the one he actually lived in—a beautiful, spacious, modern house. He was dreaming a typically vivid Neapolitan dream about a parallel house with a parallel kitchen and a parallel garden.

Gigi smiled: this satisfied him. He was persuaded that with my response to his story (and my five-dollar coat) I had risen above the generality of moral imbeciles who assailed him every day. He had decided, he said, to give me a screenplay he had recently written.

"I want your honest response to this script," he said. "I've given it everything, it's the blood of my veins."

He pushed up a sleeve and showed me his arm. It was a ropy arm, with long, knotted veins. Wincing, he fingered a vein as if to draw blood.

❧

"I would have preferred," Gigi said, with a hand floating out toward the audience, "to have been born in Sicily, where nobody talks, but unfortunately I was born in Naples, where nobody ever shuts up." He was stuttering and also mocking his stuttering, not in a self-pitying way but proudly, vaingloriously, and the crowd following his performance was in hysterics.

"Everybody has a star," he rapped out, in dialect. "Some have the star of beauty, others the star of wealth, and I have the star of *cacaglio*. Most babies when they're born go *gheeeeee!* but I just went *ghe-ghe-ghe!"*

More hysterics.

About fifty of us were sitting downstairs in Al Portico's sub-level nightclub, a vaulted cantina remodeled for entertainment by its owner, Roberto Calandra. Tall and graceful, with a broad smile, Roberto had the habit, not patronizing but cordial, of grabbing my cheek between thumb and forefinger as a salutation. He also had a certain commercial sixth sense, having recently convinced Valentina Stella, a rising Neapolitan pop star, to sing at his club, and every Thursday he held a kind of variety-evening featuring new, relatively untested acts, such as young balladeers or kids doing improv sketches. The show acquired some professional weight thanks to Gigi's clowning and an accomplished band led by a droopy-mustached keyboardist called Mauro.

But unhappily for me that night, I frequently failed to grasp what Gigi was saying. Or I'd get everything in a joke but the punchline, which was like a pizza with no cheese. My problem, as Benedetta had pointed out long ago, was dialect innuendo, and Gigi's brand of it especially had a way of cranking itself up to tremendous speed, a sort of supersonic staccato: as his listeners clutched their sides in a final agony of mirth, I would feel my smile begin to sag.

By the time Gigi's act ended the crowd had gone wild. "Carmè, Carmè," he sang at the end, and everybody joined in:

Carmè, Carmè, you're not enough for me,
I could easily satisfy three women like you . . .

After the show a group of us gathered around a table upstairs. Gigi said to me, "Well, what did you make of the screenplay I gave you? What do you say? Terrific, wonderful, rotten, fantastic? It's the blood of my veins, you know."

I told Gigi that I liked his play, which dramatized his story of

Abinotto, the concierge with the seven hundred condoms. Gigi had always been very attracted to this idea, and the script was funny, and well constructed. But I had one reservation. At the end, poor Abinotto is dragged into court and accused of a long list of misdeeds, including pandering and arms trafficking, and this struck me as overexplicit—too "pat," as we say. Could Gigi cut this one little scene?

I was secretly hoping that Gigi would cut a few other details as well, things that deprived his story of some of its irony. But as soon as I'd voiced my suggestion about ditching the trial scene, I saw that I'd made a terrible faux pas. He glared at me coldly, and explained, with a stab of his hand, why such excisions were unnecessary. Once the play was in production, he said, the director would tell the script girl to delete anything that didn't fit in, and material like that last scene could go, if necessary. I had assumed that the idea was to get the script in fair enough condition to seduce a director, but in Gigi's imagination it already had one.

Gigi stared sourly around the table as I quit my unwanted job as television critic and ordered a frittura di pesce. Roberto sat with us, and some other people who helped run Al Portico, and a raven-haired young woman called Lella in a burnt-orange lamb's-wool sweater, and Mauro the mustachioed jazzman. Then Gigi started to harangue them in high *cacaglio*. He hadn't much liked tonight's show, he said, because some of those young comics just didn't cut it. Even someone who didn't know Neapolitan could tell from their gestures that they weren't funny, that they weren't original or perceptive. A comic's very way of holding himself ought to make people laugh, he said. And besides, they were much too slow: dialect humor had to be fast, *"ta-ta-ta!"* Some people were born to this art, Gigi said, and some weren't. He told us, almost shouting, that he had been on the *Maurizio Costanzo Show,* a popular Italian TV talk program, where he had frankly told Silvio Berlusconi, who was also Costanzo's guest (though not yet prime minister), that he, Berlusconi, was not a born politician. Rising from his chair, Gigi repeated what he had said to Berlusconi, which was that some people were naturals and others were not. Maradona was a natural and Vittorio Gassman was a natural, but Berlusconi—no!

Gigi cut a strange figure. His legs, I noticed, were really quite short, and with his sporty two-tone T-shirt and gelled, dyed-blond hair he seemed a caricature of an American skateboarder. He was one of those Italians who were fed up with the Italian elegance, the Italian predictability, and suddenly he looked terribly young. It occurred to me that he was like some strange electronic contraption that depleted itself as it pulsed out humor. When Gigi ran low he recharged himself with bile, and then he pulsed out humor again. I felt a surge of sympathy for Gigi.

Mauro's droopy mustache seemed to reach its nadir as he followed Gigi's harangue. The only one who responded was Lella, the girl in the sweater. Lella had also read Gigi's script, and, as it happened, her views were not so different from mine. Abinotto was cute, she said, but he verged on being a little too cute, a little too *Neapolitan* what with his naughty pilferings and his habit of fondly swindling people, of exploiting their gullibility in that *grateful* way that swindlers had in these latitudes. Gigi's script, if it wasn't carefully staged, could end up making the Romans laugh at the Neapolitans, a typically Roman sport; whereas the real aim of comedy was to get people to laugh at themselves. And as Lella said all these things, in broad dialect—she was clutching her cigarette packet and Bic lighter between both hands in the prayer gesture, shaking her hands at Gigi, admonishing him—she looked increasingly like a Neapolitan stock figure herself.

The Neapolitans, Gigi shot back, supplied Italy with a lot of her best theatrical talent, but if you were Neapolitan yourself people typed you, they put you in a bag. Okay, you were funny, and maybe clever as well, but *competent? Dependable?* Never! "Naples," Gigi said, "is like a beautiful woman, but we don't know how to dress her."

"Gigi," said Mauro, "could you do us all a favor—"

But Gigi wasn't listening. He wasn't doing anybody any favors that night.

10

The Curiosity Shop

You realize that it's mildly epic, what you're asking? I mean, really, I don't know . . . Of course it was me who started this whole thing, but now it's made her nervous big-time. I feel so guilty, I guess it's time for a little damage control. Oh God, does that sound juvenile?"

"Tina, Tina," I said.

"Benedetta likes to say I sound juvenile. Ciro, that's my *fidanzato,* says she's a bourgeois bohemian. You should hear how he describes her, he says she's austerely luxurious and savagely domestic and residually—"

"Tina, I just want you to put me in touch with her. Is that asking so much?"

We were talking on the telephone, and she sounded like her mouth had gone dry. "In touch," she said.

"Tina! That's what I've been saying for the past ten minutes."

"I guess if I were more centered I'd know just what to do. Let me think . . . okay, okay, listen, she's not even in Naples right now, why don't you call me in a week. No, in two. Two weeks. *Intesi?*"

So there matters stood, for better or worse; and as I floundered about town I came to think of Benedetta as a missing person, like one of those whose photograph you might see in a New York laundromat, or one of Donato's fugitives from justice. In my day-dreams it crossed my mind to hire a private detective, but then I would remember that she wasn't really lost, except to me: no one could find her until she wanted to be found. I brooded over my chance meeting with Tina in the boutique, the half-truths she'd given me to swallow while I wandered peering at distant silhou-ettes, misled by vaguely familiar scents, drawn to an uplifted eye-brow, long lashes over the wrong hazel eyes. Sometimes I stopped to wonder what my meanderings would look like on a map, traced in red with a fine-pointed pen. Like loops and spirals, I supposed, scrabbled over and over the same thoroughfares; and when I decided to buy her a propitiatory gift in the hope of an eventual meeting, the retracing of my steps grew compulsive, nightmarish.

And now someone is following me in the street—*Signore, aspet-tate!*—whom I ignore until she catches at my sleeve. It's that little shop assistant, her expression so comically earnest that I allow her finally to escort me back. An hour ago I entered the place, a curio dealer's smelling of fire and mildew, and came across something I wanted for Benedetta. A *riggiola,* a decorative tile of the eighteenth century, pilfered no doubt from some ruined palazzo. How much did it cost? The girl, gummy-eyed, half asleep, didn't know; she told me the owner had stepped out for a moment. She rang him at home; no answer; and then, a minute later, he rang back. She said: Poke around a little longer, or try the bar two doors down, it's a good one; he won't be a moment, he's on his way. But the owner wasn't back after half an hour, and in disgust I departed. Now, five blocks farther along in my meanderings, Piazza San Domenico slides into view and I feel the tug at my sleeve. He's back, he's there, I promise, *ve lo giuro!* But when we enter he must have just stepped out again. Any note as to the tile's price? At the counter she thumbs through a mess of papers, scraps as ragged as leaf mold. Sorry, come back later.

Without Benedetta's patience for hunting and haggling, I'd

started to frequent the *rigattieri* because they reminded me of her and helped me pass the time. The shops clung like bats to the neighborhood of Via Costantinopoli and the district around Piazza Ecce Homo, the more expensive ones clustering discreetly in Chiaia. The bona fide antique dealers, the *antiquari,* took offense at being called *rigattieri,* yet the latter were not to be sneezed at: they often got their hands on unprovenanced treasures, which, camouflaged in the rat's nests of their shops, could be furtively sold to collectors. They were accomplished tax-dodgers and suspected of being rich. The secondhand dealers regilded imitation rococo secretaires in the street and refinished ribbon-backed chairs in their rear courts, and whenever I made them an offer for something they said, "My partner will kill me if I let it go for that," eyes full of reproach. Every Sunday morning one or two street markets also mushroomed up, swarming with dealers. There I saw wall-shrine putti and ledger-stone carvings, things never meant for trade.

Clemente Esposito, the engineer who'd descended into the underworld with the Quaranta brothers, collected just about everything and knew the *rigattieri* well. He owned considerable acreage atop a grand palazzo near Santa Maria Maggiore—the same building where Benedetto Croce, the philosopher, had lived. Esposito (grizzled beard, bulky sweater, eyeglasses on a cord) amassed rare maps, obsolete machines, fossils, pipes, seashells, panoramic views of the bay, stuffed weasels, egrets, owls; from his perch he could see enough churches to claim that he also collected the domes of Naples. He told me once that during the restoration of a nave in the old city the doors had been left open and a secondhand dealer had slipped inside. "A bad apple," Esposito snorted: the next day a stone *stemma*—a coat of arms—went missing from (if I have this right) a donor's tomb.

In Via delle Belledonne, where I was browsing the *rigattieri,* still trying to find a token to win Benedetta's favor, I saw a small woman in a dealer's vitrine. She was bent over what looked like a ledger, so I couldn't make out her face, but there was something touching about the long gentle curve of her neck and the way she caught a lock of hair with her finger and pulled it out of an eyebrow.

On the telephone I asked Tina, "Where's that dealer Benedetta works with these days? The one in Chiaia."

"Dealer? Benedetta? Chiaia?" I had caught her off guard.

"Come on, just the address of the place."

"I can't tell you yet."

"Tina, I saw her there, I know where it is. In Via delle Belledonne."

For a moment Tina was silent. Then, capitulating, she said, "Okay, dammit, she is there. Oh God, just call her there. Call her tomorrow—I'll tell her you're going to be in touch. I think it's all right now anyway. And . . . there's another thing. When you go, tell me what you think of Renzo?"

"Renzo?"

"Tell me your opinion," she said.

Tina and I were friends, of course. But I think she disliked Renzo a good deal more than she liked me.

I didn't dare just walk into that shop. For half a day I rehearsed casual-sounding ways of announcing myself to Benedetta on the phone, and then, on the spur of the moment, I called up empty-headed. No shame in that, I told myself—I *was* empty-headed, as anyone in the throes of strong emotion usually is. Hearing my voice, she didn't say a word at first; but then, in a pale voice, she welcomed me back to Naples.

"We should meet," I suggested, coming straight to the point. "Maybe in Piazza dei Martiri, when you're finished one evening." If any place might quicken her emotions, I thought, it was this square, so near her shop: beside its monument of carved lions we had begun our last drive up to the promentory of Posillipo, three years earlier. But perhaps I was too hastily emboldened, I considered a moment later, recalling Tina's remark about "Renzo."

"I would like that," she said, "but I can't." Several times she began to explain and her voice died away. She seemed to want to spare me something that pained her as much as it might hurt me.

"It's just that"—she searched for words—"*lui non lo vuole*—he doesn't want it. Not just with you—with anyone. He doesn't want me to see any man on my own."

"He doesn't want it." This was a phrase I'd never heard before, anywhere: it was too antiquated to connect with anything in my experience, and saying it had cost her something, I could tell. Nonplussed, I let it pass for the moment.

"Well, how *can* we meet?" I asked her.

"Come to the shop." She gave a little laugh. "You'll come and make yourself unhappy. And me, too."

There was no one in the front of the shop when I arrived, though a chair stood out on the sidewalk and another just inside. It was one of those densely packed Neapolitan lairs, dark and self-entangled as a tropical root system. I halted apprehensively at the threshold, figurines and devotional statuary gawking at me through the window. Then I saw her moving through the interior's blurry depths—she was threading her way up an aisle of stacked furniture. Darkened by a virtual canopy of pendant brass chandeliers, wearing a green silk top, she looked slightly haggard but lovely just the same, her eyes more deeply set, each cheekbone casting its hint of shadow; but she scarcely resembled and could not have been the pensive girl I'd followed into the cloister. As she came nearer, entering a zone of table lamps and wall sconces, I tried to decipher her expression, but it seemed, and still does as I remember it now, too varied to define. It registered threat, and perhaps a hint of aesthetic embarrassment or guardedness against my expected disdain at that crowd of Saint Anthony statues and crèche figures—protectiveness not so much of the bric-a-brac as of her association with it and by extension with its absent proprietor. Certainly the shop was an unabashed display of what she herself had once termed the *borbonico*—the conventional taste of a bygone era. And yet our meeting there didn't displease her; the smile growing on her lips was proof of that.

The air was cigarette-stale. She leaned forward for the obligatory embrace.

"So that runt got her way at last," she said, not in annoyance. But we had regained our distance.

"She's a big girl now," I said.

Benedetta's irrepressible left eyebrow arched up. She plucked at my collar, removing lint. "*'Na santerella,*" she said. A little saint. "Butter wouldn't melt."

"Do we have to talk about Tina?"

"Well, she's been quite a pen pal," Benedetta said. "And all with the best intentions, of course. No dark motive. This isn't our best stuff." I'd been looking around discreetly. "It's too bad, we just sold a lot of really good things. I don't know what you want."

"I don't want anything."

"I mean with me." She glanced apprehensively out the window, as if something or someone was about to interrupt us. "It was hopeless trying to write you," she said. "In the end I just gave up. I was furious. You changed addresses so often they filled two pages in my address book. Where are you staying, anyway? Give me your telephone number."

She wrote it down, though I had little expectation she would call.

"Oh, don't give me that half smile," she said.

"Half smile?"

"You're smiling with half of your face. It's unbearable, really—"

I began to laugh. "That's better," she said, tweaking my earlobe. "Oops, that lamp, you're going to knock it over . . . There. This wasn't supposed to happen."

"But it's happening."

"I'll never forgive you," she said, very forgivingly.

Just then, in the street behind us, somebody shouted "Mamma!" I couldn't see who it was: Benedetta was already immersed in a fast-forward recap of the last three years, how her not getting a teaching job was ultimately a relief and all for the best and so forth. I knew she wasn't being frank because her arms stayed motionless, but little by little they started to stir, and before long they were moving quite freely.

"You've hardly changed," she said. "I've put on weight—"

A bus clanked noisily by outside. "Mamma!" called the voice. "Mamma, it's time!"

Benedetta giggled and pointed over my shoulder. On the sidewalk a woman, not a year under sixty, was hollering up at a shuttered window.

"Every day at this hour . . . Don't think," Benedetta said, "that just because we're laughing here together it can be like it was . . ."

"Actually the thought hadn't crossed my mind," I said, as it occurred to me that it had crossed hers. "But what is this 'he doesn't want it' stuff? After all your talk about machismo and how insufferable men are, trying to—"

"Mamma!"

"Because," Benedetta broke in—our talk had got at cross-purposes—"I've had to accept and you'll have to accept—"

"Would you kindly explain to me—" I started to reply, but before she could finish, a man pulled up on a Vespa and dismounted.

The proprietors of such shops were always doing this, leaving their doors and returning, restless, mosquito-like, searching for finds around the city. As he took off his helmet a balding, late-middle-aged head emerged, terra-cotta-colored and jaggedly modeled, rather like the face on a crèche figure. He wore green corduroy trousers of a baggy cut then in fashion, a dark blue shirt, and eyeglasses on a cord. Tall and slightly stooped, he moved in a slow, rather somnolent way, which, I would later confirm, was habitual, as though he were perpetually condescending to rouse himself from sleep. His lofty brow might have seemed philosophically inclined but for the raddled, purplish pouches under his eyes. He nodded to Benedetta as he entered but took no notice of me, and she made no effort to introduce us.

To my amazement, she sprang into a position resembling drill-ground at-ease. Almost mechanically I sidled off and feigned interest in various objects on display, but could not make out their price, since they were labeled in code.

"Well, did it have the mounts?" Benedetta asked him.

"Yes, and they were original, but—"

"Did you buy it?"

"Of course not," he said crossly, "don't interrupt me." Apparently she and Renzo—for I assumed the newcomer was he—were resuming an earlier conversation. "The price was too high," he continued. "These *chiattilli*—they want ridiculous sums for their démodé heirlooms nowadays." In drowsy tones he began to denigrate the yuppies of Naples, and as he droned on I worked my way down a corridor flanked by two rows of doubtful antiques. On either side, furniture teetered: massive chests topped by tables or chairs which were in turn crowned by glassware or theater ephemera. At length I found myself contemplating a majolica vase, cylinder-shaped and daubed with yellow and cobalt-blue figures.

"I intuited that you would like that," Renzo rasped out, startling me. I had thought him oblivious of my presence. "I sense a spiritual affinity between you and that piece."

"It is attractive," I conceded, suppressing a smile.

He slouched down the aisle and picked it up. "Chipped around the base, but nice of its type. Capodimonte, you know. Probably from the old Jesuit pharmacy here. For storing medicinal herbs."

Rotating it in his hands, he tilted his head back and scrutinized it through his half-moon glasses. "Imagine getting medicine from a priest," he commented. "About as reliable as absolution from a doctor. Charming decoration—from a composition by Titian.

You won't find anything this good from much after 1820—Naples has been artistically inert since then. But let's be charitable to the old whore. She has many beautiful things, most of them either carefully hidden away or too openly exposed. Do you want it? I can do a good price for you."

I hesitated.

"What is it you're looking for?" he asked.

Of course, I was merely playacting the customer. But I felt I had to say something.

"I'm looking for a Caserta tureen or teapot," I blurted out, momentarily forgetting what such things cost. Caserta and Capodimonte were the only local names I knew.

"Curious," Renzo said, "that a foreigner should have any interest in such items. Compared let us say to Sèvres or Meissen. You're a person of taste, I can see." He had assumed a scholarly air. "Of course, we're talking about a period when the palette of the Neapolitan majolica painters lightens considerably."

"A lot of delicate greens," Benedetta put in. She was standing beside us, biting her lip, twisting her interlaced fingers. "Pea greens and olives. Lovely turquoise shades."

"There is something vaguely Turkish," Renzo said, peering over his glasses at me, "about much of the Caserta majolica of the *settecento*. Of course, those pieces aren't easy to come by. Things disappear in this town. This is an ignorant place, and ours is an ignorant age. But here now—I feel we have met before. Where, though? Perhaps at some auction?"

"I don't believe we have met," I said.

"I am certain we have," he insisted, still peering at me over his glasses. His gaze had grown keen and familiar. "Will you permit me to hazard a description of your aesthetic personality? It is entirely positive, I assure you. You gave off strong vibrations on entering my shop."

"I did?"

"Of course you did—such things cannot be concealed from me, I've been in this line for decades. For instance, your relations

with your family—I mean your parents. They are primarily interested in business affairs, are they not? Don't get me wrong—it's
entirely normal to take interest in such matters, look at me. But in
your case—well, I sense the soul of an aesthete. Your position is a
difficult one. You have been involved in a painful struggle with
your father, have you not, because he has failed to grasp that
beauty is more important to you than getting on in the world.
And of course the most painful part of this struggle is that you
love your father, the furthest thing from your wishes is to cause
him any disappointment, and yet—but listen to me! I can see I am
making you uncomfortable. Forgive me for prying into matters
that are none of my concern—later you can tell me whether I was
right." He set down the majolica vase and lit a cigarette, while I
marveled at the perfect inaccuracy of his guesswork concerning
my family.

"Let me reciprocate by telling you a little about my own background," he said, with no apparent logic. "You may think this
establishment is new—it is not. For years I have done my part in
championing the Neapolitan artistic heritage. My business was
formerly in Via Morelli—I have had a number of shops in the city.
As a child I began to take an interest in beautiful things, and I
even remember the moment when it all began. I must have been
twelve or thirteen—there was a religious procession in our quarter. Some bishop or archbishop came to rededicate a church or
something, and my mother took me to Mass to see this bishop. I
already knew it was all mumbo-jumbo, but I saw the pastoral staff
he was carrying and, well, I coveted it. The crook was of gold and
wonderfully wrought, and his miter was no eyesore, either. I had a
pretty good view of the ceremony, and whenever it came time to
genuflect I just sat there, craning forward, trying to make out the
embroidery on the geezer's surplice. When I kissed his ring I was
in heaven. Or would have been, if I'd been able to snitch it."

When Renzo said "geezer" I noticed how old he was—decades
older than Benedetta. Was this the man who was keeping her to

himself? I supposed he was still good-looking in his way, but the flesh under his eyes was so discolored as to look almost bruised, and his speech was disconcertingly slurred.

"It's miraculous what religion can do," he went on, "because till then I'd had no interests at all. School bored me terribly. I hated sports. And then, *voilà!* I had a calling. And it came rather early, too, as such things go—nowadays no one has a calling anymore, even the Communists are in it for the dough. Don't think, by the way, that my business is restricted to what you see before you."

"Many of the things in the window," Benedetta said, "are up front merely to catch the eye of tourists."

"I think this gentleman knows that," Renzo said curtly. "Here, let me show you something special." Grasping me by the elbow, he drew me into a storage area at the rear of the shop.

It resembled a ruin or necropolis, this area. A maze of passages, lined by ramshackle ziggurats of piled-up furniture, stretched into the gloom. At the end of one passage was a storeroom where a large ceramic plaque stood propped against the wall. It showed, in vivid colors, a nobleman's armorial bearings, girt by scrolling vines.

"The Marquis d'Astorga," Renzo said.

"A Spaniard?"

"Yes indeed. A viceroy." Tilting his head, he admired it with a sort of sardonic reverence. "How are the mighty fallen," he wryly intoned. We contemplated it in silence while he finished his cigarette. Then we went back into the front of the shop, where Benedetta, standing by a table, appeared to be arranging something.

As we drew nearer I saw that she was toying with a stone carving of a dog. It represented, as far as I could tell, a mastiff of some sort, which though probably quite beautiful centuries ago had a somewhat corroded surface. She handled the carving tenderly, and looking more closely, I saw that two small pieces were detached from the dog's main body.

"This was damaged during the earthquake," she said, tentatively fitting a severed paw onto the dog's foreleg, "the one that happened a few years back. It caused such terrible destruction and suffering around here, you wonder how people like my mother can go on believing in God. I mean, really, think about it, how could an earthquake possibly serve God? Or serve the designs of Providence, as they say?"

Renzo squinted at her. "Oh, I don't know," he said darkly, "an earthquake has its own sort of beauty. All those dramatic fissures and irregular wall fragments—they're very aesthetic in their way. Why do you think we all love to smash crockery during a good family quarrel? Or throw wineglasses into the fireplace? Why is the broken arch a staple of Baroque architecture? The truth is that man adores breakage—he probably couldn't live without it."

Benedetta frowned, so that her whole face became wonderfully stormy. "Lots of people got killed in that earthquake," she said. "Lots of families lost their houses, everything they owned."

"Oh, nobody wants his own house destroyed," Renzo said, "I'll grant you that. But somebody else's ruin can be charming to look at, hence the tradition of painting ruins, which is particularly strong in Campania. Do you know, my dear, that the Academy of Sciences of your fair city was the first such body in the world to appoint an earthquake commission, after the quake of 1783? The commission's report was almost four hundred pages long, but did it prevent a new earthquake? Of course not. Nothing has ever prevented an earthquake. But it was full of fascinating pictures. You know, yawning crevasses, toppling palaces—that sort of thing."

"All I can think about is those poor people," Benedetta said, "some of them still living in shipping containers."

"It sounds," I said to Renzo, "like you're not from Naples yourself."

"Heavens no," he said, "my father was a Roman. My mother, who is from Gaeta, committed the unpardonable crime of bringing me here when I was fifteen, so you may say I'm a Neapolitan by adoption. But this place has never agreed with me, especially the swill that these people call wine." And he drifted into another tirade, this time blasting the local vintages.

A customer entered, and after some hesitation bought a chess set, which Benedetta, who had left off toying with the broken carving, wrapped up for him and put in a plastic bag. Outside it was quieter now—the lunch hour. Benedetta and Renzo made ready to close up shop.

I had managed to prolong my visit for an hour, but it had of course been excruciating. Nothing had prepared me for the pain of seeing somebody I'd once been close to at so great an emotional remove. That she was allied in profitless commerce (for so I already suspected it to be) with this saturnine, grizzled merchant roused an unexpected access of tenderness in me. Surely this was no place for the Benedetta I remembered. Despite the strength of my feelings, however, they failed to suggest a clear course of action. For the moment, I wished only to continue to see her.

At all events, Renzo had not yet figured out who I was, but he would surely ask. And eventually, of course, Benedetta would tell him.

⤙⤚

"So?" Tina said, several days later at a café in Via Santa Brigida, near her work.

I was trying to adjust to Renzo but it wasn't easy, I confessed. That pedantry of his, that way of constantly "imparting"—it was preposterously theatrical, buffoonish.

"He was a marvelous person once," Tina said. "He was the consummate outsider—like, no overlay, just essence. But now he's destroying her. He's going to drag her down with him. You must've noticed what a wreck he is."

I hadn't really, I admitted. He'd just looked harried—a little tired, maybe.

"Tired of existing," she said, looking me hard in the eye. "*Si buca, sai. Renzo si buca.*"

I winced. I had often heard the expression in Naples, *bucarsi,* "to put holes in oneself." So Renzo was addicted to heroin—at least, according to Tina he was.

"It's no secret," she said. "We all know it. He practically main-lines"—*si fa* were her words—"in public. He ups the dose all the time. And he takes it with Roipnol, or whatever it's called. Haven't you listened to him? How he talks like he's got pasta e fagioli in his mouth? Look at his eyes!"

I really hadn't noticed anything so unusual, though the power of suggestion was beginning to take hold of me.

"I've known people who were strung out for years," I said, rather hypocritically. "Gifted people. Sometimes it's not too serious."

"*Ma che dici?* He's going to kill himself," Tina said. "He wants to. With an overdose or God knows what. Last month he got knocked off his Vespa in Via Medina. He had a gash in his leg, but he rode away out of fear he'd get busted. He was afraid they'd yank his license. Listen, don't think I don't care about him. As I said, he was a marvelous person once. With his antique business—he was a real antique dealer then, not what he is now—he connected with my sister's soul-search, only like in reverse. They had this couple-life that worked, even if she was sort of confused, like she always is. But now I hate him—well, I suppose I can't say that, it's too awful. I just hate what he's doing to her."

I asked, afraid of the answer, whether Benedetta was also using heroin.

"No," she said. "Never."

"No baby habit?"

"Of course not. She doesn't even do *spinello* anymore. But she's incredibly loyal to him, because he threw her a spiritual lifeline once. I don't know if she told you"—I had a nauseating presenti-ment of what was coming—"that they're married. That they're husband and wife. At least theoretically."

"Theoretically—what does that mean?"

"They've been married since—oh, since well before you met her. She was very young, younger than I am now. They kept the whole thing secret. I must have been about fifteen when she told me, and I think I was the only one she ever told. I guess they were deeply in love then—well, they must have been. But now he's messing up her life."

I just sat there. I couldn't think of anything sensible to say. I was trying to absorb what Tina had told me, and wondering where Renzo had been three years earlier, when Benedetta and I were together. We looked at each other in silence, Tina fighting back tears and I in a stupor of unwilling comprehension.

"I think," she said, "I know—he takes her money. He lies to her. And of course he makes her his accomplice. He humiliates her."

Though I didn't know whether Tina was telling the truth, my visits to Renzo's shop became regular. Every few days I would drop by and resume the charade of interest in pieces of Caserta majolica that might have turned up in his backwater of the antiques trade; fortunately, none had so far. I didn't know what I expected or wanted of Benedetta anymore, but I knew I couldn't keep away from her. Nor, despite her demure facade, did she seem to want me to.

And so it went, for days, for weeks. I could never tell when Renzo was being serious and when he was merely playing the idle aristocrat. Maybe he didn't know himself. He was moody, exhausted, haughty—and jealous. In time I suspected that he knew everything about Benedetta and me but wanted only to regard me as a potential customer, a possibility he couldn't afford to exclude. Soon, any day now, he would sell me one of those wildly expensive pieces of majolica. "Ah, here comes Caserta," he would murmur, whenever I arrived.

One day he said, "Caserta, you have an exotic accent."

"Well, I am a foreigner," I said, smiling, "but hardly exotic."

"Anglo-Saxon?"

"American."

"Ah, America. King Ronny. Queen Nancy." His manner, characteristically frosty, now grew unusually glacial. He surveyed me with weary condescension.

"Signor Caserta," he said, "what do you think of Gabriele Castellano?"

"Who's he?" I asked. "Somebody I should know?" I looked at Benedetta, who was looking elsewhere.

He smiled disdainfully. "Somebody you *would* know, if you had the slightest familiarity with majolica. Castellano was the finest modeler at the Bourbon factory during Gennaro Chiaiese's tenure as master of the works. But I daresay you are not uneducable. Doubtless your knowledge will progress."

"Oh, doubtless," I said.

Looking around the shop, I saw for the first time how many of the things Renzo sold had once served sacred purposes. There was the usual collection of crèche figures, a brutal bestiary of misbegotten rustics: obese, squinty-eyed, beggarly, drunken, insane. And then there were those congeries of Madonnas and Saint Anthonys, those plaster archangels and ex-votos and holy-water stoups.

"All these religious objects," I murmured, running my finger over a silver-gilt ciborium. "This place has an air of deconsecration. It's like everything here once had a more exalted role somewhere else."

It just slipped out—I actually hadn't meant anything.

Benedetta recoiled slightly.

"You're making the rather vulgar assumption," Renzo said, with lazy hauteur, "that objects look most beautiful—most exalted, as you tritely put it—in an ecclesiastical setting. This is a housemaid's delusion. With us only the serving people"—*la servitù,* he said—"have ideas like that. 'Oh, the little fellow, how beautiful he is in his first communion outfit!'—or 'How sweet that Jesus looks on the Cross!' Well, I happen to espouse the opposite view-point. I am happy that Latin has been removed from the Mass. That Latin made a mockery of the language of Virgil."

He had retreated, unaccountably, from the cusp of confronta-tion—but no, it was not unaccountable. For I knew, suddenly and with absolute certainty, that he was desperate to sell me some-thing, and that this eagerness overrode any urge to draw attention to my gaffe.

In my many visits to Renzo's, mistrust distorted our conversa-tions, double entendres cropped up constantly, and I remained uncertain of the part he was playing. Like many who have squeezed themselves into poverty, he seemed inclined to believe that others had bottomless resources, including, absurdly, myself. This led him to fantasies of finding an exorbitant piece of majolica, or perhaps something else, to fob off on me at a propi-tious moment. But it wasn't only that my appeal as future pur-chaser outweighed the taint of my past sins: I also came to suspect that he was pleased, perversely, by my presence. Despite his be-dimmed faculties, he could see that his theatrics amused me against my better judgment, and this flattered his vanity. Craving an audience, he enjoyed dishing out humorous insults, rather as a stand-up comic enjoys humiliating the very public to whose laughter he's addicted.

Addiction: that, if Tina was to be believed, was the key to Renzo's character. Tina had said that Renzo was constantly increasing his *bustine,* his doses, and if so his expenditures were probably outpacing his receipts by an unimaginable margin. The poor fellow ran the risk of ruin along with that of an overdose, and who knew what the consequences for Benedetta might be? Tina had an impulsive, not fully reasoned hope that I would rescue her sister from her destructive husband, but by now I found this idea, as she might have put it, "juvenile," or, at the least, immature.

Locked into a state of permanent indecision, I was also plagued by mounting fears. Surely I would not be able to conceal or control my desire for Benedetta indefinitely. The awkwardness between us was deadening all verbal exchange, a situation I might recklessly alter with a few heartfelt words. As for Renzo, he was, I felt, working off some obscure sense of degradation on the two of us, and though it was one thing for her to sympathize with him, it was quite another for her to pick up the contagion. Sometimes she seemed enveloped in his mortal gloom. Yet the more I meditated on all this, the less certain I was of what to do about it, and for some time the tension only continued to mount.

Doctor Candeloro

If I had entered a phase of indecisiveness, it was certainly made worse by the weather. Stifling, maddening, the sirocco was now upon us. Unfortunately, the siesta period usually found me far from my flat, searching for somewhere to cool off, and often I had no luck. One afternoon, when I sought out a place to read my newspaper in the garden of the Villa Floridiana, I came up against a row of benches claimed by desperate old folks and a lawn worn virtually bald.

In general terms I was anxious about Benedetta. But I didn't know which concerned me more, the possibility that I might lose her for good or the chance that I might recapture her. I hadn't reckoned on coming between man and wife, however unhappy they might be together. And Renzo's condition alarmed me. He was an estimable fellow in his way, and it was not for me to induce her to abandon him in hard times. I was reduced to the position of passive supplicant.

In this limbo, I fell prey to a horde of idle thoughts and dreams, dreaming as deeply as I'd ever done in Naples. One night I dreamed I had a donkey, chestnut with white markings. We were inseparable, and he let me ride him all over the city, so that I had no need to walk. Whenever he didn't know the way he would stop and crane his head around and look at me mutely with his big brown eyes, and I would nod "*That* way," and off he would go again. In the streets the crowds admired my donkey and parted ways for him, and when I awoke I regretted that he was gone.

What was the "meaning" of this donkey dream? I soon found an interpretation that satisfied me: it involved the weather and the way it affected my well-being. Walking about Naples, I perceived that in this famously sunny city the sunlight touched the older quarters only with fastidious reluctance. Even as spring melted into summer, certain courtyards stayed so gloomy that their dampness never dissipated. The humid shadows offered a grotto-like, somniferous relief from the heat, but I also began to notice the return of an ache in my spine that I'd had, off and on, since childhood. Despite walking, exercising, and swimming in the sea, I found no way to reduce this inflammation, which seemed subject to moods of its own. So my donkey, I thought, acted the way I wanted my body to act: he carried me, without complaint, wherever I wanted to go. And with this notion in mind, I began to think of consulting a doctor.

The tradition of curing ailments empirically, with plant-derived medicines—with vegetal unguents, pastilles, or drafts—is ancient in Italy, especially in Campania. The herbalist is a common feature of town life, and I'd had good luck with one during a bout of insomnia when I was living in the Quartieri. This female healer had counseled me to await the arrival of a decoction from India, which turned out to be potent enough to afford me many nights' worth of deep nocturnal sleep.

I no longer knew any herbalists, but Benedetta did tell me that she had been helped, dramatically, by a certain semiretired physician called Doctor Candeloro. She had once suffered from a virulent chronic infection that no conventional practitioner could cure, but Doctor Candeloro had succeeded somehow. Just how, she had no idea: though he possessed a standard medical degree, he also engaged in mysterious practices of his own. These were derived, she had learned after pressing inquiries, from a healing guild called the Antica Scuola Medica Salernitana, or the Ancient Medical School of Salerno, which was founded in the tenth century by followers of Saint Benedict and survived in Campania until 1811, when Joachim Murat suppressed it. Murat, Bonaparte's brother-in-law, was appointed King of Naples after Napoleon's capture of the city; why he suppressed the Scuola Salernitana—apparently with indifferent success—was something I never found out.

I made an appointment to see Doctor Candeloro, though it occurred to me that I was seeing him partly on account of Benedetta. I pictured aged curative hands touching her half-naked body, then those hands touching mine, and this fantasy was irresistible. Perhaps all this touching would by some sympathetic magic bring her closer to me, and then, when we met again, we would have something physical to discuss.

The doctor's quarters, comprising both office and lodgings, were in an antique palazzo whose tall windows overlooked, with genteel reticence, a large and noisy street market. As I arrived, the market had just awakened from the siesta, and black eggplants and red peppers were being deployed in vast regiments—their beauty struck me as auspicious. In the palazzo's inner courtyard two shrines to the Virgin stood forth gaudily from the walls, each one guarded by an ailing dwarf palm; a corner stairway, with well-worn marble treads, led up to the doctor's door. He answered the bell himself and showed me along a corridor and into his office, where he sat down behind a large desk. Tiny and swarthy, Doctor Candeloro seemed immemorially old, a holdover from a remote era, and he moved very slowly, though not, I thought, with pain. He was swimming in an oversize gray check suit, which had doubtless once fit him. His open collar revealed that he wore an undershirt, despite the late afternoon heat.

"So," he said, cocking his head and peering up at me with a melancholy smile, "you have come to me on account of a rheumatic complaint." He glanced down at a pad on which I suppposed that my name was written. "Are you German?"

"No," I said. "American. From New York City."

"Ah, from New York. Do you come from the swampy part of that country?"

"There are no swamps where I live," I said. An image of gas stations and convenience stores flashed into my mind.

"No swamps, that is excellent," said Doctor Candeloro. "And your house, what is it made of? Is it made of cement? Because that would be very bad. Cement prevents cosmic energy from entering our houses and our bodies."

I assured him that my house was not made of cement, and he looked less worried. Then he surveyed my attire. "Your shoes, you must change them, they won't do," he said, with peremptory concern. "The rubber soles interact with the pavement, releasing ions that will hurt your joints."

Doctor Candeloro's face, like that of many very old southern Europeans, appeared slightly miniaturized, as though seen through a diminishing glass. It also had the ruggedness of a Bernini sculpture. Tufts of hair shot out of his ears, and his thick white eyebrows, which shone like luminous pelts against the deep tan of his skin, suggested a pair of small Arctic animals darting swiftly apart. His office had a tiled floor and a lofty ceiling; one wall was entirely covered by a large glazed bookcase full of leather-bound volumes and personal memorabilia. An antique clock with a case and pendulum projected from another wall. Behind the doctor hung a great many framed pictures and documents, including, directly over his head, a watercolor of a kind-looking old man, with big round spectacles and a square white beard split into two points. Beside this picture was the doctor's diploma, a neomedieval hand-illuminated document in faded colors that proclaimed, in Gothic script, that Baldassare Candeloro, by the grace of His Majesty Vittorio Emanuele II, King of Italy and Emperor of Ethiopia, had received his M.D. in 1936, from the

Faculty of Medicine of the University of Naples. An aura of gen-
tility and wistful desuetude hung about the place. It had an empty
airiness to it, and I wondered how many patients still visited Doctor Candeloro.

"Please do not be alarmed if I ask many questions," he said.
"We are not in a rush here, and in any case we treat the whole
patient, not just the disease. So: do you drive a car?"

"Yes, I do."

He made an annotation on his pad. "And do you fly an aereoplane?"

"A what?" I said, startled.

"An aereoplane. An airplane, a plane, whatever you call it."

"No," I said, "I can't fly a plane. I'd like to, though. Would that
help me?"

He didn't answer, but made another note on his pad. "So!" he
said, with a flourish of his pen. "Now then, do you sleep soundly?"

"Yes—pretty soundly."

"And what sort of trees do you have around your house?"

"Let me see. I think there's a larch, and a sycamore—"

"But no walnut trees?"

"No, no walnuts."

"Good! You must never sleep under a walnut," he said, with
fierce intensity. "The ancients knew this."

All this while I had been wondering who the man in the watercolor was—the venerable gent with the bifurcated beard, whose
eyes looked so mild, so forgiving. "Excuse me, Dottore," I asked
him, "but who is that person in the picture?"

"That," he replied, "is my master, Pier Nicola Gregoraci. He
was born in 1886, in Catanzaro, in Calabria, and he founded the
movement of which I am a very modest exponent. His great aim
was to restore the spiritual element to our profession, to elim-
inate the egoism. It was a noble task—*Medicus par Deo est,* said
Hippocrates!—and Doctor Gregoraci was much loved by the
common people of Naples. But that is a very long story, so please

let us get on with my medical interview. All this is very important." His gaze had sharpened behind his thick lenses, and he
scrutinized me slyly, with mounting eagerness.

"So—do you go bathing to alleviate this problem with your
back?"

"As often as I can," I replied.

"And do you bathe in salt or fresh water?"

"In both sorts," I said. "Sometimes I swim laps in chlorinated
pools."

"Ah, but you must bathe in salt water!" he exclaimed. "Our
Roman ancestors understood these matters. In Naples, at Pizzofalcone and Posillipo, they built splendid seaside villas, and do you
know what? They installed pools right next to the shore. They
would not swim in the bay. Why? Because their diet was very salty,
they knew there was enough salt in their bodies. We moderns, on
the other hand, lack salt. You must try to swim in the sea, or, failing that, to prepare a bath for yourself using salt. I will give you
the correct proportions before you leave." He scribbled for a
moment on his pad.

Then, with unfailing patience and curiosity, he continued with
a long list of questions about my family history, work habits, and
earlier illnesses. He also inquired about my diet, bowel movements, stomach, and other internal organs.

"Have you ever had any respiratory ailments?" he asked, as the
pendulum clock struck five.

"Once, when I was living in Florence," I replied. "I had a minor
case of pneumonia."

"Oh? And how was it cured?"

"It was cured by a nun," I said. And then, with shameless
loquacity—he seemed, after all, so friendly, so benevolent—I told
him the story of Sister Anna: how I had been directed by the Italian national health service to the nunnery across the street, the
Convent of the Stigmatine Sisters, where sharp-tongued Anna
was authorized to give gamma globulin injections; how I had
dropped my trousers so she could administer her shots; how she

had recounted her struggle against the mob at the hospital in her hometown of Messina; and how when Anna asked me once what religion I professed, and for no other reason than to get a rise out of her, I said, "Sister Anna, I am anticlerical," to which she replied without a moment's pause, "Then you'd be right at home in this convent—we're the most anticlerical people on earth."

Doctor Candeloro followed this account with increasing excitement. "Aha! May I infer that you're an atheist?" he said, mischievous wrinkles forming at the corners of his eyes, then dissolving.

"An atheist?" I said, a bit taken aback. "Well, I don't know that I'd—"

"Let's put down 'atheist,' " he said merrily. "There's nothing wrong with it—in fact it speaks well for you, at least you're not worshiping a false god, like all these religious hypocrites, like Dante's Boniface, like the current pope. What do you make of the pope, by the way?"

"I haven't actually—"

"The trouble with the pope," Doctor Candeloro declaimed, his reedy voice ascending an octave, "is that he rules over an erroneous hierarchy! He is worth very little, and do you know why? Because he's certain that he has understood Christ. *Certain,* mind you!"

My lips struggled numbly to achieve a neutral smile.

"God does not command, as the church appears to believe, nor does He condemn," said Doctor Candeloro, half lifting his tiny frame off his chair in his enthusiasm. He tossed down his pen and raised a monitory finger. "God's justice is neither permissive nor punitive—it is in-struc-tive!" His thumping finger punctuated his syllables on the desk.

The doctor was glowing now, an orator transfigured by the current of his rhetoric. But worried that I might wind up on the wrong side of his theology—wherever that might be—I put on a politely obtuse expression and began to look out the window. What I saw there captivated me. Across the alley was an interior corner formed by the meeting of two vine-clad walls, each pierced by an oval window. Garlanded with trumpet-shaped blossoms, filled with the reflection of drifting clouds and also by some mysterious stirring within, these windows were as subtly animated as forest pools, so that looking at this corner where architecture melted into nature was like admiring a fragment of eternity. Not for years had I had such a vision of a world unchanged, unchanging, and I tried to figure out what made it so. Was it the windows themselves—their design perhaps, or their position? Was it the way that roof shadow traced its irregular outline on the pitted, overgrown masonry? Or was it simply the warmth of the southern light?

"Beautiful, isn't it?" said Doctor Candeloro, with a proprietary smile—he looked suddenly ageless, himself an integral part of the scene. "Do you know, this neighborhood, which originally consisted only of a few buildings, goes back at least to Dante's time. That palazzo you're looking at is one of the oldest around here, probably the oldest—at one time that palazzo *was* the neighborhood! But come now, we must find out more about your medical history."

He sat back and picked up his pen. "You are, I suppose, or have been, a playboy?"

"Excuse me?" I said. "I'm not sure I understand what you mean."

"A playboy, you know, an adventurer. Like most of the males of your generation, you have had relations with many women, have you not? This produces infections, contagions . . ."

As I began to formulate a denial, he said, "Yes, let's just put down 'playboy.' There!" He scribbled again. "So! And now I shall request you to please remove your shirt and lie back on the examination table."

I did as he asked. The examination, though orthodox, was every bit as leisurely as the interview that had preceded it, and was accompanied by the expounding of a medical philosophy as timeless as the view from his window. It went on for a long time: I recall that there was something about a "divine pyramid" and a "rebirth of the universe." When he left for a moment to fetch his stethoscope from another room, I noticed that he had a spring in his step. He practically sprinted back into his office.

Finally the doctor asked me to get dressed and be seated. Perhaps, he said, I might like to have a glance at the manual of Italian floral essences on his desk while he wrote out a prescription.

It seemed that he would never stop scribbling; again his clock struck the hour—it was six o'clock. At last he looked up at me and said, "Shall I tell you what would help you most?"

I nodded assent.

"It is to hoe," he said.

Zappare? To hoe the earth? He had lost me for a moment. What in heaven's name was he talking about?

"Sì, zappare, zappare!" he cried. "What you need is to get yourself a plot of land and hoe it—hoe it well. Hoe it and seed it. Plant something you love."

That was his final recommendation. Provided with a script that counseled salt baths, a tisane of linden leaves and raw sugar, and several remedies of the sort known, I believe, as naturopathic, I thanked Doctor Candeloro and departed. Outside, the shadows had shifted position, and a fresh breeze had sprung up. The doctor had given me directions to a pharmacy at the top of a nearby stairway, one of those long flights of stone steps you find all over Naples and climb half looking over your shoulder, admiring whatever vista may be fanning out behind you. He said that when I saw a Madonnina, a small statue of the Madonna, I would know that I had not lost my way.

I walked energetically up the steps for several minutes. Then I stopped and gazed down at the infinite city, at its domes and campanili, its wharves and gantry cranes, its hideous office towers. In the harbor, white cruise ships towered menacingly over the battlements of the Castel Nuovo. The sky, badged with cumulus clouds, resembled a table set with endless teapots, but in the far curve of the bay a streak of smog blotted out the coast: the cone of the Vesuvius floated on nothingness, like a wash brushed in with the palest of tints. I could not make out a single figure in all that sweep of geography, but somewhere was the one person I really cared about, and perhaps, I thought, with a catch in my throat, she was already drifting out of reach.

Oh well . . . One was always doing this in Naples, turning to look rearward, to sort out the old from the new, the beautiful from the spoiled, the living from the extinct. Even a visit to a doctor became a detour into the past, and strangely I already felt that Doctor Candeloro had become a distant memory. He had drawn me into a bygone era, an era of Benedictine monks or, as I preferred to think, Franciscans, people who kissed lepers and gave away their clothes and abstained from wearing shoes or belts of leather. I remembered the donkey in my dream, and I remembered, too, that Saint Francis had called the human body "Brother Ass."

Then I thought back to that moment when Doctor Candeloro had left his office to fetch his stethoscope. I recalled his elfin gait, the magical lift in his step. On my arrival he had seemed immeasurably old, but there was nothing old about him when I said good-bye—he was younger than I was. I turned to resume my ascent, and as I passed the Madonnina and knew that I had not lost my way, I realized that Doctor Candeloro's cure was already a success. I had scarcely any need to climb farther.

I 2

I'm Listening, Dear

In the evenings, awaiting a resolution to my predicament, I
had time on my hands, and often I would join friends in
some restaurant or café. Afterward I would walk to my room
through the noisy but oddly vacant streets. The nocturnal city was
remarkable that way: if Naples by day was as rowdy and colorful as
a hand of cards, by night it was as blank and secretive as the same
cards dealt facedown.

Once back, I would pour myself a glass of wine and listen to
Gennaro D'Auria, the radio soothsayer. People still cried out to
him from the whole volcanic landscape, each caller a little smoking cone of desire and frustration. Sometimes as I listened I
would try to figure out why Gennaro's show contined to fascinate
me, since the source of this attraction puzzled me a little. Partly I
think I liked him not because he was exotic but because he was
familiar. I came from New York, which, like Naples, was full of
wounded, hungry, slobby, magnetic people: just as I often felt right
at home in Naples, Gennaro would have been a big hit in Brooklyn. Besides, he had the sibylline gift, and though intellectually I

gave it little credence, emotionally I was susceptible to oracles, and never more than now.

Recently all my dreams seemed to portend something about Benedetta. I'd had a hyperreal dream that especially affected me. In it I went to a car rental agency deep in a catacomb, where the agent guided me on a labyrinthine journey not, as I expected, to a car park, but rather to a library: he showed me a big volume of freehand drawings of radiator ornaments, leonine and rather Leonardesque, and asked me which one I'd prefer on my hood. I awoke recalling my drive with Benedetta in Sandro's convertible, our happiest time together.

And then it came to me—why shouldn't I visit Gennaro D'Auria? Maybe my dreams meant something and maybe not, but he was as likely to decode them as anyone, and if he couldn't, or wouldn't, what had I to lose? So I telephoned Radio Camaldoli Stereo and told Gennaro that I was a foreign fan who wanted to meet him; and after some bafflement and annoyance he agreed, reluctantly, to see me. He told me to catch a late train out to his studio, in the suburb of Torre del Greco.

Formerly a semirural town, Torre was (and still is) served by a dilapidated railway line called the Circumvesuviana, which I'd occasionally taken in the past. The coaches, covered in graffiti, rattled through a mutilated landscape of vacant lots, warehouses, and broken windows to halt at nearly deserted stations where paper cups and pizza papers did dervish dances in the wind. That evening, as I watched the ramshackle buildings fly by, their rooftops silhouetted against livid, moonlit clouds, I thought of the Vesuvian eruption of 1794, which had all but obliterated Torre. I thought of Leopardi writing his final poem here, as he lay dying of cholera, about the brutality of nature and the doom of peoples. In the wan light of the coach old men dozed, clutching rolled-up copies of the *Gazzetta dello Sport,* and careworn women with lusterless skin fussed and glanced at their watches. On the opposite banquette, a heavily rouged seductress in late middle age tried vainly to put on a pair of pendant earrings, which dangled from her fingers like gaudy tropical fish.

Gennaro D'Auria had asked me over the telephone whether I had a special interest in magic, and I had answered, truthfully, that I did not. I told him about my dreams; I told him that I was interested in those people whom the Neapolitans called "intuitives," and in how they prompted others to pour out their souls. I did not tell him that I was a talk show fan. I did not tell him that I liked his program less for its occult than for its social content. And I carefully concealed my superstitious streak, the mental weakness that led me to play games like lotto and *scala.*

Outside the Torre railway station, in Via Leopardi, a beat-up car pulled over to pick me up. The driver, a rough-spoken man with a three-day smudge of beard, introduced himself as Salvatore, Gennaro's secretary. He drove us through a monotonous, intermittently blacked-out neighborhood to a small villa with decorative iron grillwork, where he got out and swung open a gate. A moment later I was standing in Gennaro D'Auria's studio.

He was already at work, so I took a seat opposite the podium from which he conducted his broadcast, but my attention was at once drawn elsewhere. Beside me on a wall hung a large speaker, and over this speaker the frail yet exalted voice of an elderly lady drifted in. The caller brought to mind a pale, ascetic face—the face of a nun or nursing sister, Baroque, with humid, upturned eyes, but so wraith-like it might have been floating in the sky. That voice, lunar and attenuated, spoke of all that we have to be thankful for, especially in this beloved Campania of ours, this land blessed by God: the self-sacrifice of our dear mothers, the love and trust of our children, our luminous volcanic horizon, our matchless sunsets, our lemons, our tomatoes, our Padre Pio of blessed memory . . . on and on the voice orated, in flawless Italian, never dodging the subjunctive, never at a loss for the next inspirational cliché . . . and I sat there listening, mesmerized. Every so often Gennaro would slip in over his microphone a heartfelt "of course" or "how true" or "so beautiful," in his deep, curiously nasal voice. Oblivious of what she was saying, he appeared to be sorting distractedly through a stack of recordings; and then, gliding by me, he had left the studio altogether, so that I was now sitting alone with the voice.

As the ethereal caller started to praise the wonderfully cordial and obliging Campanian people, a standard theme in these parts, I glanced around the studio. Though the lighting was subdued, the fittings looked new. Behind the microphone, a long incandescent banner sign repeatedly flashed, in rapidly moving letters, the legend RADIO CAMALDOLI STEREO and the time of day. The front panel of Gennaro's podium bore a pair of garish sculptured logos of presumably mantic significance, and a starfish-shaped neon light spread its tentacles across the ceiling. Rows of musical recordings occupied part of the wall behind the podium, and I recalled now that Gennaro sometimes played selections during his program (*The Phantom of the Opera* was a favorite); but the shelving along the other walls was wholly claimed by a populous tribe of bug-eyed figurines.

I was trying to make out just who or what they represented when the ethereal voice abruptly stopped. There was a moment of pained silence, then: "Are you there, Gennaro?" But Gennaro hadn't returned yet, and the voice, more distraught, repeated the question. Then suddenly Gennaro reappeared, went around to his microphone, and answered, "Yes, yes, I'm listening, dear." The voice resumed its paean to life, the Blessed Virgin, Padre Pio, and the land of Campania, but presently Gennaro reminded its owner that other callers were waiting, and with a wavering valedictory blessing she went off the air.

"That's Vanda, she's a doll," Gennaro told me sotto voce. Signaling with his hands, he indicated that he'd craved a smoke and so had ducked out of the studio. His hair had a peculiar shape, like a fez-shaped toupee. He was tall and strongly built, and wore an electric-blue track suit.

The next caller came on. "What's your name?" Gennaro said, using the intimate form of address.

"Alessandro," said the caller, a young man.

"And where are you calling from?"

"Naples."

"What district?"

"Arenella."

"And when were you born?"

Alessandro gave his date of birth.

"Ah, another Capricorn."

"Yes, sir."

"Okay, let's get started," Gennaro said. "I'm seeing a . . . homosexual. Who is this homosexual?"

"A homosexual? I've never had a homosexual relationship—"

"Very well, my friend, but hasn't this homosexual insisted on having relations with you?"

"Um, yes. His name is Giuseppe."

"And he put the moves on you five days ago."

"Yes."

"And? What happened?"

"Nothing."

"All right then, who is Massimo?"

"I don't know a Massimo."

"You're right, it's not Massimo. But it's Ma-something. *Maria!*"

"Maria's my wife."

"And you have one child, a boy?"

"Yes."

"Okay, we're on the right track. Listen up now, who's the pastry cook? I'm seeing a pastry cook."

"My God, that would be Flavio. You're really good, Gennà!"

"And he lived near you."

"Two flights up."

"And he died last night?"

"Two nights ago. *Mamma mia!*"

"Let's not waste time. Who has red spots all over his face? Would that be you?"

"Not me, Gennà."

"Are you sure?"

"Yes."

"Okay, now pay attention. Unfortunately, I foresee . . . no, it's happened already! Who's been in an accident?"

"An accident?"

"Yes. Who has the gray car?"

"I do, actually. My car is gray."

"With a long scratch along the side?"

"Yes, Gennà. A woman did it. She came and—"

"Alessandro!"

"Yes, Gennà?"

"That woman cast a spell on you! She's a bad woman. She's cursed you. Because—because you left her, Alessandro."

Contritely: "Yes, Gennà. It's true."

"Sandro, for the love of heaven, watch out for that woman."

"Yes, Gennà."

"She wants to hurt you, Sandro."

"Yes, Gennà."

I noticed now that Gennaro, described in his publicity spots as a card reader, did not in fact use a deck of any kind. I had always assumed that as he listened to his callers he dealt himself a row of tarot cards, examining each one the way the reader called Melissa did on TV; but clearly I was wrong. Gennaro merely closed his eyes and pressed the fingers of both hands against his temples (the Neapolitan gesture for *thinking*) and concentrated intensely. He would shut his eyes tight and tilt way over, and sometimes I thought he would fall.

"I don't need cards," he said to me, when Alessandro got off the line. "And don't ask me how I do what I do, because I have no idea. Well now"—another caller had come on—"who's this?"

"My name is Antonio."

As usual, he requested the name of Antonio's hometown or

district and his date of birth. Then he said, "What do you want to know about, Antonio? Love, family, or work?"

"Work," Antonio said.

"Work, eh? And your sign is . . . Leo, right?"

"That's it," Antonio said.

"Okay, who's dead?"

"Dead?"

"*Eh già,* you're really calling because someone died, aren't you?"

"Someone died?"

"Look, let's not waste time here, I have a large public and the lines are all tied up with people waiting to get through. Who died? Why don't you want to tell me?"

Choked up, Antonio murmured, "My uncle." And then, "I was kind of doubtful about you, Gennà, but you're good, you're really good."

"He died just this morning."

"Yes."

"Of a tumor."

"Correct."

"Okay, you're very upset, and I'll try to get in touch with Uncle for you. Hold on, who's coming into your room?"

"Coming into my room? Nobody."

"Liar! Turn off your lights! Look, Antonio, I can't get involved in stupid experiments. You know the rules. When you call me I want everybody else out of your room and the lights down low. For the love of heaven, I'm not a miracle-worker, I'm only a drop of water in God's infinite universe, and I can't help you if you won't tell me the truth. I might as well give up and go home!" Clasping his head with both hands, Gennaro began to concentrate. "Okay, are all your lights out? . . . Excuse me, but I'm seeing a red light. Neon. Heavens, a pizzeria! Hey, what's going on here?"

"The pizzeria's right opposite my apartment. I can't do anything about the shop sign, Gennà."

"Okay, okay, but who's Mario?"

"Mario's the name of my uncle who died."

"Oh, right, I'm sorry about that. Let me see if I can get in touch with him." Gennaro clasped his temples again; he said a few perfunctory words about Antonio's uncle, about how much he loved Antonio, and so forth, and then got off the line.

With an air of regret he said to me, "I needed a smoke. I just couldn't stand it anymore."

He disappeared briefly while a commercial announcement lavishly praised his extrasensory gifts. Then a woman named Rita came on the line and told him where she lived and her date of birth.

"Good," he said as he dashed toward the microphone, "but who's the prostitute?"

"The prostitute? I have no idea."

"You know perfectly well. And Anna—who is she?"

"My grandmother."

"Who is dead. I can see her—" With no warning Gennaro gave a ferocious cry. "Somebody's reading the cards! You can't read the tarot while you're on the air with me! You must stop at once."

"It's only my girlfriend," said Rita, sounding terrified. "She's sitting right here with me, consulting a deck of cards."

"All right, all right, put her on!"

"Hello, Gennaro, it's me, Nannina. I didn't mean any harm."

"Signorina, you mustn't read cards while you're on the air with me. Do you understand that?"

"Yes, Gennà."

"Are you sure? You have green eyes, don't you? Brilliant green eyes."

I heard a shriek on the other end of the line.

"And you like oral sex."

"No!"

"Yes. You're a great liar. Also . . . you're doing something you shouldn't be doing right now. You're . . . I don't know. But you're making me nervous."

"Well, I don't mean—"

"*Buona sera,* signorina." He cut her off with a snort.

There was a strange rumbling on the line. Then a young girl said, "Hello, my name is Marta."

"Marta," Gennaro said, "you've suffered a great deal of disappointment over a person you still love. Tell me, who is Enzo?"

"Enzo? A friend."

"And who is Salvatore?"

"He's my brother."

"And Antonio—who's he?"

"Let me think—oh, he's a friend of my brother's."

"Well, you've had sex in a car with somebody who has black hair. With . . . Gianni."

"No."

"Marta, I see a white car. Who owns the white car?"

"I don't know."

"You've made love in that car."

"No."

"Liar."

"No, Gennaro, I'm telling the truth."

"Marta, you are a great liar. You made love in that white car with Gianni."

"No, Gennaro. He wanted to, but I didn't. I wouldn't let him."

"You touched him down there. That's still making love."

"No, Gennaro."

"Marta, have the courage to tell me the truth. He put his hand on you down there, didn't he?"

"No."

"But I see it—he did."

"No, Gennaro."

"Marta, please don't talk nonsense. Otherwise I'm going to have to break off this call."

"But Gennaro, I've told you the truth. He wanted to, but I didn't let him. And that's all there is to it."

"I don't believe you."

"But it's true."

"You're a great liar. How can I help you if you lie to me like this. I might as well throw in the sponge."

"I'm not lying, Gennaro, I'm telling the truth."

All of a sudden Gennaro's voice softened. Very gently, almost wearily, he said, "You have a mole on your ear."

"Yes." She sounded shocked now, and chastened.

"Okay, now tell me the truth. You let Gianni touch you down there, didn't you?"

"No, I didn't."

"My God, this is useless," he said, despairing. "I refuse to go on."

"But I've told you, Gennaro, he wanted to and I didn't. Oh, maybe he came close—I don't remember."

"He touched you . . . on the outside."

"Not that I can remember."

"Ah, not that you can *remember*! But I *see* it, Marta, you touched each other's genitals. You made love in that car!"

She said, very meekly, politely exasperated, "No, Gennaro."

For a while they argued over whether, how, and when Marta and Gianni had had sex, depending on your definition of it, in the white car. The possibilities were endless. At times poor Marta seemed to give in and agree, surrendering to Gennaro's browbeating. I had never before heard anything like this on Gennaro's program, and I wondered why he was so concerned to unmask her supposed fibs instead of telling her future. Did it have anything to do with my sitting there? I certainly hoped not.

Finally Gennaro replayed Marta's account for her over the air, like a prosecutor trying to trip up a witness, and every now and again he nodded buoyantly at me, with an air of vindication. "See?" he whispered. "See? She did it. She really did do it."

At last, worn out, both litigants gave up. "Listen, Marta," Gennaro said, "just tell me who's your boyfriend now. I see a uniform."

"That's Filippo. He's a policeman."

"Well, he's not nice, he's no good for you. You'll only have sex with Filippo, he'll never love you, he'll never give you what you need. Do you know that he whores around? He goes to clubs every night."

"He does?"

"Of course he does. But this young fellow Tommaso—who's he?"

"Tommaso? I don't know any Tommaso."

"Well, you'll meet him over the summer. And he'll make you very happy."

Caller after caller came in over the air, and on the big computerized sign behind Gennaro's head I watched the passing of the hours. As the time wore on, his craving for cigarettes overmastered him completely, and leaving the room for a smoke, he ordered me to field the incoming calls. Sit up there, he said. Put on the headphones. Ask them some basic questions. In essence, I was to play the magician's assistant.

What's your name? I had to say. Where do you live? When is your birthday? Is it love you want to know about, or family, or work? Sometimes I would chat with the speaker for a few minutes, allowing Gennaro time to smoke a whole cigarette, and for me these intervals were enlivened by the vision of a million ears glued to the radio. I pictured callers in San Sebastiano, in houses perched on the hardened lava of the Vesuvius; I pictured them amid the malodorous alleys of Forcella and the clotheslines of Secondigliano and the crime-infested housing projects of Scampia. Most of the callers asked whether I was thriving in Naples. They wanted to know if I liked real Neapolitan pizza and maccheroni al ragù. They wanted to know what was best about their city. Aren't we cordial? they wanted to know. Aren't we obliging?

Then a voice said, "I'm Francesca, and I don't want to talk to you. Can I talk to Gennaro, right away?" She was clearly a lady of a certain age, and she sounded frantic. I called in a whisper to Gennaro, and he bounded back into the room.

"Tell me, signora," he said, gently.

The lady told Gennaro in a trembling voice that she had a serious medical problem. Something was wrong with one of her eyes. She had had an operation in Naples but it hadn't been successful, and she worried that the same condition might afflict her other eye.

Gennaro asked her whether she was telling him everything— I'd never heard him sound so concerned. She described her condition and her operation, and he told her that she should have gone to Rome. There was a hospital there, he said, that would have done a much better job. "Signora, they've ruined your eye," he said. He sounded miserable. "They've botched the procedure and ruined it."

Her stifled sobs were audible. She told him exactly what her doctor's diagnosis had been, and he said, "Signora, did it all start with a drop of blood on your pupil?"

She said that it had. And now she wanted to know what would happen next. She wanted to know what she should do.

A moment of terrible silence ensued. Gennaro said, sadly, "There are times when I wish I didn't have this gift. There are times when I curse it, I really do. And I wish I weren't seeing what I'm seeing now. I wish it wasn't so clear." For a moment he stood speechless. "I'm sorry about what I have to say, signora, I'm really terribly sorry, but . . . isn't there something you haven't told me?"

She didn't answer.

"Signora, I hope this isn't true, I really hope it isn't, but what I am sensing here is that you have recently lost your sight in the other eye as well." He screwed up his face. "You have already lost your eyesight—isn't that so?"

There was a long silence.

"It is so, Gennaro," she said, in a faint quaver. "With my good eye I can see large shapes, bright lights, but they're getting weaker. I—I—" Her voice failed her.

Gennaro heaved a deep sigh. "I'm so very sorry," he said. His vocal organs sounded narrow, constricted. "I'm really so very sorry. To lose one's eyesight is—well . . . listen, signora, do you have any children?" For once there was something he didn't claim to know.

"No," she said, despairingly, "I don't have any children."

He cast about for some source of consolation, but her answers soon made it plain that there was none. An order of misery had intruded which was many times greater than the transitory problems most listeners called in to discuss. In any case, the lady had no option but to consult, without delay, the best ophthalmologist available, and a secondhand melancholy came over us in the studio.

Earlier in the evening, Gennaro had offered to drive me back into the city—or, rather, to keep me company while his secretary did so. Now he felt pressed to close down and get started, and I supposed that he would also turn off his psychic receptivity, like a shopkeeper shuttering his shop. Seeing this, I remembered why I had come here in the first place—I remembered the dream I had wanted interpreted, the future I had wanted foretold. In truth, I had been seeking a sort of cultural entertainment, which since our encounter with the blind lady's suffering seemed decidedly superfluous, even larky. On the other hand, I decided, it would not be unseemly if I asked him succinctly what the coming months in Naples might hold in store for me.

I told him I had a question for him.

"Yeah, sure, anything," he said.

There was, I said, this dream I'd had whose meaning I wanted to know.

"Uh-huh," he said. He was playing with a complicated switch panel, trying to turn off the lights in the studio, but only one had gone off.

In the half shadow I told him about the rental car agency in the catacomb and the beautiful book full of drawings of radiator ornaments.

"Cars in a catacomb? . . . Drawings of radiators?"

He hadn't been listening. He flipped another switch, but no lights went off. "This panel is such a nuisance," he muttered.

"It was a *dream,*" I said. "I got my choice of radiator ornament. They were beautiful lions, drawn in ink—like Leonardo's drawings."

"Catacombs, lions—that's a very significant dream." His mind was still on the switch panel.

"Okay, but what does it *mean?*" I said. "Does it tell me anything about . . . the future?"

"There's a trick to this thingummy," he muttered, fiddling. "There!" The lights went out. "Okay, it's late, let's get going." He stepped halfway into the corridor.

"About my dream," I said. "Why a catacomb? And why all those ornaments for the hood of my car?"

In a flash all the lights in the room bounced back on, and in the dazzle the hundreds of glassy-eyed figurines seemed to jump out of the shadows.

"Damn switch," Gennaro said. "This thingummy does this sometimes." He had both hands on the panel now. A moment later he pulled a lever, and this time all the lights went out and stayed out.

"Gennaro," I said, "doesn't the catacomb—"

"Oh, yeah . . . well, your dream's about Naples."

"About Naples," I echoed, as we went down the corridor to the front door.

"Yeah, those lions—it means everything'll go well for you here." He fished in his pocket for his keys and called for Salvatore.

"That's it? That's all it means?"

"Yeah, everything'll go great."

"Oh."

"We'd better hurry."

As I was letting myself into my room the telephone rang.

"God, how are you? Are you okay?"

"Of course—never better."

"What a relief! I was so worried." It was Benedetta. "Tina told

me where you were going. You really had me in a state. Those psy-
chics are such crooks, who knows what they could do to you? And
then, Torre del Greco! It's a no-man's-land—you were taking your
life in your hands. I would never go there by train, much less get
off at the station. Nobody from here would do that unless they
absolutely had to."

She fetched a sigh of relief. "At least you're back," she said.

"Gennaro drove me," I said.

"Gennaro, he says. So now you're best buddies."

"Actually Gennaro doesn't drive." I said. "His assistant drove
me."

"Well, that was decent of them," she conceded. "But then, I'd
have expected it. After all, they're Neapolitans."

She was contradicting herself, but I was used to that. On the
subject of Naples, most of her pronouncements were contra-
dictory.

"I don't know if they're proper Neapolitans," I said. "When
they got to Naples they didn't know what anything was. Gennaro
asked me what the Maschio Angioino was—you know, 'What are
those big black towers?' and so on, like he'd never seen them
before. They got lost and had to ask me for directions."

"Ma che bello!" she said, laughing. "A psychic who can't find his
way around Naples. Who doesn't know whether to go left or right
at the next intersection. That's what I call seeing into the future.
Oh yes!"

"What about that poor lady who was going blind?" I said.

"Lascia perdere. That was the saddest thing I ever heard."

"Gennaro does seem very intuitive."

"Mmm, super-intuitive. I adore those initial questions of his,
like 'Who just died in your family?' or "Who's this homosexual
I'm seeing?' Somebody has always died in every family. Everybody
knows someone who's gay. And then, those names he asks about.
'Who is this Enzo?' 'Who is this Antonio?' Who doesn't know at
least one Enzo or Antonio! Why not 'Who is Ernesto?' or 'Who is
Ascanio?'" I could picture her hands moving as she spoke.

"You know, it's funny," I said, "how when he put me on the air—"

"I heard you. You overworked your subjunctives."

"I did? But I thought—"

"I'm sorry, forgive me," she said softly. "I'm always correcting people. I wanted to be a teacher. I guess on some level I still do."

Now it dawned on me fully that she'd taken out time to tune in to the show for my sake. There were even moments when she sounded like the old Benedetta. The spontaneity, the tenderness, the sweetness mixed with fieriness—it all brought back memories of the times we'd spent together. "Well, anyway," I said, feeling buoyed by her concern, "when he put me on the air and I was questioning the callers?—'Where do you live?' 'When were you born?' and so on—it was amazing how much I could tell about them from their answers. A mind reader could get very far with a little information like that. I could see that all of a sudden."

Silence at the other end of the line.

"When you asked for their birthday they told you their sign," she said at last, as if ending the discussion.

"So?"

"Well, isn't it obvious?'

"Isn't what obvious?"

"They told you their sign. Automatically, automatically you're going to know a lot about them."

"I am?"

"Of course you are."

13

The Red Guitar

After my visit to Gennaro D'Auria, I listened to his program far less often. For a while, I was haunted by the episode of the lady going blind, the sheer sorrow of it. Her pretense that she could see, even as Gennaro was cursing his second sight, was like something in a Greek tragedy. It was like being given the run of the House of Atreus and seeing all the most frightful things.

So I would lie in bed at night with the radio off, listening to the sounds of the city, crockery crashing, sopranos practicing scales, anonymous laughter. And I would wonder why it is that we often begin to understand our obsessions only as we grasp our powerlessness to erase them. When I had first glimpsed Benedetta in the shop in Chiaia, for instance, I had seen her afresh. For that instant, she was just a small southern Italian girl, no longer quite young, rather swarthy, with startling black eyebrows—not at all the sort of girl you'd find in *Amica* or *Vogue Italia*. But she was, to my eyes, more enthralling than ever, and now I began to see why. Yeats says somewhere that a man falls in love with a woman because of her way of scratching her head, but he neglects to acknowledge that head-scratching, when a woman does it, may be a fine art, and one with a glorious history: I remembered a Pompeiian painting of a woman scratching her head. Benedetta raking her hands through her mane in fury was one of the more spellbinding, and intrinsically Neapolitan, gestures I'd witnessed, the product of centuries of cultivated femininity. Such a stylish fusion of seduction and righteous indignation in order to shame a man—what would the good abbé de Jorio have said about that?

Several days after my outing to Torre del Greco my telephone rang and I heard Renzo's voice. This was unsettling: he had never phoned me before and so I expected the worst.

"This is not a hostile call," he said, without announcing himself.

"Good, I'd prefer that," I replied.

"Your preferences don't interest me," he went on, in his worldweary manner. "Myself I enjoy making hostile calls. I like to keep myself in training for quarrels with my relatives and my dearest friends. This time, however, there will be no attack—I can reassure you about that. I have a straightforward proposition to make you. If you could see your way to dropping by the shop about five this evening? Of course your little friend with the huge eyes and pretty eyebrows will also be there. That ought to be a sufficient inducement."

I agreed, but with irritation. Against all reason, I regarded Benedetta's facial features as forming a secret canon of beauty perceptible only to myself, and it was irksome that her eyebrows charmed Renzo as well.

On my way to the shop for this confrontation I was reminded, ironically, of why I loved Naples. Great shafts of sunlight slanted along the frontages, and streets slipped into view from impossible angles. Rustic-looking housing balanced atop gigantic archways, and boulevards coursed along on multiple levels. In a sense, I thought, the Baroque here had only confirmed a preexisting confusion. All the space was convoluted, like a coat turned inside out, and the inhabitants were obliged to behave accordingly.

On arriving at Renzo's shop I found him and Benedetta seated on rush-bottomed chairs just inside the doorway. Benedetta was talking with some animation; Renzo, who scarcely appeared to be listening, drew up a chair for me and gave me a searching but illegible look. The pansy-like contusions under his eyes, along with various purple blotches on his brow, had intensified in color, leaving his face somewhat mottled.

He said, "Just as you came Benedetta was in the midst of teaching me something. Apparently she has discovered that my education is defective. She wants to add the final polish, don't you, darling? And I am sitting humbly at her feet. Why don't you share your thoughts with our honored guest?" Rolling his head around toward me, he yawned openly. For an instant he seemed on the verge of slumber.

"It's not important," Benedetta said.

"But it is," Renzo urged. "Instruct us."

"I've forgotten what I was saying," she said listlessly.

"But I haven't," he said. "It is etched on my memory."

His truculent insistence prevailed, and Benedetta began to speak in a careful and subdued tone, as if any livelier rhythm might physically shatter Renzo, as if he were made of china. Now I thought I grasped what she had meant by the expression *lui non lo vuole*—"he doesn't want it." She hadn't meant that she was obeying Renzo's strictures—no, no, far from it (who even knew whether she was faithful to him?). What she had meant, I suddenly saw, was that she didn't want to do anything that might pain or distress him. Her words might have befitted a nurse speaking of an invalid in her care.

She was talking, rather speculatively, about visitors to Naples. "Take Stendhal," she was saying, "there you have a man of the north who comes down here and stays for a while in Naples and takes up residence in Civitavecchia and for whom Italy is, simply, another word for happiness. Stendhal's mother died when he was little. His father was a brute, a horrible man. Even if you read that novel of his, well, in the novel Julien's mistress, what's her name—"

"Madame de Rênal," Renzo breathed, his head flung back in affected boredom.

"—right, Madame de Rênal, well, she's so much older than Julien, so nurturing, she's really just a mother figure. And what seems true is that like Stendhal, so many of the people who end up here, especially those expatriates on Capri, are actually in need of some sort of mothering, and this culture provides it for them, which in a way is silly but also rather wonderful. Even our food, you know, is sort of like their nursery food—or at least they can take it that way. The Anglo-Saxons come in the winter with their lovely warm clothes, their tweeds and plaids and porkpie hats, they have their cappuccino in the morning, and at lunchtime they have a pastasciutta and another cappuccino, and then for an early dinner a pizza I suppose—"

"Ah, but our friend here is an Anglo-Saxon," Renzo put in. "My wife, as you can see, is a remarkable anthropologist. What do you make of her theories concerning the northern people's love of Italy?" He stared at me quizzically with his bruise-encircled eyes.

"I'm not a northerner," I said, infuriated at the reference to "my wife." "New York lies on the same latitude as Naples. For that matter, I'm not an expatriate. So I cannot claim expertise on this matter."

"What a forceful debater you are, my dear fellow. It seems to me that you have just cried uncle. I'm afraid we shall have to put you down as yet another visitor in need of mothering, in need of swaddling by our culture. Do you wander about with Leopardi in your pocket, humming Rossini, exclaiming over the altarpieces in every church you enter? Because if so—"

"Listen, Renzo," I said, bristling at his presumptuous pigeon-holing, "you said you had a proposition of some sort. I can't wait to hear what it is." No doubt it was an offer I'd decline, but at least his stating it would cut short this maddening chatter.

Renzo closed his eyes for a moment of long, freighted silence. "I'm coming to that," he replied at length, in the voice of one whose patience is being insufferably tried. "Indulge me."

Resting his watery gaze on Benedetta, he began, at first softly, then with greater force, to contradict all that she had said, decrying in his pseudo-aristocratic manner everything about Campania that might naturally appeal to an expatriate or enthusiastic foreigner. Pompeii was crowded, the Vesuvius had stopped smoking, the uncouth Neapolitans could not even pronounce the word *súbito,* and on and on. "But the big problem with seeking poetic sustenance on our Virgilian shores," he insisted, "is what has become of them since the American bombardment of 1943. Oh, I know, I know, our Leopardi-reading romantic here is not to blame for the destruction of Santa Chiara, one cannot exactly see him as a bold bombardier, but the Americans burned it to a cinder anyway, along with half the city, and look what has happened since then. Imagine what the galleys of *pater* Aeneas would find today, arriving off the shores of *umíle Italia?* Black water, hepatitis water, water full of condoms, sewer runoffs emptying into the Gulf, children covered with dermatosis, condemned foundries, collapsing tower blocks . . . an inferno!"

As I listened to Renzo, I wondered why I had never noticed in Benedetta's speech the echoes of his intellectual conceits, especially the contempt for Naples and the anticlerical stance. With Renzo, I considered, all this probably amounted to more than a pose. With her, though, it seemed partly youth's mimicry of an admired elder and partly an attempt to camouflage a contrary impulse: her deep (and therefore defenseless) love of her homeland.

"Well, all I am claiming," Renzo concluded, "is that there is a terrible irony here, which perhaps should be communicated to the peoples of the misty north. And the irony, the historical joke, is this: that those who come to Campania, to the land of Homer and Virgil, to throw themselves into the warm embrace of a life-giving *madre* will find only a *madre profanata*—an old whore, pathetic and dishonored."

Benedetta sat impassive through all this, her expression suggesting that she was inured to such performances. Indeed the couple seemed peculiarly spiritless. If Renzo's mock-insolent condescension was what Tina had meant by his "humiliation" of Benedetta, she gave no sign of any pain: she might have been attending a mediocre comedy seen many times before. Now her left eyebrow twitched up and she said to Renzo, "May I tell our friend where we'll be spending this Sunday afternoon? Unless it's one of those rare occasions when I have leave to visit my parents."

"Of course you may," said Renzo, with a wave of his hand.

"At precisely one o'clock this Sunday," she said, "as on practically every other Sunday, we shall arrive at Renzo's mamma's house, in Posillipo, which has by the way a hideous view of the Gulf and the islands, to enjoy our Sunday dinner. So you should know who is ridiculing the mother figure here. You should know who's mocking the northerners, those ingenuous northerners deluded by the *madre profanata.*"

Renzo's jaw tensed. "Mamma makes excellent paccheri al ragù," he said to Benedetta, "among other things. I've never heard you complain about her cooking."

Casting around for some object on whose mercy I might throw myself, I sighted a handsome vase in a corner. It was one of those tall ceramic canisters called *alberelli,* and as I got up to inspect it I heard Renzo heave his long frame out of his chair. He shambled to the rear of the shop, to reemerge a minute later carrying a large manila envelope. This he handed to me.

I stepped into the light of the doorway. From the envelope I drew a color photograph of a rococo tureen whose lid, if I recall correctly, bore the design of some Oriental gentlefolk feeding animals in a garden. The tureen was indisputably a museum piece—something for the Villa Floridiana.

"Are you offering to sell me this?" I asked.

"Not exactly," he said, narrowing his eyes. "But I intuited that this is the sort of thing you admire. Only someone of your cultivation . . ."—and he began to flatter my "exquisite" taste.

"Well, if you're not selling it," I said, "just what are you proposing?"

Renzo explained that the piece, a Caserta *zuppiera* from the late 1750s, would soon be up for sale in another provincial city, but that he could not afford to purchase it by himself. He suggested that as co-devotees of such objects we should acquire it together. Later, either one of us could buy out the other—indeed I could buy him out soon afterward, if I so desired: this would start me off as a truly superior collector of majolica. He would even undertake, he promised, to resell me his share at a good price. He spelled out all sorts of guarantees as to the authenticity of the piece and the refundability of my investment, but what it all boiled down to was simple enough: I was to float him a loan for his share.

When he named the sum, I believe that I kept a straight face.

I need hardly point out that I had neither the means to collect eighteenth-century majolica nor any knowledge of the field. But I also wondered whether Renzo really thought that I did, considering that I'd scarcely mentioned the matter for several weeks. Only he had kept alive, with occasional sprightly remarks, the hope that I might purchase some treasure from him. So his offer seemed merely bizarre, until a moment's reflection suggested a motive for such a gambit. Perhaps his proposition was simply a snare, a jealous man's devilish use of the proof by contradiction, a demonstration that I wasn't what I said I was. For I had never dropped the pretext, thoughtlessly established at our first meeting, of being some sort of collector, and from his point of view, if I was going to sail under this false flag, he had every right to strangle me with it.

Standing with the photograph in my hands, I felt acutely embarrassed. Not because I transparently cared for Benedetta, not because I had refrained from declaring my passion outright, but because I had never decided on any course of action, and she and Renzo knew it. I had never known what I should do about her, and my morbid indecision lay exposed: any other man, I sadly suspected, would have acted more forcefully than I. Yet when with a sidelong glance I tried to measure her response, I saw that she wore the same blank expression as before. And I said the only thing left for me to say.

"Renzo, may I have some time to think this over?"

"But old fellow, you *should* take some time. After all, it's an important decision. A very important decision about a very beautiful piece."

Was he laughing at me? Sneering, with those strange, bruise-like eyes? That is how I seem to remember it, but in truth I can't really say.

"Only don't take too long," he added. "The sale comes up in two weeks."

I was never to see him again.

That same evening, Benedetta telephoned me. "Don't you dare take him up on that offer," she said.

"I couldn't if I wanted to," I said, "I don't have the money. Why, wouldn't I get it back?"

"It's not that," she said. "It's just that . . . I can't explain it. He does this sort of thing sometimes. It's part of his—well, his weird sense of humor." Talking in riddles, she conveyed only her resignation to Renzo's eccentricities. And then, as if by accident, she told me that she'd let me take her to dinner.

My hope that we'd be able to meet in private had been so long deferred that I responded with astonishment bordering on alarm. I no longer knew what I wanted to say to her, or what I wanted to come of it. But she relieved me of the anxiety by stipulating that we would meet merely as friends. And knowing the city far better than I did, she insisted that she choose the restaurant.

This might have seemed forward, but Benedetta's bossiness, I had come to see, was skin deep, masking a deeper resignation. Whatever Italic god, at the beginning of time, had wound up the clockwork of Naples had also made its women this way. For countless generations they had born five, six, ten, twelve children, who had to be fed, clothed, washed, and reared. So for a woman to assert her domestic autocracy was only a roundabout way of confessing her preparedness, within well-fortified boundaries, for a life of submission. Yet Benedetta, that evening, also had a conscious motive in choosing our place of rendevous. In the past, whenever we had gone out to eat together, she had always embraced the restaurant's proprietor on entering and inquired at some length after his family before settling down to order. This time she did not even know him, and I concluded that the spot was unfamiliar to her, one that she never patronized with Renzo.

Tonight the proximity of several noisy, hungry families allowed her to pour out her heart as excitedly as she wished without fear of being overheard. We ordered the standard municipal antipasto of salami, marinated anchovies, *polipetti* or tiny octopi, olives, potato croquettes, and pickled zucchini, of which she selected several morsels, only to push them idly about with her fork while she refuted every idea that Tina had ever advanced concerning her relations with Renzo. Her adorable *santerella* of a sister, she told me, raking an olive to the edge of her plate, certainly had the best of intentions; but not being lodged in Benedetta's matrimonial nest, she was hardly in a position to speak knowledgeably about Renzo's health, the couple's finances, or any other domestic detail. Banishing an anchovy from her plate to mine, she characterized Tina's information as essentially fanciful, and her luring me back to Naples as an embarrassment to all concerned. Listening to this, I found in Benedetta's fascination with her beautiful sister a self-sustaining, almost demented vitality. Like some magical thornbush, it had crept into every corner of her mind, and I perceived that the only point of this evening's tête-à-tête was for Benedetta to discredit Tina. I sat back and listened, without saying a word; we were drinking a pleasant wine called Greco di Tufo, and I decided I could do worse than enjoy it.

And so Benedetta, still tormenting her food, went on disabusing me of all the preposterous ideas Tina had put in my head. Yes, of course Renzo had a habit, she said; everybody knew that, but he wasn't sponging off her. Mostly, in fact, it worked the other way around: he had, over the course of time, turned over so much of his stock to her in compensation for cash advances that the shop was effectively hers. And not only that, she added: practically nothing of real value that crossed its threshold was actually acquired by him these days.

"Renzo has a great eye," she said, "and he taught me almost everything I know. In the beginning, before I worked for him, I used to go to these auctions, these estate sales where all the bidding seemed to be rigged. I wondered what was going on till one day he explained it to me: those sellers were people who'd gone bankrupt for tax reasons and arranged to have camorristi buy back their property for them. Then Renzo took me on and taught me about porcelain and majolica, and then glassware and old silver, and he explained the value of a lot of stuff I didn't personally care for but had to know about. He was very kind, and very patient—I admit he's lost some of those qualities by now. But I have to tell you that even greater than Renzo's eye is his vanity: he's incredibly vain of his taste and his knowledge. So I just keep on jollying him along, pretending that all my purchases are really his purchases, based on his recommendations. Though a lot of what I buy and sell he doesn't even see anymore. It's all done, you know, by appointment. What you see in that shop is the shadow of his former shop, the husk of his old business. I guess you could say that he's ruined himself, but he hasn't ruined me by any means. And I don't believe he'll stay ruined forever. He has serious problems but he's the most brilliant man I've ever met."

I nodded politely as Benedetta sang the praises of Renzo, on and on. Unmoved by this paean, I studied her face: her large, mobile eyes had always attracted me, but I noticed now that their slight asymmetry had increased with the years and that the pupils lay more deeply recessed, more mysteriously shadowed beneath the upper lids. Her lips, too, had gained definition, a tiny ridge having appeared in the upper and a cleft in the lower, which now, being moist, caught a capricious spark of light. She wore a single string of pearls over a white silk blouse, and her hair was caught up in a knot on her head, and she gazed at me with such tender, con-

fiding concern as she aired her many anxieties that I decided not
to believe a word she said. As far as I knew she didn't tell lies—no
more than most of us do—but she was so given to confessions that
she had probably told Tina all sorts of things, only to forget them
later. Familiar with her generous nature, I doubted whether she
knew what she owned at this point, or whether her odd duck of a
lover—husband—whatever he was—knew either. Some lawyer
could make a meal of it, if it came to that. She nattered on without
stopping, and though several times I had a question in my mind,
each time I somehow misplaced it.

"Benedetta," I said finally, "how come you never told me about
Renzo when we were together."

She let her head droop for a long while, caressing the stem of
her wineglass and then taking a sip. "When Renzo got heavily into
roba," she said, "I tried and tried to talk him out of it. Then I got
scared and, well . . . I walked out on him. I just couldn't stand it
anymore. And the reason I never told you I was married is that I
sort of never admitted it to myself. I didn't see it as real. We got
married in secret, Renzo and I. I never even told my parents, until
after you left for New York. There was no church ceremony, we
never once talked about children or even mentioned the marriage
to each other."

"But Benedetta, why?" I asked.

"Because he wanted it. And because I wanted to make him
happy. My body, this girl that you see, wanted to make him happy.
Even though inside was a smaller, harder girl that didn't care so
much. That didn't particularly want to do it. But I wouldn't listen
to that other, harder girl. Unfortunately. You see, I believed . . . I
believed in him *so much*."

"And how old were you then?"

"Eighteen—"

"You can do that here? In this Catholic city? Without parental
consent?"

"Sure you can. Anywhere in Italy. You just walk in and—"

"And you never let on to anyone?"

"No—not till three years ago. Oh, to Tina—eventually. I told you that. I was secretly hoping you and I would find a way to be together. But when that fell through—well, not only because of that—"

"Why didn't you tell Gemma and Beppe?"

"*Dio mio,* isn't that obvious? Renzo was over twenty years older than I was. And already he was, you know—well, you know, *un maledetto bucomane*—a goddamn smackhead." She fell silent.

"People—it's disgusting—they have no patience with addiction, no compassion or understanding at all. Well, anyway, I'm telling you . . . I didn't even admit it to myself, how could I have told Mamma, who frets about everything, who worries about the dresses I wear, the water I drink, my lousy politics, contaminated shellfish—how could I possibly have told her? Anyhow, in a way we weren't really married. Marriage is a social arrangement, don't you think? A secret marriage doesn't really exist, except perhaps in the church, and ours wasn't blessed by the church." She laughed bitterly. "It was just something I did to make him happy. Because he loved me so much. He was devoted to me, that's why he's given me all these things. Okay, I admit it, he's owed me money now and then, but most of what he gave me he just gave me. Because, you know, he wanted to. That's how he is."

She still hadn't taken a bite of her food; all but an olive had ended up on my plate. I said, "Benedetta, I think you let Tina speak for you more than you admit. I mean, in some secret, unconfessed way. The things you don't dare say you let her say, and then you question her truthfulness to people. It's a little strange, isn't it? I mean, you love her more than anyone else."

Tears welled up in her eyes. "I'm not at all good, if that's what you thought," she said, biting her lip. "I'm not a good person." Her voice had grown hoarse and she took a long drink of water. "Do you know what that sound is?" she said.

"I suppose it's an ambulance," I replied, letting her change the subject.

"It's a black Maria," she said, smiling sadly. "It's coming up this street as fast as it can with its siren blaring. It's going through all the red lights, it doesn't dare stop, and do you know why? If it paused at one of the intersections—"

"Benedetta," I said, "these tales about the camorra, do you really expect me to believe them? Maybe twenty years ago, maybe ten, all that was true. Not now—"

"Not now! What do you know? Do you think this place ever changes? Do you think it improves? Every ten years it has a so-called renaissance, with beautiful quarters secured and great churches restored, and two Milanese journalists write articles about it, and then it slumps back where it was. The streets cave in. The trash piles up. Little kids get shot in the street. Half our auto accidents are staged by clowns, and we pay the highest car insurance of any region in Italy. But you of course wouldn't know that, Joe—you never stay here long enough!"

"Joe."

"Do you remember?"

Did I remember! Remember how I became the anonymous Yank at little Marisa's wedding . . .

"What I mean is, it's all cyclical," she said. "But if you never stay here long enough to experience a full cycle, you don't go through the incredible letdowns, the disappointments . . ."

You never stay here long enough . . . Feeling bad, I began to compliment her. My sense of her beauty was troubling me, and I was tired of keeping it a secret. I reminded her of her resemblance to Pontormo's country girl at Poggio a Caiano, and then I went on to thank her for showing me Ribera's *Marsyas* and for making me lie down on a pew at Santissimi Apostoli so I could see Lanfranco's martyrs, and for taking me to Eduardo's *Napoli milionaria!,* even though she didn't like it and thought it a poor sublimation of terrible sorrow and we had quarreled about it. Once I'd got started, I went on for some minutes without letup. It was my first unrestrained expression of gratitude to her, and my last.

After a while I noticed that she wasn't looking at me anymore. She gazed pensively off to the side, pursing her lips, squinting into the middle distance, as though in calculation, as though pondering the pros and cons of some practical decision—we had, for a moment, lost contact. Then abruptly she stood up and counted out some ten-thousand-lire notes from her purse and laid them on the table. "Come on," she said sternly, "we're leaving."

"We are?" I said, bewildered.

"Yes."

"Then let me pay." I supposed I was being punished for something I'd said. The lone olive sat forlorn on Benedetta's plate, and I eyed the wine bottle with regret.

"I've already paid," she said. She grasped my elbow firmly and led me toward the door.

"Are you all right?" I asked, when we stood outside.

I felt a warm breeze against my cheek, but it was not a breeze—it was her palm. "Where's this place you're staying?" she said.

Loneliness is commonly represented as a sensation of absence, but my loneliness, in the days following this occurrence, crowded in on me as a keen, almost unbearable presence. There was no curve of Benedetta's limbs, no cadence of her voice, no article of her clothing that I could not call to mind with hypnotic clarity. Her image never left me, yet with each hour the reasons for staying clear of her became more compelling. I would like to say that we made a clean break, and parted as lifelong friends, but this would not be true. What is known as a "messy" situation ensued: disputes, further embraces, rebukes, a resurgent sense that the affair was framed in the subjunctive mood, a matter of "woulds" and "mights." No renewal of our old attachment seemed likely to succeed, and in the following weeks, as I prepared to leave Naples—not to return for many years, as it would happen—a tacit understanding grew between us to refrain from all manner of seduction. Both Tina and Loredana seemed to know of the rekindling of our intimacy, and each in her way fanned the guttering flame; but I managed to dampen their kindhearted hopes.

In the meantime, a new thought began to console me; though not in itself a reason for giving Benedetta up, it was a plausible vision of her future. It came to me when I thought again about the time, just before little Marisa's wedding, when in jest Benedetta had called me Joe. Joe was the familiar nickname for American men around here—it harked back to the "G.I. Joe" of World War II, the years of the black market, of mass prostitution, of duplicitous marriages—and it told me what a cliché I'd become. Three years earlier, when I had so often been in Naples, I had not known a single person who spoke English, and I had assumed that I did not belong to any social category. I was beyond category: a free agent who happened, for now, to be hooked up with a girl. It had not occurred to me then, as it did now, that during the Allied occupation, in the mid-1940s, practically all American males had been free agents, and practically all their Neapolitan girlfriends had been tied down by a dense web of loyalty to family and friends. I had thought of my interlude with Benedetta as coming out of nowhere, like Venus rising from the sea, whereas actually it came at the tail end of a lurid chapter in the social history of the city. Had it awakened a lingering memory of injury in her or her people? I didn't think it had: I had never detected any resentment. But as I thought over the whole situation, my vaunted independence felt decidedly shopworn to me.

And Benedetta? In the catalogue of *napoletane,* women of Naples, which would be organized (as it would for men) according to district, Benedetta was a *popolana,* literally a "woman of the people," or, in the word's contemporary connotation, a female denizen of the quarters of the old city. Naturally, I'd met women from other, more fashionable or suburban districts, *posillipine, vomeresi, puteolane,* etc., but none I'd known very well. About *popolane,* however, one might say this: a big happy family—including a reliable mate and beautiful children—was generally conceded to be their innate aim. And I felt that Benedetta would very soon set about realizing this aim, doubtless in competition with the redoubtable Tina. Then, with the same backhanded practicality whereby she had become proficient in the low end of the antiques trade, she would discover that she needed a life very different from the one she had hitherto pursued. I pictured her conventionally housed with some sturdy artisan or small businessman, perhaps no more than a few blocks from where she had grown up.

With this picture of Benedetta's reversion to type I salved my conscience. For actually I had no idea what would become of her, and the one who reverted to type was me. But by now, at least, the obfuscation of emotion was gone. She couldn't have doubted how I felt about her.

I have never had so many friends anywhere as I then had in Naples, but I could not say good-bye to them all in one day. As I arranged my farewells, I was left with intervals of time on my hands, and for a week I knocked about the city, saddened by the imminence of my departure. Once you have decided to leave a place, you might as well be gone at once.

Thankfully I was still able to lose myself now and again. There was a bus I took at dusk for no other reason than its way of dawdling up and down the narrow, slanting streets of Pizzofalcone, and from my seat the merchants in their shops looked like actors in a row of pocket theaters: portly, gesticulating sellers of sausages, poultry, baccalà, mozzarella. Watching them, I wouldn't be reminded of my own existence again until nine or so, when the city fell vacant and there was nobody to look at, nobody but the urchins under the glass dome of the Galleria, slamming soccer balls at one another in a ghostly flood of light.

One evening I spotted Gigi in a café, sitting at a table with Graziella. Our paths hadn't crossed for weeks, and I was pleased to see them. They greeted me warmly, but again Gigi surprised me. I had known him as a theatrical blond, with bristling porcupine hair. Now he had given himself a new look—he was *rilookato*. His hair was dark and fell about his temples, and he wore a red silk scarf and picked softly at a red guitar.

Graziella and I drank white wine while Gigi sang a love song to his red guitar. Then he sang a song about an octopus. An octopus's life, according to Gigi's song, was no bed of roses—it was, as he put it, *una vita di cacà*. The worst of it all (he plucked an arpeggio) was that when the poor octopus was caught and put in a restaurant tank (arpeggio), he wasn't even served up as a tasty morsel, but secretly replaced (arpeggio) by a frozen octopus. So he had to carry on in ignominy as a sort of front man for the unscrupulous restaurant. Gigi sang of the frustrations and grievances of octopus life with a dolorous and impudent air.

Then he asked me whether I could teach him to sing his song in English.

"Sure he can!" Graziella exclaimed. "He'll just put down the sounds of his English version phonetically and—"

"Graziella, shut up," Gigi said. "You don't know what you're talking about, you don't know anything. I only need the syllables written out so I can pronounce them."

Graziella's face relaxed into bored passivity. "You ox," she said, "that's what I was trying to tell him."

None of this embarrassed them, or me. I had long ago concluded, perhaps optimistically, that Gigi's surly outbursts were to be taken as tokens of affection—*I vouchsafe you the dregs of my soul*—and anyhow I had already started jotting something down on my spiral notepad. "How's this?" I asked, handing him a slip of paper with a title printed across the top:

DA LAIF AV DA OCTOPUS

"That's just what I need," Gigi said. "Can you write out the whole song like that?"

I looked forward to the assignment, which made me feel a little less footloose; but my enthusiasm was wasted, for soon Gigi was singing about something else. We sat there far into the evening, amid an ever-changing circle of friends, drinking wine and listening to the red guitar.

I 4

A Parting Glance

After that sojourn, I did not return to Naples for more than a decade. Eventually I would resume my visits, staying once for the better part of a year, but I would never hear of anyone who fit Benedetta's description in any branch of the antiques trade. Nor would I come across her, as I half expected to do, in the backstreets of her old neighborhood; perhaps she had changed course in life, or, contrary to my imaginings, moved to some other city. Of course I continued to miss her, but in a new, more mellow way. She was like a sonata that echoed in my mind, but which I would never hear played to the end.

And my other friends—both those I have written about and those I have not—were they "typical" Neapolitans? I doubt whether there is such a thing. They obviously didn't correspond to the familiar ethnic stereotype of thief or slacker; no one in Naples ever stole from me, and in fact people continually gave me things, pressed them fervently into my hands. There was a good trattoria I hesitated to enter because the owner refused to accept my money. It is true that some of my friends could sing *canzonette* with the trills and mordants of the Neapolitan vocal style, but there were foreigners who could sing the same songs just as well.

Actually my loss of belief in a specifically Neapolitan character, indeed in national character as such, predated my first meeting with Benedetta. National character, I thought, was a set of signs—a code. Wherever you happened to be, this code rendered universal human impulses palpable, and it also changed with the times. A failure to crack the code when you were living in a foreign country only betrayed your own laziness. Being embraced effusively in Naples did not mean the same as being embraced effusively in London, and if you could not figure that out, the fault was yours.

I was curious, nonetheless, about how the Neapolitans saw themselves. Of course they were happy to tell me. In public squares, by the waterfront, in cafés, at the dinner table, I watched their dark eyes, their rueful smiles, their gestures of disclaimer or disenchantment as they tried to explain the persistent corruption and clan violence in their city. I also heard over and over that they were an unusually "humane" people, largely out of plain Christian decency but also out of a sense of vulnerability—they made no bones about that. For most of the last two thousand years, they had been awed and cowed by superior force, obliged to curry favor with one or another band of armed ruffians. Yet this relentless currying of favor was tinged, they intimated, with ridicule. The derisive Neapolitan flattery verged upon paradox, as with the Cretan who tells you he's a liar: most outsiders hardly knew how to take it. Yet I remembered it in my bones, from childhood: for the play-world of New York children had its own conventions of soft-soaping and leg-pulling and self-mockery, which could be traced, I suspected, to the great immigrations of the early twentieth century. Those conventions probably owed more to the Neapolitan ethnic strain than anyone suspected, though I would not have known how to prove it.

The Naples of several decades back was a place full of children and food aromas, and children stampeding toward food aromas. It was, above all, a place where you could get by with very little money and were not expected to have much more. Those with more lived elsewhere. One dollar bought a meal or several bottles of wine, and I remember joining a group of strangers at their café table in the Quartieri and sharing their repast before realizing that it was not a café at all. They had merely moved some tables and chairs out in front of their *basso* and roped in the first unusual-looking passerby for a little spirited conversation. Those days have passed; yet much of the coarse old hospitality remains.

It is common to praise the resourcefulness of the poor, less common to praise their good taste. Yet nowhere else have I seen such elegant poverty—a chastening lesson to those who, like me, are always shabbily short of funds. Nowhere else are the down-and-out so beautifully dressed, so deliciously fed, so even-tempered and courtly and frolicsome (one suspects some Faustian bargain). I think I mean to say that a deeper elegance can come from the capacity for fellow feeling. Shortly after I said farewell forever to Benedetta, I happened to pass two masons during their lunch break. They were sitting on crates at the threshold of a door, facing each other, their knees almost touching, with a wooden board stretched between their laps like a bridge, and on the board they were playing a game of cards. It was a haunting picture, an ideogram of the sort of companionship I have never enjoyed.

An amalgam of equivocal beauty, vestigial beliefs, betrayed resolves, and half-concealed secrets, Naples still largely eludes my understanding. I cannot fully explain why I'm drawn to the place, and I suppose I keep returning to find out why. Certainly I like the coffee, so inexpressibly perfect; and the perfumed Amalfi lemons, with their sweet overtones; and fennel at the close of a meal. I like knowing that even if I enter a restaurant alone I will not end up eating alone, but with companions new or old. I like the kaleidoscopic views from the funiculars as they rattle up to the Vomero, and popular festivals that still serve their sacred purpose, and stumbling on great paintings that nobody seems to have heard of. I like the fact that every conversation lasts at least three hours, that the absurd awaits me around every corner, that extravagant silliness is encouraged (and sometimes, as in Totò's movies, enshrined).

As for the lingering notion that the afterlife is easier to contact from this spot than from elsewhere on earth, I do not know what to make of it; Signora Perna, for instance, is a rational person, and I believe in the stories she told me. What cannot be denied is the dominion of the dead over the municipal imagination. Everywhere and in every age, the decisions of the dead have made up the better part of those governing the living, but in Naples those decisions can be seen and touched. Like the columns of the vanished Roman Temple of the Dioscuri, which still frame the portico of San Paolo Maggiore, or the branching corridors of the underworld, exposed by gaping fissures after nearly every rainstorm, the dead are immanent as architects of the present, and the living ignore them at their peril.

From this visible condition it is only a hop to the notion that the dead reveal lottery numbers to us in dreams. I am superstitious enough to suspect that this may be true, and here I believe I have Dante on my side: the goddess of fortune was the only heavenly agency that he regarded, metaphorically, as a deity. No human intelligence can match hers, he contended, and she disposes of her realm like any other god:

> *Vostro saver non ha contasto a lei:*
> *questa provede, giudica, e persegue*
> *suo regno come il loro li altri dei.*

This is Dante the betrayed politician, who was forced out of Florence for no good reason and came to terms with his unjust fate; he would have understood why the revolving Wheel of Naples so hypnotizes the city's people. Naples juxtaposes grinding poverty with antique and ornate splendor—crowds of the unemployed milling around in front of cinquecento palaces—and it is just the strangeness of that juxtaposition that gives rise to the passion for games of chance. In the piazzas of Naples I came to understand that fortune rules the lives of ninety-nine percent of humanity, and that "destiny," defined as a fate you pursue with your willpower, is so rare a privilege as to be almost a fiction.

All this may explain why, whenever I return to the city, to my room overlooking that steep, narrow street, I make sure that my nightstand holds a copy of the *smorfia*. As I gaze down at the old ladies fanning themselves in chairs along the sidewalk and wonder what dreams will come tonight, I am soothed by the knowledge that this bible of Naples has some hold on those filmy visitations. For with time I have come to feel that our dreams determine our waking life. Naples, the city of nocturnal din, accords a sovereign power to dreams, because its noises conjure them up and keep them aloft through a strange aural wizardry in the sleeper's head. In Naples I abandoned the idea that dreams were a sort of running commentary on events, like the sports section in the evening newspaper, and embraced the opposite idea: that I was trying to work out in my waking life what I'd dreamed about at night. I knew that some poets had made this claim, but it ceased to be merely literary for me and became real in Naples, where the most elemental feelings that had pulsed through my dreams drove me forward during the day. In Naples I caught a glimpse of the old Italian idea, which is also a Shakespearean idea, that life can be a kind of romance in which the errant brain, led by fancy alone, seeks out whatever scenery best mirrors its vision of joy.

AUTHOR'S NOTE

The characters in this book are real, but it bears mentioning that I have used some pseudonyms and have altered descriptions of several persons in order to protect their privacy. Though this is a work of nonfiction, I have taken some storytelling liberties, particularly with regard to chronology. Where the narrative strays from strict fact, my intention has been to remain faithful to the characters and to each event as it happened. All the reported conversations took place in Italian.

ACKNOWLEDGMENTS

I thank George Andreou, my editor, for his excellent structural suggestions and commitment to every word in the text; and Robin Reardon for her unfailing assistance.

For believing in this project and steadfastly helping me to realize it, I am grateful to Andrew Wylie and Zöe Pagnamenta.

My gratitude is also due to my friends Daniela Villani and Luigi Tavassi, and to Eugenio Blasio, for their day-to-day support and advice.

For friendship, help, information, or counsel along the way I am indebted to Enzo Albertini, Arturo Assante, Gigi Attrice, Mario Avallone, Mirella Barracco, Wima Caniglia, Clemente Esposito, Dr. Joseph Fetto, Flavio Fierro, Raffaele La Capria, Raimondo di Maio, Nunzia Perna, Salvatore Pica, Salvatore and Alberto Piccolo, Eleonora Puntillo, and Alain Volut.

Finally, my thanks go to all those who, under their real or assigned names, appear in the pages of this book, especially the Quaranta brothers, Michele and Salvatore.

A NOTE ABOUT THE AUTHOR

Dan Hofstadter is the author of three previous books. His most recent, *The Love Affair as a Work of Art,* was nominated for a National Book Critics Circle Award. He has written for most national magazines and was for eight years a regular contributor to *The New Yorker.*

A NOTE ON THE TYPE

The text of this book was set in Requiem, created in the
1990s by the Hoefler Type Foundry. It was derived from
a set of inscriptional capitals appearing in Ludovico
Vicentino degli Arrighi's 1523 writing manual,
Il modo de temperare le penne. A master scribe, Arrighi is
remembered as an exemplar of the chancery
italic, a style revived in Requiem Italic.

COMPOSED BY
Stratford Publishing Services,
Brattleboro, Vermont

PRINTED AND BOUND BY
R. R. Donnelley & Sons,
Harrisonburg, Virginia

DESIGNED BY
Iris Weinstein